The Murder of
LEHMAN
BROTHERS

An Insider's Look at
the Global Meltdown

JOSEPH TIBMAN

Brick Tower Press

Brick Tower Press
1230 Park Avenue
New York, NY 10128
Tel: 212-427-7139 • Fax: 212-860-8852
bricktower@aol.com • www.BrickTowerPress.com

The Brick Tower Press colophon is a registered trademark
of J. T. Colby & Company, Inc.

Library of Congress Cataloging-in-Publication Data

By Joseph Tibman
The Murder of Lehman Brothers

ISBN-13: 9781883283711
LCC#: 2009927654

First Edition, September 2009
Includes index.

Copyright © 2009 by Joe Tibman

Typesetting by The Great American Art Company

10 9 8 7 6 5 4 3 2 1

Contents

For my wife and children

Prologue

While I was not present for what I describe below, the story is true and, at Lehman, was legend, especially among us lifers who broke bread in the executive dining room. On this one page, I have allowed myself reasonable poetic license. Still, as I have known and observed both of the men I describe, I believe I have nailed the tenor of this event.

Piled high with the usual paperwork, Allan Kaplan, an old-school senior executive, whom many came to regard as the "conscience of Lehman Brothers," sat as his desk. Dick Fuld, one of the fixed income[1] traders, appeared in his office door.

Kaplan, as always, continued methodically working through the piles stacked and arranged in perfect right angles before him. He glanced expressionlessly in Fuld's direction, returned his gaze to the work on his desk. Kaplan acknowledged the figure in his office doorway, just loud enough for Fuld to hear, and then ignored him as he continued his progress through the great volume of paper that required his attention, his sanction.

Fuld was unable to shuffle his feet in the threshold of Kaplan's office for very long, and like a shark that must keep moving to live, strode to the senior executive's desk, announcing that he required a signature so that he

---

1. A security that pays a fixed return, such as a bond, commercial paper, or preferred stock.

could complete a profitable, time-sensitive trade. Kaplan lifted his head, placed his half-smoked Cohiba in an ashtray and blankly looked at the impertinent, headstrong Fuld. Moving only his lips, he informed Fuld in crisp words that seemed to disappear into the pile of the carpet, that he, Kaplan, from his mile-high aerie, would consider approval of Fuld's trade *once his desk was clear* of the many piles.

Fuld, his veins filled with adrenaline rather than blood, could not sit on this trade. Every second that passed increased the risk that he would lose it. For Fuld, it was all about the moment. In this one, as in so many others, he saw the purpose of his very existence and that of his firm as one: to make money. It was written in stone that no one wanted to rub Kaplan the wrong way. To do so could precipitate unpredictable wrath. But Kaplan was increasingly an anachronism. Time would not stand still to accommodate the outdated approval process that tied Fuld's hands.

To consummate the trade, Fuld required Kaplan's immediate sanction. Making the situation doubly frustrating was a clear expectation, undoubtedly shared by Kaplan, that the trade would be quickly approved once the titan's eyes fell on the paperwork. Slam-dunk. But Fuld was tangled in the red tape of this powerbroker, known for his traditional, understated manner, as well as limited tolerance for hotheads who came to him half-cocked, ill-prepared, or disrespectful of *the process.*

Still there was a monetary bottom line and it flashed neon in Fuld's eyes: the trade will not wait. Kaplan, still ignoring him, had become an intolerable brick wall. And so, acting on pure impulse and instinct, the very innards of the best traders, Fuld cleared Kaplan's desk with a single sweep of his arm, scattering the exalted one's neat piles around his desk. Sucking in his breath, Fuld told the implicitly fearsome Allan Kaplan that now he could approve the trade; his *desk was clear.*

If Kaplan flinched, it was not visible to the human eye. But he did fix his stare on Fuld, eyes widening, this, the only discernible reaction. Fuld's cheeks filled with blood as he awaited his fate. Inwardly, Kaplan smiled puckishly. Yes, he was amused and impressed. This Fuld had potential. Kaplan silently reviewed the documents requiring his approval of the insubordinate trader's transaction, and with dispatch, delivered his signature.

Fuld rotated on heels of wing tips, utterly in the dark as to what the poker-faced Kaplan had in store for him. Would he even have a job the next day? But Fuld was in the moment, like the best of traders, the risk takers, and held the authorization to trade in his hand.

Many years later, in May of 2003, Dick Fuld stood before a packed chapel of mourners, including numerous employees of the firm that Fuld, now CEO, transformed into a major force on Wall Street. He lauded and joked affectionately about Kaplan, making great mention of his deceased colleague's integrity and ethics, and about the suit pants Kaplan belted so high—Fuld affectionately chuckled—that they reached Kaplan's chin. Until a week before, Allan Kaplan had been fully engaged at Lehman, despite a festering illness, serving the firm he had made his second home for thirty-six years. In summing up Kaplan's tenure, Richard Fuld, the hard-assed titan, one of the most powerful men on Wall Street, always bursting with testosterone, choked tearfully on his closing words: "Allan was my friend."

Fuld would later honor Kaplan by naming the auditorium on the lower level of Lehman's majestic Time Square tower after him. *He wanted to do something.* And it was a fine gesture. But the man called *the conscience of Lehman* had expired.

Introduction

I t was a Friday like no other. September 12, 2008. Just one day earlier, I was somewhat concerned about the hammered Lehman Brothers (LB) share price and the persistent rumors about my firm, but I had been here before. Well not exactly here. But I was sure Lehman would survive as an independent firm. I knew it. And this was the consensus, not universally throughout the firm, but among most people with whom I spoke. We were not panicking. Were my colleagues and I deluding ourselves? Had we overdosed on the Lehman-distributed talking points for client damage control? Or were we simply in mass denial? I cannot even pretend to know. I slept well that Thursday night and woke up on Friday refreshed. But this was a Friday, the memory of which is hard-wired in my brain. Soon after I arrived at my office in the Lehman headquarters at 745 Seventh Avenue on the north end of Time Square, it was clear my world, and that of all those around me, was spinning off its axis. The word was out. The Federal Reserve Bank (Fed)[2] and U.S. Treasury were in the building. So were Bank of America and Barclays Capital. Or were they? Were they meeting elsewhere? *Shit.* What did it matter where they were? This was it. Two of our competitors, far weaker in investment banking,

---

2. The Federal Reserve Board, the chairman of which is currently Ben Bernanke, is charged with monitoring the U.S. economy and is responsible for monetary policy, i.e., utilizing tools such as setting interest rates, managing money supply, etc., to optimize economic health. Under the Board are twelve Federal Reserve Banks, that issue currency, maintain reserves, and lend to member banks, providing them with a source of liquidity that is intended to help maintain stability in the U.S. financial system.

1

were negotiating to buy us. By the end of a day fraught with innumerable rumors, minor incremental truths, and speculation, no agreement had been reached. Negotiations were set to continue through the weekend. And what a weekend it was; a lost weekend, where time became a blur as if I had gotten lost on a bender. All I can remember, even after just a couple of months, is obsessively trading Blackberry messages with similarly restless colleagues and perpetually scanning television general and business news channels for just one more sliver of incremental info, for hope. But the big takeaway was that negotiations had stalled. My world had stopped rotating. This much was certain: my firm, Lehman Brothers, was coming unwound. I felt powerless, like a child, hands tight around the bars of a Lehman rollercoaster I could not remember boarding. It seemed about to careen from the tracks at any moment. In a word, *fuck.* Our Blackberries seemed to be continuously humming this same word throughout the weekend as non-stop emails expressed the collective freak-out. Then suddenly a bombshell dropped. Merrill Lynch was to be acquired by Bank of America in a government-brokered deal. We were toast. We would fail. If there were to be a Lehman deal, it would have been announced at the same time. *Fail.* This was surreal. On Sunday, many of us rushed to the office to retrieve personal possessions, just in case we were locked out on Monday. The firm had not yet been pronounced dead, but the Lehman I had long made my second home was teetering on the brink. And by Sunday night, the news was unambiguous. My Blackberry began to load up with farewell messages. All that was missing was a coroner's report. And we did not have to wait long for it. A talking head on the widescreen TV said Lehman would file for bankruptcy under Chapter 7, a full-blown liquidation of the firm. Operations would immediately cease. Dust to dust.

Monday morning was a mindbender. Lehman had filed, was officially bankrupt, but, sipping my morning brew, the voice on the kitchen tube said Chapter 11—reorganization, not 7—liquidation. Something had changed. I arrived at the office, and made my way through the encamped media outside Lehman's headquarters, where a handful of ambulance-chasing headhunters[3] were handing out business cards. Monday was long. Bar-

---

3. Slang for executive recruiters or employment agents.

clays was back in the building, along with the government, and the news filtering from the boardroom pushed our spirits up and down throughout the day. By Tuesday, the outcome was announced. Lehman was no more. But most of our jobs were safe, at least for the time being. On Tuesday morning, I walked through the doors at 745 Seventh Avenue and entered a new reality: Barclays Capital. *Man, life can be strange.* A week ago, I had been a Lehman banker. Then exogenous forces had rocked my world. I had been jobless. A dead man. But, now I had been resuscitated as a BarCap banker, or so I thought.

* * *

I was proud to be a senior Lehman investment banker. In fact, I am still proud to have been part of the Lehman phenomenon—despite the fact that Lehman has disintegrated, and that our sterling name, along with that of our once-exalted CEO, Dick Fuld, has tarnished, together with names of select others, such as John Thain,[4] who are now at the epicenter of popular vernacular for greed and excess on Wall Street. Barclays acquired most of the former Lehman's North American operations for mere pocket change—in fact, a fraction of the employee bonus payout required at year-end to maintain parity with other bulge bracket[5] firms—an imperative if Barclays is to retain the franchise that walks in and out of the office every day. Back then, when I temporarily morphed into a senior banker for Barclays Capital, the investment banking unit of British behemoth Barclays Bank, I tried as hard as I could to muster optimism that my pride would regain its footing and endure. It helped that the Lehman Brothers investment banking team was largely intact and running the combined North American investment banking business. Still, it was not

---

4. Chief Executive Officer of Merrill Lynch who approved massive bonuses for the firm's bankers in a hugely unprofitable year, just ahead of the firm's already scheduled acquisition by Bank of America.

5. The leading investment banks placing the largest amount of underwritten securities with investors. Until recently, there were five such independent firms: Goldman Sachs, Morgan Stanley, Merrill Lynch, Lehman Brothers, and Bear Stearns. There are other large players in the same markets that are part of larger financial conglomerates.

easy to be optimistic; not with the ongoing trickle of departing colleagues I would soon join, and the market-data horror flick playing on all our screens. Those still at Barclays are busy, but the intense flurries of activity, even with an occasional seven figure revenue payday, are a meager semblance of years past.

A loyal, long-term veteran of the firm, I was at Lehman when it was, bluntly, a pile of shit, *i.e.,* owned by American Express and welded to other American Express broker-dealer[6] acquisitions, Shearson and the failed Hutton. I witnessed firsthand, indeed lived through, American Express's separation and disposition of Lehman and Shearson. After suffering a financial black eye, this first-class issuer of credit cards, travelers' checks, travel services, etc., abandoned its quest to become a broader financial supermarket. Yes, I was there for the spin-off of Lehman under terms extremely favorable to American Express and onerous for Lehman. We were all glad to be rid of American Express. They did not know how to play master to a Lehman. It was essentially a dysfunctional parent-child relationship. They failed to extract value. In fact, they achieved the reverse. And *that* was the bottom line. It was extremely liberating that again we were an unshackled, independent firm, despite the financial arrangement with Amex. Its terms were a ball and chain requiring Lehman, if we were profitable, to give Amex a large slice of the pie for some years. But we were in the moment. The struggle ahead was to restore Lehman to its grand stature, its proudest days as a preeminent Wall Street house. And as Dick Fuld was anointed and took charge, in the most upward of climbs, good things began to happen.

I was there for the historic, defining, Lehman IPO[7] (we all got tee-shirts which proudly displayed a Lehman stock certificate) and the seemingly irrepressible ascent of the share price, enriching us all—on paper—and peaking well beyond anyone's expectations those many years ago. I still

---

6. A firm in the business of buying and selling securities for its own account and for others.

7. This is an initial public offering of shares to the public by a company privately held, or by a subsidiary of a public company. Typically, the shares then trade on a stock exchange, such as the New York Stock Exchange or NASDAQ. The IPO of a private company is at times also referred to as *taking a company public* or *going public.*

have the tee-shirt. And even in its bedraggled condition it is worth more than the pennies of a bankrupt Lehman share. Yes, the defunct shares. My hat is off to those who sold. Many of us held on to most of what was allotted, running counter to what we had all learned back in business school Finance 101 about diversifying. *Shit,* you would learn how important it is to diversify in the first fifteen minutes of an adult education class on personal finance. But then, we were Lehman. We were almost Goldman. We had just as much bravado; maybe we had more. We were on the up. We were invincible. We always bounced back from a downturn, from the rumors of insolvency, stronger than ever. *Right.* And even all this is ironic. Before joining Lehman, back in the day before its ascent, I had been ambivalent, because the firm was such a steaming pile of shit.

As for my purpose in writing this book, it is most obviously to tell you what it felt like within the belly of the beast, during the unimaginable unfolding of events at my office-home that have indisputably impacted the world. All this occurred under the mass media's unforgiving glare, but I will tell the tale from an intensely personal perspective. Also, I have been in finance for a very long time, and as I have only one life, why not take a stab at launching a new career, something totally unanticipated and never contemplated until this juncture? I certainly do not know that investment banking will ever again be what it was. And in certain ways, I pray that it will not. In the best of cases, even with ripe optimism, I cannot count on a return to a reinvented semblance of the good old days. Fuck, no. So, instead, the time may be ripe to shift gears completely and leap from Joe-the-Investment-Banker to Joe-the-Author. And so, I intend to relate this story through my utterly personal, and therefore, by definition, subjective, biased paradigm. Because Lehman's demise is so recent, it would be impossible for me to attempt a different sort of telling.

I hope also to impart a sense of the mentality, the culture, the adrenaline that is investment banking. Along with a very few other professions, ones like private equity,[8] my business was capitalism in its most purely

---

8. Private equity firms raise funds to invest in and hold shares of companies that are not listed on a public stock exchange. They most typically, though not always, gain full control of companies that if not already private, are usually taken private by tendering for all outstanding public shares.

distilled form. And because in this rarified world, what matters most is
this year's bonus (most of an investment banker's compensation), at times
we capitulate to faulty, flawed judgment. And when these lapses occur, we
are often found rationalizing that the great risk inherent in contemplated
business is a trifle. When the lucid point this out, we characterize them as
buzz killers. It is this mentality that sometimes leads to disaster.

Finally, you could Google away for months and just skim the surface of
Wall Street meltdown content littering the World Wide Web. And wherever you turn—on-line, print, radio or TV—the media are describing a
rasher of troubling new developments. Yet few people seem able to get
their arms around all that sank our financial sector and our economy to its
current nadir (at least I hope it is a low point). I am constantly asked why
Lehman Brothers was the only firm permitted to fail. There is no succinct
explanation. Simplistically, it can be attributed to timing. But there were
many forces that collided to cause the collapse. Examined one at a time,
these factors are not complex. And that is what I will do, explaining them
in plain English (relying to some degree on footnotes to clarify unavoidable jargon), so that no prior knowledge of finance or economics is
required to understand precisely what happened to Lehman, our financial
markets, and the global economy. I am sure that for any non-financial type
who cares to read what follows, the true causes of the meltdown, as well
as the sequence of both relevant headline and more subtle events, will
become clear. Still, there is one mystery about which I can only conjecture:
how the many intelligent people who played a role in the grand debacle,
some at critical junctures, made the choices of blind, unthinking fools.
Because this factor figures so prominently in Lehman's death, I do not consider the firm's murder calculated or premeditated. Rather I believe it was
an act of involuntary manslaughter, of criminal negligence. Once Lehman
was in an ICU, there were those who deprived The Brothers, writhing on
its deathbed, of critical life support that would have ensured its survival,
perhaps only through a merger with a stronger financial firm. At this critical juncture, there was a misguided, but deliberate, thoroughly considered decision by a very few to martyr the dying firm as a cautionary lesson
to others of its kind.

In telling my story, there are certain Lehman executives who have been prominent in the media, and are therefore open game. But this book will not criticize by name anyone who the media has not already splayed and nailed to one of their Walls of Shame. There has already been too much pain among all former Lehman staff. I will not add to it.

It is mildly ironic, since I feel my tale is so entirely a personal one, that I have chosen to crouch behind the pseudonym "Joseph Tibman." And because I wish to remain anonymous, primarily to preserve maximum viability of working in finance, there are stories that, with some frustration, I must withhold. In any case, as I first sat down to write this account, I chose the pseudonym "Joe-the-Investment-Banker," (later morphing to Joseph Tibman) in large part because the final chapter of the Lehman story played out against the backdrop of a historic presidential campaign. This was a campaign in which the *Joe-the-Plumber* and the *Joe-the-Everyman* monikers were ceaselessly invoked by the presidential candidates and their running mates to convince the American electorate that their priority was the average American, the average Joe—the many, who, during his eight years in the White House, were strangers to George W. Bush. And while investment bankers, at least financially, are anything but average, and by no means strangers to "W," among my own much maligned kind, I easily fade into a sea of finely tailored grey pinstripe Joe-the-Investment-Bankers.

I also chose this name because it directly ties the Lehman tale to the late days of the Obama-McCain campaigns. When my firm collapsed, this presidential contest dominated American thought like no other in my memory. It was during this historic time that the LB collapse set in motion panic and dislocation in global financial markets and a gloomy global economic environment that may have decided the outcome of the election; and if not, surely the landslide margin of victory and the mandate Obama now carries in his breast pocket.

The murder of Lehman I am quite certain has hurt us all. And yet, certainly, there are many in our country and our world that are only vaguely aware, if at all, of the Lehman name, people hurting far more than most professionals on Wall Street as the financial market and economy dissolve. It is not surprising to me that many of those most responsible for the mayhem come away from it with bruised egos and bank accounts, but continue to live with their coffers massively overstuffed. Given my own losses, I do not fit into either of those extreme groups. But for me, like so many others at Lehman who are not the cartoon characters popularly represented as evildoers driven by seething insatiable greed (though Lehman had a distinct share of these objectionable types), well, it is personal.

CHAPTER 1

The Brothers:
A Family Business

*"The report of my death
was an exaggeration."*

—MARK TWAIN

I t was said of Lehman Brothers that the firm had more lives than a cat.
Indeed, how could any firm, especially a financial one, by definition a
risk-taker, endure for more than a century and a half without the ability to undergo major surgery, swapping out failing vital organs for healthier replacements? Only in this way could a finance shop keep rubber on
the road in an evolving, often unpredictable commercial biosphere. Still,
Lehman has returned from the brink more than most. Until recently, like
any cat, no matter how twisted its body and jolting its circumstances,
Lehman repeatedly somersaulted and landed on its feet. In recent times—
since the intense and enigmatic Dick Fuld took charge—we bounced back
stronger every time we were down. Our proactive management team, as if
by sheer will and a canny display of muscle, muted the Frankenstein
movie mobs, torches ablaze, that relentlessly gathered for our public evis-
ceration. Death was never an option. Our management's long infallible,
awesomely nimble maneuvering through minefields was a high testosterone source of pride for us all—in both our firm and our leaders. So great
was our confidence, that we generally saw negative market rumors that
prompted our top management to toil aggressively, 24/7, to dispel them,
as an opportunity to buy more of the invariably plunging Lehman shares.

And every time we did this, we won, adding to our paper fortunes when our stock price rebounded. Some of these gains, however, were pure dumb luck; not every Lehman rumor was pure fiction. Fuld's executive team was long adept at managing both internal and external perceptions, such as during the Mexican tesobonos[9] crisis when Lehman's health was truly threatened—a brush with death not widely known to either Lehman insiders or outsiders. Still, for Lehman veterans, these buying opportunities, and, even more so, the gains in the value of our existing Lehman holdings, often easily exceeded concurrent record years' compensation. Our stock price, again and again, hit stratospheric new highs, driven by the only occasionally interrupted momentum of our surging performance. We became, in our minds, invincible. We were Lehman. The Brothers. In hindsight, we were also like a teenager who believes he will live forever. At least until September of 2008, *i.e.,* the meltdown, when in an electronic world we could not even utter the cliché that our shares were no longer worth the paper on which they were printed.

Again, I get ahead of myself. This chapter is meant to be a brief history of Lehman; a tall order, as this saga reaches as far back as the period leading up to the Civil War. And while the state of Lehman/Barclays, my former employer, and that of today's markets, has me wholly in its thrall, to appreciate and understand what has been truly lost requires a historical sketch of the path Lehman blazed. Lehman was frequently a pioneer. And while LB quite often stumbled, and ultimately crashed and burned, the firm did much that was good—not only for the bank accounts of its tabloid-defamed rainmakers as well as its clerks (who I pray sold lots of their shares a couple of years ago), but for the development of business and commerce in our country. Of this, I am proud.

Lehman's long history can be divided into two distinct periods: Acts I and II, if you will. Act I began with the formation of the first Lehman enterprise in the mid-nineteenth century and endured for more than a hundred years until the death of Robert "Bobbie" Lehman in 1969. Throughout this period, Lehman's chief executive was always a Lehman family member. In fact, it was not until Bobbie's tenure that non-family

---

9. Detailed later.

members rose to the status of partner in large numbers. Bobbie reigned by birthright, like an epic monarch, for 44 years. Upon his death in 1969, the year that Dick Fuld joined Lehman as an intern, Act II began, with the Lehman family fading from the scene. Bobbie Lehman's death precipitated a corporate identity crisis. The firm, now led by commoners, faltered but reinvented itself. At other times, the firm rebounded from defeat, and excelled beyond all expectations.

For the many years that Lehman was a family business, there was continuity that can only exist when such an enterprise's leadership is passed from one generation to another, and fortuitously for Lehman, these leaders were more than up to the job. Of course, this sort of dynasty is an anachronism in the modern world of large corporations, high tech financings, and raucous, no-holds-barred, kick'em-in-the-balls competition. What emerged from the Lehman of Act I was a Lehman that continued to change tactics to adapt and to cope, but now a firm whose altered stripes often led to undesired consequences.

* * *

In 1844, Henry Lehman, a German Jew, emigrated from a town in Bavaria to Montgomery, Alabama where there was a small Jewish enclave. The timing of his arrival was both auspicious and unfortunate. The good news was that he preceded the great wave of immigrants whose numbers swelled a few decades later, and so had opportunities that may have later been absent. For his first several years in the Antebellum South, Henry worked as a peddler. By 1847, he had saved enough money to open a modest business selling dry goods and other wares to the surrounding community of cotton farmers. He prospered sufficiently enough that letters to his family across the Atlantic enticed his brothers Emanuel and Mayer to join him. In 1850, the dry goods business adopted the name Lehman Brothers. Still just a local business, it grew. But as tensions between the North and South grew, and the local economy weakened, Emanuel and Mayer began to accept cotton, in effect, "barter," as payment for their wares. Unfortunately, Henry, who had first planted the Lehman family flag in America, died in 1855 from yellow fever. He was thirty-three. But his two surviving brothers soldiered on, and with substantial bartered cotton, evolved to

become a full-fledged commodities broker, buying and selling. They surely possessed no electronic screens, but soon enough the commodities trading business grew so large that in 1858 they established an office in New
York.

As mentioned above, Henry's timing in establishing the Lehman base
in America had many downsides. Having died from yellow fever, he was
in the wrong place at the wrong time. And just as his two surviving brothers' commercial empire was moving rapidly up a moneyed trajectory, the
Civil War erupted. From a purely commercial perspective, this was a difficult time to be a cotton broker; the business suffered. Still, as would be
the case for nearly another century and a half, Lehman Brothers was
resourceful, and to survive, merged with another, more resilient cotton trader.

In 1867, venturing into capital markets[10] and municipal finance, areas
where the firm carrying their name would later consistently distinguish
itself, the Lehmans lent money to the post-bellum State of Alabama, a
state that like others in the defeated, ravaged South, was in exceptionally
dire need. In return, Alabama made Lehman Brothers the state's fiscal
agent. And Lehman sold Alabama state bonds, the proceeds of which were
necessary for Alabama to participate in reconstruction. A devastated
Alabama's risk could not have been an easy sale to bond investors in the
aftermath of the Civil War, but team Lehman, like today's investment
bankers, seeing a profit opportunity in the Southern states,   quickly
pounced. And the value of the two Lehman brothers' Alabama investments and assets ballooned.

* * *

In 1870, the two Lehman brothers revived the firm, again in New York,
and became pivotal players in the establishment of the New York Cotton
Exchange, the nation's first commodities futures trading organization.
Ever ambitious and creative, Emanuel and Mayer diversified into other
commodities, and in the 1880's were instrumental in the establishment of
more exchanges, including those for coffee and petroleum. They began
selling and trading securities and in 1887 joined the New York Stock

---

10. Markets where long-term funds, both debt and equity, are raised to finance companies, and where these financing instruments subsequently trade

Henry Lehman

John M. Hancock; Robert Lehman July 1, 1945

Lehman Brothers partners John M. Hancock (L) and Robert Lehman sitting in front of clock. (Photo by Herbert Gehr/Time Life Pictures/Getty Images)

In the Lehman Brothers "partner's room," seated in the foreground is Paul Manheim talking with Philip Isles. A few paces to the rear Robert Lehman (L) is chatting with Paul Mazur (C) and Monroe Gutman. January 1, 1957.

(Time Life Pictures/Getty Images)

Exchange (NYSE). Before long, they ceased to be a pure commodities player, dipping a toe into varied financial dealings. In 1889, Lehman Brothers engaged in its first underwriting, assisting the International Steam Pump Company in issuance of common[11] and preferred shares.[12] LB also became active in financial advisory.

All this was a warm-up for the early twentieth century, when in 1901, Phillip Lehman, Emanuel's son, became president of Lehman Brothers and decisively transformed the family business from a commodities player, with a broad range of other far lesser interests, into a full-blown underwriter. In turn of the century American society, unsurprisingly, the Jewish Lehmans could not gain access to the club of Gentile financiers, such as J.P. Morgan. However, other Jewish financial houses were also on the rise and Phillip forged an alliance with Goldman Sachs (ironically the firm whose former chief, many decades later, as Bush's U.S. Treasury Secretary, let Lehman die). Beginning in 1906 and continuing for about twenty years, LB and Goldman underwrote more than one hundred new securities issues. Indeed, the House of Lehman knew how to grow. Together with Goldman, the firm saw opportunity in burgeoning American consumerism, and so focused much of their joint-underwriting on rapidly expanding retail chains, such as Macys, Gimbels, Sears and Woolworth.

Robert "Bobbie" Lehman, a third-generation Lehman chief, and Phillip's son, took the reins in 1925, the year after the firm promoted a non-family member to the partner level for the first time. He would be the last Lehman family member to run the company. At this time, Bobbie was in his mid-thirties and led for a remarkable forty-four years, until his death in 1969. (By comparison, when Dick Fuld was the longest serving CEO at a bulge bracket Wall Street firm in September 2008, his stewardship spanned a comparatively truncated fourteen years.) Bobbie's forty-

---

11. Shares representing ownership in a company.

12. Technically represent partial ownership in a company, but typically lack the voting rights of common shares and trade based more on their fixed return than on a company's performance. Preferred shares rank ahead of common in liquidation and the fixed dividend normally represents a higher return than common dividends, but preferred shares do not possess the same upside in their trading price as do common shares.

four years were, by all accounts, a dictatorial, often harsh reign, but also a time when Lehman rarely faltered.

During Bobbie's years, non-Lehman family members increasingly populated positions that had previously been the family's exclusive domain, with more of the best and the brightest eventually elevated to the rank of partner. At the same time, and to an extent, incongruously, he fostered an intensely competitive internal environment, generating heretofore unparalleled, toxic infighting. Bobbie, however, made this work. As divine absolute ruler, when he chose to intercede his directive was always the very last word.

Early in Bobbie's run, as for his father, growth of consumption and production was front and center in his strategic brain. So Bobbie's Lehman placed a bet that the firm would be rewarded by focusing its resources on new or rapidly evolving sectors, including, for example, the entertainment industry. In 1927, Lehman advised on the merger of the Orpheum and Keith-Albee theatres, creating the country's largest vaudeville circuit. In the 1930's, Lehman had a role in financings for several of the major studios, underwriting capital that enabled their rapid expansion during that decade and later. It also backed the funding of RCA and played a role in the emergent auto industry. Many traditional, more conservative Wall Street Houses, such as J.P. Morgan, balked at financing companies in emerging industries, but Lehman's well-calculated success in this arena yielded enviable returns, and rather quickly placed it among the elite of Wall Street.

During the late 1920's and 1930's, with the country devastated by the Great Depression, companies lacked the easy access to capital markets that had existed until the stock market crash. Resourceful and creative, Lehman was among the first firms to develop private placements,[13] today a common source of funds. In the 1930's, Lehman typically arranged these financings for blue chip companies that were starved for capital. A key fea-

---

13. The private sale of a security directly to an institutional investor. Such investments are not registered with the Securities and Exchange Commission (SEC), the government entity charged with regulating securities markets, and are not traded, but are held to maturity by institutional investors. Because the securities are not registered, the documentation governing them is not publicly filed.

ture, providing lenders with necessary comfort in an extremely harsh and uncertain economic environment, was the inclusion of terms that protected them against loss.

It is normal practice, today, that large bank loans to non-investment grade[14] companies include these protections, commonly referred to as covenants. Of course, since the subprime market meltdown began to impact broader capital markets in 2007, covenant requirements, that had become quite lax, did an about-face and are now far more restrictive for any borrowers able to tap wary loan markets. Following Lehman's failure, borrowing for non-investment grade companies, already almost dead, fully shut down. While investment grade[15] borrowers were, in most cases, still able to borrow, whether in bond or loan capital markets, as of this writing, interest rates for these companies are still at higher levels than the rates available before the current crisis.

Also during the Depression, Lehman Brothers embraced venture capital.[16] By connecting investors with entrepreneurs, Lehman was able to invent another source of revenue. On the whole, Lehman's resourcefulness during this challenging economic period enabled the family business to generate sufficient revenues for The Brothers to survive at a time when many other financial enterprises failed.

The Lehman family probably had money enough by then to disband the business and cut coupons on Easy Street, USA, for generations. Instead, as driven capitalists, they maintained the ability to enrich themselves further, provided continued employment for many earning a spectrum of

---

14. A company rated lower than Baa3/BBB- by Moody's and S&P, indicating that it does not possess the financial flexibility of the most sound companies. This is, however, a broad category, including both companies that are unlikely to default on their obligations for the foreseeable future, as well as companies that are on the verge of bankruptcy.

15. A company rated at least Baa3/BBB- by Moody's and S&P, indicating that it is very sound financially, with substantial flexibility to weather difficult operating environments. All blue chip companies are investment grade, though not all investment grade companies possess characteristics strong enough to place them among blue chips, the very strongest of companies.

16. Generally, seed funding for new start-up companies or very small businesses with high growth potential.

wages, and kept afloat or breathed life into enterprises that would have otherwise died or scraped by, diminished.

Clearly, there is a fundamentally different dynamic between executives who by chance find themselves on the same team and executives who break bread together at family gatherings. But Bobbie, by fostering rivalry, even as a tactic to propel productivity among his army of bankers, undoubtedly laid the groundwork for internal fracture that would later bedevil Lehman Brothers and threaten its survival, as there was not until the reign of Dick Fuld, an equivalent iron-fisted boss who could assert control as had Bobbie.

Though the Depression had been a challenge for all financial firms, the first half of the twentieth century was a period when the U.S. economy evolved, with a number of industries gaining footing and then expanding exponentially. Oil exploration, for example, skyrocketed. Lehman, always keenly building business ties with growth industries, played a major role in funding this. Even today, the Lehman legacy natural resources and energy business, under the Barclays Capital banner, has maintained a best-in-class position among its competitors, with bankers from this practice frequent recipients of the Investment Banking Division's (IBD's) "Big Deal" awards.[17] In fact, Skip McGee, head of Investment Banking under both Lehman and Barclays, began his climb as a rainmaker in this business.

Lehman also carved out a financing role in the rapidly expanding electronics and computer industries during the 1950's. But of greater significance, at least for the firm, was Lehman Brothers' substantial expansion of its capital markets trading capabilities during the 1960's. Lehman became a leader in the commercial paper[18] market, a business that grew substantially at the expense of the commercial banks, as the largest companies

---

17. Lucite award introduced by Lehman IBD head, Skip McGee, distributed to all deal team members in recognition of work on transactions that generate high fees. More on this later.

18. An unsecured obligation (backed not by collateral but only by the integrity of the borrower; opposite of secured) issued by a corporation or bank to finance its short-term credit needs, such as accounts receivable (money owed to a company by its customers) and inventory.

eventually all found this short-term capital markets funding instrument more efficient than the traditional revolving credits long utilized to satisfy working capital[19] funding requirements.

During the 1960's, fundamentally altering Lehman for its remaining years, the firm became a powerful force in both sales and trading of corporate and government bonds, and was appointed an official dealer of U.S. Treasuries.[20] In the best and worst of times that lay ahead, when some Lehman businesses deteriorated and recovered, leadership in debt capital markets was a constant.

This new sales and trading business at Lehman quickly grew, accounting for an increasing portion of the total Lehman revenue pie. While this surge was certainly good news for Bobbie and all the firm's partners, increasing all their wealth, two distinct and largely incompatible cultures developed. The bankers were ensconced in wood-paneled digs, with elegant dining facilities and a clubby, posh old-world environment at One William Street. The traders and salesmen were initially situated in an

---

19. In financial terminology, current (short-term, *i.e.*, less than one year) assets less current liabilities. Put more plainly, it's the excess of items like cash, inventory, and receivables from customers (money owed to a company for goods and services it has provided) over short term obligations, such as trade payables (money owed to other companies, such as an auto manufacturer's parts suppliers), and short-term debt (borrowed money due within one year). During the course of a year, or at different points in an economic cycle, Company X's inventories of goods may rise or its receivables increase. Company X only spends to build inventory, and when sales of this inventory spike and are transformed into receivables, cash payment has still not been received. If Company X is low on cash, it must borrow to finance the inventory and receivables. As the cash comes in, if inventories or receivables subside, the proceeds will typically be used to repay the borrowings that financed the build-up.

20. Debt obligations of the U.S. government, such as Treasury bonds (long-term) and Treasury bills (short-term). These are considered the most low-risk securities traded in U.S. capital markets, and their pricing, *i.e.*, the interest rate an investor yields on these at any given point in time, is often used as a benchmark for pricing of other debt securities. These other debt securities always pay interest at a spread above treasuries, since any company's obligations are considered at least somewhat riskier than Treasuries. Even the most creditworthy, highest rated (Aaa/AAA from Moody's and S&P) companies pay a narrow spread over treasuries. In today's rocky markets, investors have fled from corporate bonds to Treasuries, pushing up spreads of even the most creditworthy corporate obligations to levels unseen during my decades in finance.

entirely separate, far less extravagant building: from their point of view, like serfs. The investment bankers wore finely tailored suits, crisp white shirts, cufflinks and elegantly knotted ties. The traders' ties were often loose at the neck and their sleeves rolled up to their elbows. The bankers were Ivy League alumni; the traders often had less prestigious diplomas. Dick Fuld and Joe Gregory,[21] both Lehman traders during the next decade, under the infamous Lew Glucksman,[22] graduated, respectively, from the University of Colorado and Hofstra University on Long Island.

Over time, the divide led to an increasingly bitter rivalry between the bankers and the traders. Many of the traders considered the bankers stuffy and pretentious, while many of the bankers considered the traders uncouth. Even today, across Wall Street, this stereotype, to at least some extent, lingers.

At Lehman in the 1960's, as the profits from trading began to account for a heftier portion of the total earnings pie, many traders grew resentful of their plainly inferior status. Though by now, the rank of partner was filled with non-family members, judged solely on their earnings contribution, traders were severely under-represented, while the bankers increasingly profited from the success of sales and trading. In the culture of rivalry that Bobbie cultivated, there was now poisonous division, not only within Investment Banking, but also between the bankers and the traders. Lew Glucksman, a leading trader, who over time played a major role at Lehman, is quoted as saying, "Bobbie seemed to be the mildest of men but he was like a Mafia don who could be nice because he could send people out to do his dirty work. Bobbie's speciality was keeping people at each other's throats."[i] Still, this was manageable, and Lehman remained a Wall Street leader, while Bobbie remained firmly in charge and unchallenged.

Then, in 1969, Bobbie died, leaving behind an heirless financial empire. The dynasty was finished, not an uncommon development among privately held firms. But no one within LB possessed sufficient stature and concentration of power to unify the firm, to fill the larger-than-life void that had suddenly materialized. On the contrary, what Bobbie Lehman left

---

21. Lehman's former number two and President, under CEO Fuld.

22. Glucksman died in 2006, age 80.

behind was a divided firm filled with festering resentments and vicious political infighting, but no referee. The man with the whistle had exited the building.

Also in 1969, Dick Fuld, with no particular fanfare, started at Lehman as a college intern from the University of Colorado, trading commercial paper. Years later, Fuld would say of Bobbie Lehman, "He got people to work hard, but it took all the glue out of the partnership."[ii]

And so, with the firm in an uncertain and fractured state, the curtain fell on Act I of the Lehman Brothers saga.

* * *

As Act II of the Lehman drama got under way in 1969, the firm was more a war zone than a business poised for a bountiful future. To boot, it was operating in a soft economy. A power struggle ensued. Once it played out, Frederick Ehrman, who joined Lehman in 1929, ascended to the top spot, chairman of the executive committee. Soon thereafter, a number of partners left, taking with them a portion of their share of the firm's capital. (Partners traditionally left firms taking all of their share of equity capital paid in cash, but Bobbie Lehman had changed this policy some years earlier, probably because the Lehman family's position in the firm had waned. Bobbie's revised rules allowed partner withdrawls only over time.)

By the late 1960's and early 1970's, capital had become increasingly critical to an investment banks' success. Lehman's expertise in advisory activities did not require capital, although underwritings did, while new issues of securities were growing increasingly large. Partnerships were starting to become anachronisms, as sizable permanent capital increasingly improved a firm's competitive position. On the other hand, firms like Lehman, that built large sales forces, had the upper hand in distributing underwritten securities. Still, Lehman's performance during Ehrman's time deteriorated, and in the early 1970's, the firm was even censured for substandard back office practices. LB's performance continued to weaken, registering operating losses, until finally, in 1973 Ehrman was ousted.

Pete Peterson replaced Ehrman. Peterson's biography reads like a tale of the great American dream realized. He was raised by Greek immigrants. His father was a dishwasher. At age 34, Peterson became CEO of Bell &

Howell, a large supplier of media products. He served in the Nixon administration, most notably as Secretary of Commerce. After Nixon's resignation, Ehrman convinced Peterson to take a senior position at Lehman Brothers. With the expulsion of Ehrman, Peterson ascended to the top Lehman spot after a couple of months. The tenor of this change in leadership further marked the extent to which Lehman Brothers had ended any direct association with the Lehman family. It was also apparent that the long period on old Wall Street when firms were either Jewish or Gentile was a phenomenon of the past.

The former Commerce Secretary's portfolio as Lehman chief was straightforward, though no easy task: to rescue LB from its deep, potentially fatal malaise. Over a relatively short period, albeit one where other firms were at times under pressure due to a challenging operating environment, LB, for the first time, became an industry laggard. Fortunately, for Lehman, Peterson, during his tenure which ran from 1973 to 1984, successfully led the firm out of its doldrums. By 1975, Lehman was again profitable, and ultimately racked up five consecutive years of record results. Pete Peterson was truly well-connected, given the positions he had held before joining Lehman, and compiled a record as a highly effective marketer of the firm's services. Indeed, he diligently prepared himself for client meetings and colleagues widely admired his ability to close deals.

At the same time, many inside the firm perceived him as an elitist, a quality that surely repelled many of the traders. Of course, *elitism* is certainly not a rare quality in the world of investment banking, but at Lehman, even haughty bankers found Peterson distant and imperious. Moreover, while the deal-making of investment bankers is generally a protracted and grinding process, bursting with verbose exchanges between the players, (the polar opposite of the moment-to-moment transactional character of sales and trading), when Peterson began to speak, many partners and their minions, on both sides of LB, groaned and braced themselves for a protracted, erudite speech.

In light of Lehman's resurrection and with it the return of fat year-end bonuses, Peterson's off-putting personality was necessarily tolerable. According to some old-timers, they found Peterson insufferable, but they were all getting richer, and so were pleased enough to have him in charge.

Still, beneath the surface, the insidious, tenacious rivalry and ill will between the investment bankers and traders intensified. In 1980, with Sales & Trading and Investment Banking still occupying separate buildings, Peterson tried to address the schism by moving the entire firm to 55 Water Street. It was an honest effort to pull the firm together, but more than geography fueled the acrimonious divide, and so predictably enough, the move to one building did little to quell the resentments between the firm's two halves. At least some of the bankers, due to the internal political threat posed by the bulging profitability of sales and trading, were cheerleaders for Peterson, fully supporting his tight grip on Lehman's reins. He was a deliberate, deep-voiced, trim, authoritative figure. Despite his aloofness, self-absorption, and pathological name-dropping, the bankers at least found him presentable and credentialed, in marked contrast to their view of most traders and salesmen. Of course, these precise Peterson characteristics repelled the traders. How could they not? He embodied, in its purest form, everything, and then some, that they detested about investment bankers. Plus, while as noted, the firm's investment banking business had recovered and grown healthy, the earnings of the sales and trading side of Lehman by now had begun to boldly roar; so much so, that it would not be long before the latter's profits eclipsed Investment Banking's as the primary earnings driver.

Lewis Glucksman joined Lehman in 1963, six years before Bobbie Lehman's death, and rapidly rose through the ranks of sales and trading to become its head. In 1976, the firm promoted him to chief operating officer, in part to heal the rift between the firm's two halves, but more because this recognition became unavoidable if there were to be any hope of holding the firm together.

Like his traders and salesmen, Glucksman could not have been more different from Peterson and the social elite of investment banking. Peterson was a man ensconced in New York society while Glucksman never strayed very far from his second-generation Hungarian Jewish roots. He was a short, scrappy, heavyset proletarian workaholic who arrived before six most mornings. He normally eschewed the elegant partners' dining room for lunch at his desk. When not eating, he habitually clenched a chubby cigar between his teeth. From an investment banker's perspective, the man was a barbarian. Even to those around him, particularly those who worked for him, he could be gruff and at times explosive. On one occasion, on a tirade, Glucksman removed the shirt that covered his expansive torso, threw a breakfast plate at the wall and a phone at a colleague. Yet this was only one side of him. Unlike Peterson, he demonstrated, in both his actions and words, genuine care for all of his people, engendering stalwart loyalty.

Despite his rapid success at Lehman, Glucksman, like most of the traders who eventually all reported to him, often felt like an outsider. He considered the late Bobbie Lehman and other Lehman family members as climbers, chameleons, or both: German Jews who acted like old money WASPs. In fact, he felt that the bigotry of even German Jews had long kept Jews with an Eastern European heritage from prominent positions on Wall Street.

In 1973, when Glucksman, based on his trader's instinct as to the direction of interest rates, placed a disastrous bet to hold commercial paper rather than sell it, Lehman lost big. Many pressed for Glucksman's abrupt dismissal. Peterson backed him, seeming to figure that the man who had helped build Lehman's fixed income franchise into a powerhouse was the same man who could mend its fixed income misfortunes. He probably also feared that firing Glucksman could well spark the departure of the lucrative sales and trading franchise. Whatever Peterson's precise reasons, his retention of Glucksman was surely pure business and a decision he considered a political necessity. There was no love lost between Peterson and Glucksman, and Peterson was not adverse to cutting headcount when necessary. In fact, reducing staff numbers was one of his early tactics to turn Lehman around after he took over as CEO.

In 1974/75, as Lehman was recovering, it acquired Abraham and Company, and in 1977, acquired the prestigious, long-respected Kuhn Loeb when that firm was on the ropes, struggling to survive on its own.

In 1982, Lehman led the pack in Wall Street merger and acquisition assignments. Despite this, it was in 1983, with Dick Fuld now heading all of sales and trading at Lehman, that IBD's[23] stellar performance

---

23. IBD is the Investment Banking Division.

accounted for less than half of Lehman's profits. Investment bankers worried about Fuld's propulsive rise. Seemingly overnight, a man many considered an inarticulate barbarian now ran businesses that accounted for the majority of Lehman's profits. Moreover, without compunction, he openly and heatedly complained about investment bankers. At operating committee meetings, Fuld, like a man afflicted with Tourette syndrome, was known to rave about "those fucking investment bankers"[iii] who pocketed most of the firm's wealth, though the traders generated the majority of it.

Fuld's resentment of bankers may have been noisier than others', but he was following the lead of Glucksman, the man who did more than anyone to develop the sales and trading gold mine. Glucksman plainly bristled that Peterson seemed to get all the kudos. With Fuld lip-syncing his sentiment, Glucksman agitated for redistribution of the annual bonus pool to those generating the lion's share of the profits. And so it became entirely obvious to Peterson that not only could he never fire Glucksman, but, in fact, would now have to share leadership more equally. Given Peterson's pride, self-importance and personal dislike for Glucksman, he probably held off on addressing this imperative for as long as he could, but now conceded that a more meaningful gesture than any to date was unavoidable. So Peterson crossed the Rubicon, shattering any vestige of the Lehman family's absent genteel grip, and made Glucksman his Co-CEO. Peterson probably told himself this was the most magnanimous of gestures.

Once Peterson had elevated Glucksman, he took a delusional, cheeky pride in what he believed was a transformation of Glucksman into a more couth figure. Glucksman had lost a whopping seventy pounds. He began to dress more like an investment banker. Peterson thought or hoped that he had tamed the rotund shrew. In truth, the Glucksman for whom he had long harbored so great a distaste, a man Peterson saw as a creature with attributes somewhere between his own cultured self and Bigfoot, was fundamentally unchanged. The reality was that Glucksman could not be subtly castrated and reinvented as a Peterson knockoff. There was simply no way he would, or even could, be transformed into a member of Investment Banking's rarified, clubby society world. Glucksman was not a man willing to act the part of someone he was not.

More to the point, all that mattered to Glucksman was that he finally was receiving a meaningful portion of the personal recognition he considered long overdue.

Once promoted to Co-CEO, Glucksman immediately began to make unilateral decisions and, rather than act in a manner Peterson considered appropriate to Glucksman's elevated position, he grew even brusquer. The illusory bloom was off the rose. And with their man now equal to Peterson, traders, such as Dick Fuld, became bolder. Accordingly, the investment bankers' worries intensified. Glucksman was rocking their staid, cultured world.

Then the unthinkable happened. Only weeks after Peterson named Lew Glucksman Co-CEO, the new co-top gun bluntly told Peterson he was no longer satisfied to share leadership. He wanted Peterson to leave the firm under Glucksman's sole control. This coarse pronouncement startled Peterson; a five-hour meeting ensued without resolution. On the surface, Glucksman's audacity might seem presumptuous and brazen, but there was more behind his demand than a one-dimensional desire for absolute power.

Most of all, Glucksman was extremely concerned that Peterson planned to sell the firm out of self-interested greed. Indeed, Peterson's wife later said that it was her husband's secret desire to sell the firm before he was 60 (three years hence) so that the couple would then be free of any worries about money. A sale of the firm was out of the question for Glucksman. Like Dick Fuld years later, he would do whatever it took to prevent the loss of Lehman's independence. From Glucksman's standpoint, given Peterson's background, the latter man would have numerous options if he left Lehman. Conversely, for Glucksman, Lehman was his life. More precisely, an *independent* Lehman was his life, an obsession foreshadowing that of his star protégé, Dick Fuld.

In any case, Glucksman believed his abrupt move to rid Lehman of Peterson was likely to succeed. Otherwise, he might not have been so bold in his approach. He sensed the genteel Peterson was not a man with an appetite for a street fight, and lacked endurance if drawn into one. Moreover, Glucksman was a man on a roll. Peterson, after nominally resisting, capitulated and agreed to leave, tucking his golden parachute under his arm. Notably, Glucksman and Peterson struck all the arrangements for Peterson's departure without consulting the firm's partners, who certainly had both a business and personal financial stake in the terms under which Lehman cut Peterson loose. In fact, the partners first heard of this extraordinary change in leadership only after it was approved by a submissive board. Peterson announced his retirement in an unexpected, impromptu partner meeting in Lehman's auditorium that stunned many present. Once Peterson completed his announcement, Glucksman, landing one last kick to Peterson's ribs, said, "Would you now leave and let me be with my partners?"[iv]

Many in sales and trading were euphoric that Glucksman was taking over, certainly believing that they would finally be treated with the respect they believed their revenue contribution warranted. Dick Fuld, grossly understating his true feelings about Peterson's departure said, "It didn't bother me."[v] How could it? His mentor was now the sole chief of the overall firm. Even some of the bankers were pleased to see Peterson leave, as they believed that despite the firm's turnaround, his major failing was his inability to create a true sense of teamwork at the firm. This teamwork, the creation of a unified firm, was something that Dick Fuld, in his time, would recognize as imperative and pull off far more successfully.

For his part, Peterson went on to co-found the Blackstone Group, one of the country's most successful private equity firms.

Unfortunately for Lehman Brothers Kuhn Loeb, further record earnings did not materialize after Glucksman's triumphant coup. While, as noted above, some bankers were glad to see Peterson out of the picture, many were not. Glucksman, as the investment bankers had feared, distributed larger average bonuses to traders than to investment bankers, causing numerous discouraged banker defections to other firms. The internal environment remained politically charged—if anything more so than in the recent past—ruining any chance for the long-absent teamwork the firm desperately needed to create if it was to succeed under its new sole leader. And so, Lehman became increasingly dysfunctional.

As early as 1983, the same year that Glucksman took full control, there was already internal pressure to consider a sale of the firm. In this sulfurous environment, Glucksman tapped Fuld to make a Board presentation at a meeting on Lehman Kuhn Loeb's capital position. When asked precisely how sales and trading had generated its strong revenues over the previous five years, as well as plans for the next five, Fuld's numbing response was, "I don't know how I made it over the last five years. We've hired some people . . . to study how we're going to do it over the next several years."[vi] Fuld added that the study would extend over the next two years.

Many were floored by Fuld's, "the Gorilla's"[24] vacant response. Could this man who oversaw[vii] operations accounting for a solid majority of the firm's profits be as empty-headed as he appeared to be during this meeting? Glucksman, predictably, later defended his lieutenant, Fuld, with an explanation in which there was much truth: "Dick had a problem communicating with other members of the Board. Dick tends to be fast-thinking and somewhat impatient. He talks a lot in shorthand. He did not communicate well what he did. Very few Board members could understand Dick when he was talking."[viii] For many of these Board members, the enigma was that numbers do not lie, and those posted by Fuld proved him a superb trader. Nonetheless, they increasingly wondered whether he was out of his management depth and might, at any time, crash and burn.

By 1984, the year following Glucksman's victory, the firm was in precipitous decline. There was feverish talk that LB had racked up substantial paper trading losses. (Because The Brothers was a partnership, such information was not a matter of public record.) In fact, rumors raged that Fuld was taking on massive, wholly imprudent risk positions to generate a massive trading gain. This he hoped would boost the firm's profits and capital base sufficiently enough to solidify Glucksman's hold on the firm. (This again foreshadows events of 2008, when, under Fuld, Lehman placed huge bets on commercial real estate that would ultimately kill The Brothers.) But between October 1983 and March 1984, the firm took trading losses of $30 million, dwarfing the $8 million of trading losses that had nearly cost Glucksman his job in 1973. Fuld, at the time, disputed the figure, again foreshadowing discrepancies over numbers in Lehman's late days, noting that actual 1983-1984 losses amounted to a far lower $5 to

---

24. Investment bankers' nickname for Fuld, derived from what they regarded as the simian personality of a man who spoke in grunts.

$10 million. Neither calculation was absolute fiction. Fuld's sum counted only the actual trading losses themselves, excluding both the trading operations overhead expenses as well as diminished revenues in certain sales and trading areas—all included in the higher loss figure. In the end, the calculation one used was unimportant. The bottom line was that net profits suffered a major reversal. Unsurprisingly, Fuld denied that he had taken on massive risk to strengthen Glucksman, commenting, "I take it as a personal failure to lose money."[ix]

This much is undisputed: traders took large positions, betting interest rates would fall. Instead, they rose, and the positions were held far too long, inflating the ultimate size of the accumulated loss. This supports the contention that Fuld was betting the bank to strengthen Glucksman. Following his true trader's instinct, Fuld would have known when it was time to cut losses and cash out. Instead, positions were held as losses mounted, with Fuld playing a zero-sum game. Further clouding Fuld's credibility, he claimed all securities were marked to market daily,[25] while the firm's then-CFO flatly contradicted him.

Glucksman came under additional pressure to sell the firm, as the partners learned that ConAgra might be interested in buying it for $600 million, which would permanently enrich each of them. The Board appointed a committee to explore "capital alternatives."[x] Unsurprisingly, there was a basic disconnect. While Glucksman and Fuld viewed the committee's mission as a quest for a plain vanilla capital infusion, a majority of the Board viewed the committee's task as a search for a buyer. Fuld, on the one hand commented that he "was not thinking along the lines of a partner or a merger,"[xi] while another Board member conversely said "people wanted to get their money out."[xii] His position fundamentally weakened, the Board eventually forced Glucksman's hand, voting for a sale of the firm. By then, as Lehman's fortunes continued to sink, the firm was worth less than what ConAgra had offered, and Lehman came to terms in a fire sale to American Express, for a far lower $380 million. Dick Fuld, despite Lehman's weak position, believed the sale was a mistake.

Indeed, years later, Dick Fuld eerily retraced the footsteps of his mentor.

---

25. A security is initially booked at its cost. If a security is marked to market daily, its value is adjusted in a firm's books according to fluctuations in its daily value.

On many occasions, Fuld, both publicly and privately, made clear his intention that Lehman remain independent. Having lived with both an independent Lehman and one owned by American Express, his clear preference was for the former. In fact, despite Lehman's absence of options, Fuld felt betrayed when The Brothers was sold to American Express; particularly as this occurred under Glucksman's leadership and with Glucksman voting, albeit reluctantly, in favor of the sale. Fuld on the other hand was in the small minority on the Board that voted against the sale, despite Lehman's effective lack of options. This vote foreshadowed Fuld's reluctance to sell when he became CEO, a misstep with Biblical consequences.

During Lehman's last months, weeks and days, Fuld stubbornly refused to consider a sale of the firm while he was in a position to do so at a decent valuation. He only considered this when it was too late to strike a deal with any semblance of favorable terms, if a deal could even by then have been struck at all. Fuld's reluctance to sell would play out like a Greek tragedy, toppling both the man and his firm. In the early period of Fuld's long career, when he actively managed traders, one said that "he thought he could intimidate you out of losing money."[xiii] This persistent belief in the power of his unbendable will was indeed Fuld's tragic flaw.

Following the 1984 sale, Peterson walked away with $23 million, Glucksman with $15.6 million. Fuld received $7.6 million (no petty sum, but an amount dwarfed by the wealth he was to accumulate years later). Other partners also received sizeable payouts, but far less than what would have been attainable had the firm been sold earlier. Of course, they walked away with a great deal more than most Lehman rank-and-file senior bankers following the firm's 2008 bankruptcy filing. Had Glucksman sold earlier, he would have received a better price. Still, unlike Fuld in 2008, he did sell before the firm's position and financial standing was so weak that there was no value available to those who had dedicated their careers to Lehman, to the shareholders who had believed in the firm and its management.

American Express, during the 1980's, launched a strategy of becoming a financial supermarket. At first blush, after extensive consideration by its board and its management, this strategy, at the time, seemed to make great sense. "Cross-selling" has long been a mantra of the corporate world and one of many bases for acquisition of one company by another. From Amex's perspective, buying Shearson, the second largest retail brokerage seemed a natural adjunct to its credit card business, as it would enable the combined company to function as a one-stop shop for credit cards as well as a broader range of personal financial services. Certainly, Shearson's vast retail office network would augment Amex's and thereby improve distribution of the two firms' products. Lehman Kuhn Loeb, in turn, was a natural fit once Amex acquired Shearson, as the Shearson network would provide a vastly expanded, huge conduit for distributing the securities that Lehman underwrote and traded. In particular, the combination with Shearson would augment Lehman's position in underwriting those securities that appealed most to retail investors. Merrill Lynch had been successfully executing just this strategy for some time. Amex believed a combined Shearson and Lehman would, at the throw of a switch, present a formidable competitor for Merrill, which at the time, faced no similarly positioned rival. The subsequent acquisition of Hutton would only add to the scale, breadth and name recognition of the powerful new combination of companies. When Shearson American Express absorbed Lehman Kuhn Loeb, Dick Fuld stayed on as a vice-chairman and board member of the merged broker-dealer, and also filled the number two slot of the merged company's trading operations. Though now number two in trading, Fuld remained influential. Indeed, Peter Cohen, Shearson's young CEO (and a future central character in *Barbarians at the Gate*), had breakfast with Fuld, once the terms of the sale were set, to discuss how they would manage the two firms' combined trading operations.

As American Express would learn over a painful decade, plans run amok. For starters, Amex's management soon realized they had no stomach for the cyclicality that typifies the brokerage business, as compared to their still cyclical, but more stable, credit card mainstay. Given the wild swings and successive reversals of fortune that were intrinsic to every broker-dealers' trading activities, it is safe to assume that American Express experienced something close to motion sickness, or worse, in that Lehman remained an underperformer. Credit card bad debt is largely predictable in the context of a particular economic environment. But the volatility of a moment-to-moment, deal-to-deal, capital markets operation was the Wild West for businessmen with constitutions better acquainted to the less jolting, milder swings of Gold Cards and travel-related services.

Exacerbating the unavoidable visceral discomfort for Amex's management was the naked fact that the performance of the multiple units it pasted together was abysmal by all broker-dealer measures. By 1989, the junk bond market was in deep trouble. Ugly problems at Hutton—Amex's worst mistake in the Shearson Lehman Hutton amalgamation—had shown their true faces. The Lehman investment bank, under youthful CEO Peter Cohen, had suffered a humiliating, reputation-bruising defeat in its RJR Nabisco leveraged buyout[26] (LBO) adventure, one in which it ultimately failed to secure any role. If this was not enough, the War of the Roses between the investment bankers and the traders raged on, and then, in a climax of underperformance, for the first quarter of 1990 the brokerage business suffered the then-largest quarterly loss in Wall Street history. (That loss has since been surpassed by many, including Lehman itself in two of the three quarters it reported in 2008.) Part of this loss was the result of severance packages for the large number of broker-dealer employees Amex had made redundant, but even so, the track record this business compiled was anything but encouraging. Just to keep the limping patient alive, American Express had to prop it up with substantial cash infusions. As for the bottom line in the Lehman portion of the business, specific numbers were not publicly broken out from those for the overall, combined company, but clearly, this arm of the American Express financial supermarket was underperforming broker-dealer peers. Talk of divestment and further lay-offs was by then constantly circulating. This caused many of the best investment bankers and traders to leap to more stable, better performing firms.

In 1993, Harvey Golub became American Express CEO. For him it was clear that Amex would have to rid itself of the financial firms that were

---

26. Acquisition of a company using a high level of debt to finance the takeover.

wreaking havoc on its performance. He sold the Shearson arm of the business to Primerica, Hutton had ceased to exist, and Dick Fuld and J. Tomilson Hill stayed on as co-presidents of the remaining Lehman portion of the Amex brokerage business, with American Express planning to sell or spin this piece within about a year. But before the disposition was to take place, American Express cleaned shop at LB's top level. J. Tomilson Hill was out and Dick Fuld became sole president of the soon to be resurrected Lehman.

Why did Hill go so suddenly? Tom Hill had only spent a portion of his career at Lehman, while Fuld had been a lifer. Hill was running investment banking and Fuld, the more profitable fixed income division. But most importantly, Hill had rubbed many people the wrong way. He was the archetypal cartoon of a despotic, self-important, haughty investment banker. There was little question that he was an accomplished dealmaker. But people within Lehman, and likely at American Express, were not fans.

I recall a Monday Morning Meeting, long a tradition at Lehman, well before we introduced "Big Deal" awards. We occupied the bottom half (of course) of the American Express Tower at the World Financial Center. These meetings frequently began a few minutes past the 8:30 A.M. scheduled start time. Hill had become frustrated that bankers were not arriving punctually enough for the meetings to kick-off, undisrupted, at 8:30 on the dot. Eventually, he sternly told his army of investment bankers, scolding them like schoolchildren, to make it their business to arrive on time. He further mandated that the doors to the auditorium, where the Monday Morning Meeting took place, be locked exactly on the half hour. One week, not long after this policy was in place, as Hill was speaking to a quiet crowd of bankers, all could hear the sound of someone struggling to open an auditorium door. Once it was clear the door would not yield, unbelievably, the latecomer began to gently knock. The knocks grew progressively louder and more persistent. Hill, at the podium, smiled broadly. At last, he smugly stage-whispered, "Why don't we open the door and see who it is?" A hushed, nervous laugh traveled through the ranks. I was already cringing for the person on the other side of the locked door, while at the same time wondering why in the world he or she did not simply disappear. Whoever was there would not be missed. Then the door half opened and a senior banker's secretary appeared. Apparently, there was urgent client business that required his immediate attention. Hill looked disappointed, not to mention a bit foolish. He had been virtually salivating at the prospect of humiliating a late-arriving banker. But Hill was soon gone, due to incidents such as this one that simply caused people to dislike him. Whatever Harvey Golub's exact mix of reasons for ridding Lehman of Hill, Fuld was now in sole command of the firm, with Chris Pettit, a Fuld confidant who was already functioning as a chief operating officer, additionally charged with closely managing the Investment Banking Division (IBD). Fuld has since described his short-lived panic when he found he was to be sole captain of Lehman, though no one in the firm discerned this brief bout of nerves. On the contrary, Dick assumed his new role projecting absolute authority. Hill may have been arrogant and demeaned many around him, but Fuld was by no means a pushover. No, he was the polar opposite. As CEO, he would later say to a group of Lehman Managing Directors, "Every day is a battle. You've got to kill the enemy. They tried to kill us."[xiv] Indeed, Fuld's sense that Lehman was in daily hand-to-hand combat, at all-out war with competitors, would influence events that would unfold throughout Lehman's independent life.

As planned, in 1994, Lehman was spun-off through an IPO (and as mentioned earlier, we all got tee-shirts displaying the imprint of a Lehman stock certificate that I still have). We also got the opportunity to buy in on the cheap. For some years thereafter, Lehman remained a laggard in the investment banking industry. Indeed, early losses reduced the ratio of capital to assets, a key measure of a financial institution's soundness, to a flimsy two percent, fueling worry about Lehman's survival. We remained primarily a fixed-income shop. In this, we were a powerhouse. Our investment bankers originated[27] the deals and our sales force distributed them. Our traders continued to bring in revenues. Many of these activities were

---

27. To create a new security or loan.

supported by a fixed income research[28] group that ranked number one almost every year according to *Institutional Investor's*[29] annual survey (though our ranking at our low point under American Express temporarily slipped precipitously). This ranking is the most important industry barometer for measuring the quality of a firm's research. Also, in contrast to bankers at some other firms, we at Lehman could not count on our research analysts to compromise their integrity to support an Investment Banking Division transaction. They provided honest, independent opinions. This frustrated some bankers, but was both ethical and ultimately enabled Lehman to avoid difficulties that later proved disastrous for some of our peers.

As Dick Fuld got rolling, profits at Lehman tended to move directionally with the rest of the Street,[30] but we slowly made inroads into a number of businesses. It would be a number of years before Lehman reclaimed its position among leading firms. Missing from Lehman were leading practices in M&A,[31] asset management, equities underwriting and trading, and other lesser businesses. The absence or relative weakness of these businesses fundamentally undermined the firm's prowess and solidity. These areas were, in general, the more profitable ones for our industry. Asset management was also a source of relatively stable revenues, as firms collect fees from clients in down markets, so long as they continue to manage their clients' funds.

---

28. Analysts covering fixed income capital markets obligations, typically recommending whether investors buy, hold or sell the instruments. Fixed income research is an important, if not essential part of the broker-dealer business. With an analyst team ranked high by *Institutional Investor* (an important finance industry magazine), based on a survey of investors, research recommendations gain instant credibility. These rankings fundamentally support the marketing of debt a firm underwrites or only trades and sells. Lehman's policy, during my tenure, was always that research remain independent of banking. As a result, when Eliot Spitzer conducted a broad investigation of Wall Street analyst research, finding that many firms improperly influenced research analysts to recommend stocks or bonds to help secure lucrative underwriting mandates, Lehman walked away much cleaner than most. Lehman did pay a comparatively small fine, but was never in the headlines as one of the firms that was disreputable in the functioning of its research team.

29. A leading financial publication read by many in the industry.

30. Wall Street

31. Mergers and acquisitions advice

Moreover, many of our professionals were simply no longer of the same quality as those at the leading firms. To address this, during the nineties, Lehman was unrestrained in its layoffs when the market was in the doldrums. More notably, on at least one occasion when the markets were healthy, Lehman instituted a round of lay-offs in which the firm culled the weaker performers.

Chris Pettit's elevated tenure at Lehman was ultimately limited. At our Monday Morning Meetings, he was an effective, animated force, speaking like an evangelist whipping up a congregation. However, rumors circulated that his relationship with Dick had grown tense. Certainly, this was no more a basis for longevity than it would have been to work at cross-purposes with Bobbie Lehman in the old days. Time passed and the relationship between the two executives progressively soured. Pettit's final undoing was an affair with a senior-level woman who reported to him. The press has always reported this as "alleged," but within Lehman, this was an unquestioned truth. Indeed, there seemed to be little attempt at pretense. Pettit was forced to resign in 1996, and when he died not long after in a freak snowmobile accident, there were many who openly offered condolences to the woman with whom he had had the "alleged" relationship. While I will leave her nameless, at the time she had a high profile at Lehman, heading a key unit.

Also in 1996, Fuld created Lehman's executive committee. Aside from Dick, himself, it included Joe Gregory, who you will read much about in later chapters. Among this original inner circle, no one had the usual Wall Street Ivy League credentials or similarly elite degrees, reflecting Fuld's visceral aversion to the same elitist snobbery that Glucksman had perceived among investment bankers on the whole.

Following Pettit's departure, Brad Jack, who had joined the firm in 1984 in Fixed Income, like so many of Fuld's chosen leaders, was tapped to co-head Investment Banking with two others, who ultimately resigned in what appeared a coup for Brad. Like Pettit, Jack was an inspirational speaker, and though he had no experience in the investment banking half of LB's business, he quickly ramped-up and proved himself adept at both managing IBD and navigating internal politics. During Brad's time, investment banking began to make serious inroads, ascending among our competitors. It was during Jack's tenure, with Fuld's full support, that the firm went on a spending spree, and began a highly successful effort to lure top investment banking rainmakers from other firms. Gradually, Lehman continued to upgrade its capabilities and post improving results, reflected, in turn, in strong performance of our stock. In part, we were simply rising with the tide of Wall Street boom years and catching up with our competitors. It was not until the twenty-first century that Lehman truly began to distinguish itself, starting down a road to reclaim a long-lost position at the front of the pack.

For me, a particular peculiarity of Lehman's advance was the man to whom it is attributed, Dick Fuld. He was the first leader since Bobbie Lehman who always had the last word. Though like any public company CEO he formally reported to a board of directors, his control was largely absolute. While certain key members of the executive committee were influential, at least until his final period as CEO, it was mostly Dick's thinking, and otherwise certainly his final stamp of approval on matters of any importance that were always credited as the single greatest factor in Lehman's growing success. Even externally, the financial press lauded him as one of America's most effective CEOs. Without question, he operated with extreme intensity. His mind rarely strayed far from matters concerning The Brothers. At the same time, his face was forever ashen, unanimated, and he often appeared locked in his own head. When Dick spoke before a large group, it generally looked like he was vacantly shouting words displayed on a teleprompter. In sum, my sense (with one exception I discuss in the next chapter) was that he had long ago misplaced any human personality and replaced it with tirelessly grinding internal gears, managing the firm like a machine that never idled. Colleagues who were at Lehman when Dick joined in 1969 (before I became an employee) and observed him through the early eighties when he rose to head sales and trading, recall that he hardly spoke to anyone, despite the fact that by the end of this period more than twenty managers reported to him. When he did speak, he was monosyllabic. For this he was nicknamed "the Gorilla," and, thumbing his nose at the affront, placed a stuffed life-sized one in his office adjacent to the trading floor. For the most part, old-timers recall an image of a man fixated throughout the day on a green screen[32]. Even years later, the first time I was in Dick's office after he became CEO, among a small group, his communication skills were notably limited. His eyes continuously moved between those speaking and the market data on his computer. In fact, he seemed to be in another time zone, responding to conversation that had come and gone. The firm was improving under his leadership; yet there we were in his office to discuss developments with potentially meaningful implications for Lehman's health and he hardly seemed to find the topic of interest.

---

32. For readers too young to remember the early days of computers or simply not exposed to them before the advent of Apple and Microsoft Windows, the computer screens we veterans used for a number of years displayed only green text on black backgrounds.

CHAPTER 2

One Firm

*". . . the only thing we have to fear is fear itself—
nameless, unreasoning, unjustified terror which
paralyzes needed efforts to convert retreat into advance."*
—Franklin D. Roosevelt

It was a Tuesday. In fact, it was the United Nations International Day of Peace. But it was also 9/11, a day so completely unexpected and devastating that my memory of it is a discombobulated pastiche of images and fraught moments I have made no effort to preserve. In the immediate aftermath of the attack, every second of that day fixed in my head with the clarity of a high pixel photograph. Once 9/11's stranglehold on my temporarily obsessive thought began to fade, I packed it all away like old clothes stuffed into an attic trunk I had to sit on to close.

In short, I will not tell you my 9/11 story in granular, gory detail. To do so would, for me, feel trite, particularly by comparison to what happened to those who suffered the worst and those who were heroes. So I will not exploit what happened. No falling bodies.

Lehman on 9/11 was independent, though still living and breathing in the lower half of the American Express Tower at the World Financial Center, directly across the street from the World Trade Center's North Tower. Due to this proximity, we, like quite a few other companies, were an entire firm with a ringside seat at the devastation. Every eyewitness has a singular 9/11 tale. And like others in the area—at least those with options—we at Lehman made individual decisions about when to flee, though once the South Tower collapsed any stragglers who felt safer inside our old building than outside amid the madness, hurriedly departed.

It was earlier, however, when the second plane hit, that it became at once clear that our lives were taking a detour. Everyone has a story about their endless hike home. Or about the bar where they cooled their heels because mass transit was turned off. And, of course, few were able to reach the most important people in their lives because the transponders carrying mobile phone signals were insanely overloaded with people trying somehow just to say, *yes, I am alive.*

The roughly six thousand Lehman people in our Three World Financial Center global headquarters, and all but one of the Lehman hundreds working out of the couple of floors in the World Trade Center itself, made it home by late that night or the next day. Others from Lehman were stranded on the road. Planes were grounded. The head of investment banking at the time, Brad Jack, was with a Lehman team on the West Coast; they rented a bus to get back. Others rented cars, if they could, and drove nonstop through the night. Family and friends rallied for us all. Stepping through our front doors was an invariably emotional homecoming.

The worst was over, but the drama had legs. Events had altered my sensibility. The profession that I often think chose me was no longer just a job. Within a day of the assault, when a number of offices were shorn off our building, I found I cared far more than I had realized about my colleagues. My *real* life had always been outside the office. After 9/11, what mattered was the plain fact that I and the people I knew at Lehman had survived.

In the days that followed, Blackberries buzzed regularly, though unlike the weekend when Lehman fell, no one got in touch to share or receive information about our firm. We were more like a family that needed to remain connected. People I had never called at home, I called. Others called me.

How the fuck are you?

Same.

Like everywhere in and around New York, friends gathered, drank beer, and watched the talking heads on the tube. Everyone was shell-shocked. Still, mildly at first, and then with outright laughter, we began to kid one another, as if at an Irish wake. The dark cloud above all who worked at Lehman shifted as we heard a report that our Three World Financial Center headquarters might soon collapse. What would this mean? Would Lehman be erased? In the context of what had passed, the answers to these questions seemed a trifle, and I found myself surprisingly numb to all of these reports. In any case, it turned out the reports were untrue. Three World Financial Center was damaged, for some time uninhabitable, but still structurally sound.

I do not remember how many days passed, but it was sometime the following week that, by Blackberry and cell phone, we circulated the word that IBD would gather at one of the two midtown Sheratons on Seventh Avenue. Brad Jack talked. We listened. He had always been the inspirational speaker at Investment Banking gatherings, the opposite of Dick Fuld, who only spoke to IBD very occasionally, with minimal impact.

This time, Brad was the one who was somehow off-message. All I remember, because it seemed to sum up his perspective, is a single comment amidst his call to arms; he had not seen what we had seen on 9/11 (since he was traveling on the West Coast).

My expectations for Fuld were low when he entered the Sheraton ballroom to address us. But I immediately saw that the usual ashen pallor of his face was ruddy, imbued with blood, alive. What followed was Fuld's finest hour. I know that others in the hushed, rapt ballroom wholeheartedly agreed. This man, who was Lehman in human form, spoke with both gravity and passion that connected from his first utterance. Today, I remember little of what he said, other than, *those bastards got one of us.* Still, his oratory was a passionate rallying cry. His tone, his demeanor, had everyone in the room experiencing both his call to arms and his empathy as intimate and personal.

I have no clue as to what makes Dick Fuld tick on a day-to-day basis. He has puzzled, alienated, and at times impressed me, though I was mainly impressed by what I heard and read, not what I saw of him first hand. Still, I believe that on that day he spoke to us not simply as a leader who badly needed to lead, but as an unguarded man. Fuld was both shaken and resolved, cared deeply about how we were all coping. When Dick finished talking, we were all on our feet—definitely not a response this one-time trader, our "Gorilla," had ever elicited when he spoke to IBD, with the exuberance of a metronome.

I recall that it was at this precise moment, as the ballroom thundered with the collective cries of all those present, that Lehman's survival, success and prosperity took on new purpose. Sure, everyone was worried about having a job. Much more importantly, though, we could not dissolve due to the circumstances that had left us temporarily homeless. Each of us, it was clear, had to do whatever it took. We owed this not just to ourselves, and the families most of us supported, and not just to each other. We also owed it to our country. No one came out and said it, but Lehman's survival was now a patriotic imperative.

It was also at this moment that the tense demilitarized zone between the traders and the bankers forever disappeared. For some time, hokey little cardboard cubes painted with Lehman's motto—One Firm—and other platitudes that seemed canned, had occupied haphazard space on each of our desks. Dick understood more than anyone that the remnants of the historic division between the firm's two major halves was Lehman's tragic flaw and its obstacle to fulsome success. Yes, at last, we were one fucking firm. All that it took to accomplish this was 9/11.

By the time we met at the Sheraton, we, in Banking, found ourselves awed by what our leaders and others at Lehman had already accomplished while most of us were home with our families, in an effort that swiftly began after we were effectively evicted from our old home the previous week. The techies, typically wholly behind the scenes, and often the recipient of verbal abuse when systems do not function as needed, this day stood for an ovation, no longer unsung heroes. Yes, before us was a phalanx of technology geeks smiling ear-to-ear, as they were proud to be recognized for the sleepless days of work they had tirelessly invested to ensure that Lehman would be up and running when financial markets resumed operations. Before leaving the Sheraton, our Lehman office that day, in an incredibly orderly process, we received portable technology, enabling us to work seamlessly from remote locations, as well as a game plan for the days just ahead.

Before 9/11, Lehman was a firm with an ordinary corporate mission: in our case, to rise from the ashes of our American Express days and reinvigorate the franchise. But now the task was not simply about ascending to the top ranks of Wall Street. It had become a personal, moral imperative for all of us to deal the terrorists a *fuck you*. We had to answer the attack by delivering a message that al-Qaeda could knock down buildings, even kill a lot of us, but we would not shrink or cower.

Though this book does ultimately characterize Dick Fuld as tragically flawed, he deserves huge credit for that day, the sole moment during my time at Lehman when he fully connected with the bankers as a group. Absent Dick's inspirational appearance, it is likely that we would, nonetheless, ultimately have put our house back in order. However, we may not have rallied down a path that is more meaningful for me than anything I have done within the trappings of business before or since. With a different bravado than I was accustomed to in investment banking, we were determined that Lehman not be defeated. Following the events of 9/11, we set about the task of building our business as if waging war.

It would be a number of months before I would see Dick Fuld again.

* * *

We knew in IBD, as throughout Lehman, that 9/11 threw down unprecedented obstacles to the healthy future of our franchise, a franchise that we had, before the attack, moved decisively to resurrect. If we were to succeed, Job One was clearly all about the practicalities.

We were down a couple of buildings, workplaces for around 6 thousand people. On the days the various markets reopened, my private office downtown, on the fringes of Ground Zero, was full of dust and debris. Access to the American Express Tower was impossible, restricted. The lobby on the day of the attack, and just after, was actually used as a morgue. So I and others were relocated to the dingier of the two NY Sheratons on Seventh Avenue. I shared a room with a colleague. I found it emptied of all hotel furniture, instead outfitted with two folding tables that would serve as desks. There was a computer and the required Ethernet hook-up was already live. The necessary office supplies were on my table. I had my Lehman-issued cell phone, Blackberry and even running water. Most of us occupied the six hundred plus guest rooms. Capital markets pitched their tent in the cocktail lounge. In the lobby nearby, tables were in place to deal with every simple technological task that was no longer at our fingertips.

Seeing how immediately well oiled we proved under these absurdly con-trived and challenging physical circumstances was nearly as inspiring as Dick's talk; so much so that this one time only I really did want to pound my chest like the most pumped of investment bankers. Virtually upon our arrival at the Sheraton, deals that went dark during the days that followed the World Trade Center trauma, returned with what seemed a flip of a switch. There were only two very slow elevators to transport the invest-ment banking occupants of the dreary old hotel, now feverish with activi-ty, but who the hell cared? Up and running, baby. That is all that mattered. Accordingly, our clients were also amazed. Many reached out to offer help and support. For the most part, we did not need it, but the compassion, in the typically dispassionate, mercenary world of investment banking meant a lot to all of us. Yes, we were fucking awesome.

Investment bankers' morning travel to the office; *i.e.,* to the then-run-down Sheraton Manhattan, was not very different from our commute to downtown. We had merely moved several miles uptown. For some, this resulted in a bit shorter morning trek, while for others a somewhat longer one. But sales and trading took a major commuting hit. Lehman's man-agement had located space in Jersey City that could be quickly wired for trading. Not an ideal location, but the pickings were slim, and location was irrelevant if you lacked the required infrastructure to light up the screens. For the handful of people who commuted from nearby Jersey sub-urbs it was no big deal, but for the guy commuting from Westchester, or worse still, the wealthy suburbs of Connecticut, travel to and from work became a daily multi-hour ordeal. Still, in less than forty-eight hours, our debt market warriors hit the market running as they fully resumed activites the week after the attack. Our equities team was in front of screens when equity markets[33] reopened on September 17th.

For our clients, from the outside looking in, they saw little textural change in trading or conferring with Lehman after 9/11, despite our phys-ical circumstances. This is all the more impressive in that we were tem-porarily located in many more than the couple of makeshift nerve centers I have thus far described. Fixed income alone was at one point located in

---

33. Stock markets. Equity is synonymous with ownership.

eighteen disparate spots. In total, the New York part of the firm was in some forty locations. As Bart McDade, then our Equities head, and more recently the man to fill the president's shoes described us, we were "Bedouins for eight months."[xv] Still, how did we manage to piece ourselves together and conduct business as usual with nary an audible hiccup? Sweat, teamwork and a management team that was fast on its feet.

Once we were up and running, the appearance of normalcy, or something very close to it, was critical. While in the company of the myriad CEO's and their lieutenants with whom we had painstakingly nurtured relationships, Job One was to dispel any concerns. We did not seek sympathy. On the contrary, we were intent on dispelling any perception that the absurdly challenging job of reassembling Lehman's broken pieces, without missing a beat, had dented the quality of our operations. In essence, if it looked like business as usual, despite our patchwork of operating locations and props, our clients would be reassured, and we would preempt any flight to safer investment banking harbors. The biggest mistake possible would have been to play the pity card. This would have elicited a perception that we were struggling. What brings down a financial institution, and quickly, is a systemic loss of confidence. Fortunately, reassurance that we were as healthy as ever was a feat our management team had managed before, though they were clearly in uncharted waters. Still, in the end, our seamless continuity, from the moment the opening bell signaled the resumption of all capital market operations, deeply impressed our clients. Beginning on the day we in IBD occupied our fortress-office in the New York Sheraton, we worked more purposefully than ever, and in fact, in a soft market, would see gains in market share. And these gains were not charity. On the contrary, they were testament to our strength under adversity.

After 9/11, some of our competitors unwittingly shot themselves in the foot, helping Lehman pick off business at their own expense. More than a few rival investment bankers told our clients that we were finished as a firm, that we had no headquarters, would be prevented from reoccupying our old space for the foreseeable future. In short, they tried scare tactics to convince our clients to dump us, based on fears that we would go under and be unable to complete any work they had directed our way. This consistently backfired, with our clients appropriately offended by these slimy assaults. And our competitors, incredibly, sometimes performed an encore, shooting themselves in their other foot, by pleading to at the very least move us from the left to the right of offering document covers.[34] But this stratagem, too, failed miserably. In fact, our sickened clients were the first to tell us about the unseemly machinations of our counterparts at other firms. When we heard this, in our heads we said *yes,* mainly because the bastards got what they deserved, but also because they had in some cases handed us revenues on a platter, business that we were the dark horse to win. I suppose the difference between the bankers who tried to play the fear card and the bankers at Lehman was the absence of human, emotional intelligence that is so critical to success. Irrespective of your pedigree, causing people to hate you in the extreme is bad for business. I do not go so far as to drink my own Kool-Aid and tell you that no investment banker at Lehman would have ever pulled such shenanigans. Still, I can honestly say that we played the crazed investment banking game a whole lot cleaner. Like all good investment bankers, we at Lehman were unrelenting and opportunistic. But especially after 9/11, the culture was aggressive, not savage.

Many of us realized that if the 9/11 attack occurred twenty or thirty years earlier, we would have been screwed. Large companies have remote

---

34. This is an allusion to placement of Lehman's name on an offering document for any marketed security. Deals underwritten by investment banks generally have several tiers of underwriters. At the top of the pecking order, and raking in most of the economics (*i.e.*, euphemism for the money) are the book runners. Just below are the lead managers, followed by co-leads, *et. al.* In the past, there were many sole-managed deals, meaning one book runner. But over time this changed, so that for a number of years, most deals have two book runners, and occasionally, for a mega-deal, three or more. Book runners are listed on the cover of the offering document above everyone else. The coveted spot is on the left, indicating that you are deal quarterback. Economics for joint book runners are often the same, but everyone wants to be in charge, to occupy the number one spot. There's no shame in being on the right; you are still a book runner. Just as there's no shame in being runner up at the Miss America pageant. You hug and kiss numero uno, but you'd like her to take a spill down the stairs. Some might even give her a sneaky push in order to replace the true winner, now in a full body cast. The chemistry between joint book runners is different on every deal. But any investment banker who's satisfied with a permanent position on the right is in the wrong business.

NEW YORK, NY - SEPTEMBER 18, 2001: Hotel room mattresses are piled high on the sidewalk after being removed from guest rooms in New York's Sheraton Hotel 18 September 2001 in order to make room for the Lehman Brothers brokerage firm who has rented all the rooms on the 5th through 22nd floors for temporary office space. The firm lost its offices in the terrorist attack on the World Trade Center 11 September. (TANNEN MAURY/AFP/Getty Images)

NEW YORK, NY - SEPTEMBER 18, 2001: Workmen stack boxes of work tables outside the Sheraton Hotel 18 September 2001 to be installed in converted guest rooms to be occupied by Lehman Brothers brokerage firm who has rented all the rooms on the 5th thru 22nd floors for temporary office space. The firm lost its offices in the terrorist attack on the World Trade Center 11 September. (TANNEN MAURY/AFP/Getty Images)

system back-up at a second location that runs at least nightly to replicate everything that sits on the servers where our entire work product is located. A generation earlier the firm may very well have died with the tattered innards of our wounded headquarters. But in 2001, regardless of geography, all our screens, all the data, all the emails and documents were on our desktop PCs when we reported to work after 9/11. Without this back-up, we would not have been flawless with our clients. We were barred from the mess that was the American Express Tower, unable to recover anything from offices with mostly shattered windows, filled with debris. In fact, by the time we did get back to our old home at Three World Financial Center to recover office contents, we found that vandals had beat us to our desks and pocketed anything electronic or other items with potential street value. This was the first time in my life that my personal insurance carrier paid without an adjuster, no questions or pushback.

Another key to our stunning success was that Dick Fuld, our surprisingly human commander-in-chief, did not squander the goodwill and admiration for courage and steadfastness under fire that Lehman had elicited from our long list of existing clients as well as those we targeted for new business. Moreover, if there was a silver lining in Lehman's 9/11, it was that Fuld's determination to make us One Firm got the boost it needed. And so, in the period after 9/11, Dick Fuld led his nation state with far greater success than did America's chief. Al-Qaeda could not stop The Brothers. Hell, if the government handed us the mandate, we would have captured Bin Laden. In fact, in the quarter that included 9/11, we registered healthier results than the competition. How ironic, that a presidential administration that turned global post-9/11 goodwill toward America on its head, almost seven years later to the day, proved equally inept in managing the financial crisis that brought down Lehman, and moments later, the world's financial infrastructure. At last, a weapon of mass destruction.

Despite all the energy and determination, Lehman was still in a state of diaspora. No one knew whether we would move into our old quarters or find a new home. Then the word came that we were moving into a new building a few blocks south of the Sheraton (a hotel in need of a makeover before we set up camp—even more so after months of use by investment

bankers). Our new digs were a spanking new building, nearing comple-
tion. Morgan Stanley (MS) had commissioned it as a second major New
York location. In the aftermath of 9/11, they had misgivings. The building was only a couple of blocks away from their existing headquarters. In
the new world of global terrorism, they were loath to have their two main
buildings so close together, on the same power grid. I also suspect that
they realized markets would slow after 9/11, and with the abrupt end to
the buoyancy that had characterized the years just behind us, MS management probably questioned the sanity of expanding their office footprint.

With Morgan Stanley desperate to sell, and Lehman, in the person of
Dick Fuld, desperate to buy, the stars had aligned. Dick was hesitant to
wait eight months, if that was even the real number, to return to our old
location. The Morgan Stanley building was of course designed with an
investment bank in mind, so it was fully wired not only for the relatively
low technology investment banking floors, but also for the traders and
salespeople. Downtown in our old building we would sit adjacent to a
cacophonous worksite for an indeterminable time. And I will never know
whether this was a factor, but in Dick's mind this might have represented
an opportunity to get literally out from under the fucks at American
Express who occupied the top half of our old building. (Amex waited and
returned.) But most importantly, the decision on our location eliminated
uncertainty about our future home and our spirits quickly lifted. Lehman
paid $700 million for the building (less than Barclays paid, so at least we,
or to be more precise, our creditors, came out ahead on something). About
a year after 9/11 we sold our fifty-one percent of the downtown digs for a
paltry $158 million, though this was the biggest real estate deal in that
area since the attack. There were those who criticized us for abandoning
lower Manhattan, but there were few, if any, inside Lehman who questioned the choice.

The move from the Sheraton began once the new building was fit to
occupy, though cosmetic odds and ends of the construction were not yet
complete. From January to March 2002, we ferried any useful recovered
office contents from Three World Financial Center, and department by
department, moved into the new space.

At last, Lehman was truly One Firm. No matter how each felt about their job, we were a band of brothers and sisters. Perhaps not linked by blood like the Lehman family, but nonetheless sharing a bond and purpose that was larger than each of us, we no longer suffered the divisions that had for so long characterized The Brothers.

* * *

Following 9/11, I recall a televised tape that al-Qaeda posted so that we in America and others would air it. Subtitles translated a conversation between Bin Laden and a high-ranking cohort. He spoke with obvious relish about the success of the 9/11 attacks. A trained engineer, Bin Laden noted that he expected the planes that tore into the towers would topple those floors above the point of impact. He had not contemplated that the extreme heat of the resulting inferno would melt the steel beams that supported the two skyscrapers, resulting in the total implosion that he delightedly watched with a stunned world. In fact, this was not the first time that Bin Laden's war against America delivered the unexpected. Intimately involved in events that drew the U.S., under Clinton, into Somalia, he was both surprised and disappointed that when the going got tough, the U.S. quickly withdrew. His intention was to mire us in a protracted bloody quagmire. While he had failed to realize that goal, the weakness he perceived surely further emboldened him, perhaps leading him to conceive an attack as audacious as the 9/11 assault. But again, what he did not foresee, was that the American president, and those he had appointed, would ultimately react with so little wisdom. He could not have foreseen that "little Bush" would become so simplistically focused on an unwinnable victory in Iraq; that he would squander taxpayer funds as well as the world's profound sympathy. He could not have anticipated that instruments of government oversight and regulation would be dismantled or simply atrophy to so great a degree that financial markets in America would evolve into a Wild West without a sheriff. No, he could not have known that this inadequate president would so unwittingly set the stage for the perfect storm that resulted in the worst economy since the Great Depression. America was at its weakest, and as Bin Laden originally planned, our financial markets and economy in shambles.

CHAPTER 3

Subprime and Substandard

*"The chief weapon of sea pirates . . . was their capacity
to astonish. Nobody else could believe, until it was too
late, how heartless and greedy they were."*

KURT VONNEGUT, *BREAKFAST OF CHAMPIONS*

"Subprime" is not a word I thought about much before the summer of 2007. And I barely knew what a CDO[35] was. But subprime mortgage securitizations were to have a completely unforeseen, devastating impact on not only my world, but also the fate of Lehman and the state of global markets and economies. In fact, once subprime collapsed, and I learned more about it, I was stunned that so many had believed the risk in these securities was close to zero.

What really eats away at me is Lehman's part in all of it. And admittedly, there is a certain justice that Lehman, and for that matter Bear Stearns, paid the ultimate price as leaders, at least among investment banks, of an insidious market phenomenon that proved so destructive. I do not know what internal decisions led Bear to the precipice from which it tumbled. At Lehman, it is clear that while various professionals weighed in, only a very few people on Lehman's top executive thirty-first floor were responsible for the ultimate decision to accumulate a massive position in real estate assets at the very worst of times. In fact, it is clear that there

---

35. Collateralized debt obligation.

were important, experienced voices that objected to the real estate build-up, believing this ballooning real estate position was overly risky. But, in the end, it was the imprudent decision of a very few, deaf to rational internal misgivings, that would ultimately decide Lehman's fate.

How did this happen? In general, the subprime assets and real estate assets were generating hefty returns. A top management team long satisfied with the moderate amounts of the most toxic—but highly profitable— paper on LB's balance sheet drank its own Kool-Aid, upping the real estate ante in an effort to further buoy profits in an environment where other revenue generators were lagging. Opposition to the build-up was discouraged. In fact, all those who openly opposed the firm's top level management real estate strategy or even questioned the bet quickly disappeared from the firm or woke up the next day in smaller, windowless offices.

The day it became clear to me that we had placed a foolhardy bet on real estate, I felt utterly betrayed. In large part I was angry that my internal radar, until now always alerting me to incoming, had failed. I, of all people, was foolish enough to swallow the widely distributed, popular Lehman doctrine. And this was bullshit; an elixir I believed I was savvy enough never to swallow. I completely believed that over the years we had learned important lessons about risk from several brushes with death, and was absolutely certain we had become extremely risk averse, among the most prudent of investment banks. I found comfort in our lesser exposure to some of the problems that hobbled or destroyed other firms. When Eliot Spitzer, New York State's attorney general, investigated the conflict between investment banking underwritings and research recommendations within the various Wall Street firms, substantially damaging the franchises of several, Lehman was relatively clean and paid associated fines that were a fraction of those paid by the major offenders. When the dot-com bubble burst, we lost a revenue stream, but not our shirts. We were free of the Morgan Stanley management discord and upheaval that was well documented in the press. As has been much discussed, internal fracture hurt Lehman and undermined performance years earlier. But now it was the exalted Morgan Stanley that saw its once unblemished reputation sullied by such matters. Instead of Lehman, Morgan Stanley was for some time reduced to a tabloid brand, with a media-spun perception from which it has never fully recovered. Even after subprime melted down, with the fallout spreading across broader credit markets, Lehman appeared, in a by now familiar pattern, to fare better than our peers. In hindsight, I drank the Lehman Kool-Aid by the pitcher. Sure, we had great risk management. Rumors would always surface, and would always prove groundless. But the proof was in the numbers we posted. We would unquestionably emerge from a downturn less damaged than others, picking up market share, and increasingly the envy of our less-nimble peers.

If anything, I am now embarrassed that I not only fell hook, line, and sinker for the steaming, odorless corporate bullshit, but that I confidently spouted the same sound bites as ultimate truths. When those close to me, outside the office, would express concern about what they were reading of Lehman in the papers or hearing on the nighttime news, I largely responded with Lehman management's talking points. Clearly, the time has come to move on, to put all this behind me, but I will always feel some despair about what Fuld and Gregory did to Lehman. The two of them steamrolled all dissent. Fuld, quite early in his career was unashamedly aggressive and combative; an openly intimidating and dictatorial figure who clearly thought dissent was overrated. Gregory, however, acted the part of the far left, touchy-feeler, the man who most championed diversity at Lehman, a down-to-earth, approachable, warm and fuzzy guy. But in truth, he, like Fuld, tolerated little dissension. If you crossed him, you were fucked. And this down-to-earth dude commuted to work in a helicopter.

The ultimate frustration in all of this is that Fuld and Gregory were largely uninvolved in the day-to-day management of the investment banking side of the business. And the Investment Banking Division was indeed outperforming others in a tough environment. Absolutely, we were One Firm, and that is a large part of the reason that we enjoyed swan-song prosperity. But while our franchise thrived, the decisions of a few ex-traders who grew up at Lehman in the culture of the Glucksman-Peterson era would destroy The Brothers' financial soundness. Sure, Dick had much to do with the improvements in banking, or at least the allocation of massive dollars to lure top bankers to our shop. In the end, though, the nearly universal acclaim he received as a master CEO blinded him, so that he believed there was no hole out of which he could not dig himself, *i.e.,* his company.

The question many still ask, and that I myself asked at first, was how did we—and not just Lehman—get into this mess? Also, why is this so much worse than other instances of flawed financial wizardry? The short answer is that there was a perfect storm. Many played a role: Bill Clinton, George Bush, numerous congressional members of both major political parties (most prominently Senator Phil Gramm during his tenure as chairman of the Senate Banking Committee), the Federal Reserve under Greenspan, the Securities and Exchange Commission (SEC)[36], investment banks, commercial banks and other mortgage lenders, mortgage brokers, investors—generally institutional, the major U.S. rating agencies, the subprime borrowers themselves. All told, few are blameless who might have done something to staunch the subprime bubble. Of course, no one meant this to happen. In the end, some drank the doctrinaire, free market Kool-Aid. Some were unaware of the implications of their actions or inaction. And there were certainly those who were just plain greedy. Yes, early in this book when I have championed capitalism, I have all but quoted the line in the film, "Wall Street," that "greed is good." But greed, or capitalism, or the drive to make money—whatever one calls it—will ruin us all if unchecked and unregulated.

* * *

What are subprime mortgage securitizations? Why did they spark the financial meltdown? The only way to explain this collapse to anyone not steeped in finance is to begin with a quick primer.

For most of America's history, banks and other credit providers funded home purchases and kept these loans, and the associated risk, on their own books. They carefully weighed the risk as to whether a borrower could

---

36. The primary federal regulator of the securities industry, whose mission is to promote and ensure full required disclosure by issuers of securities as well as protect investors against fraud and manipulation in securities markets. The SEC specifically is charged with oversight of broker-dealers, mutual fund managers, and investment advisors.

repay the loan. Just in case the borrower became insolvent, and as happens from time to time, real estate market prices dropped, they never lent against the full value of the home. In this way, if a borrower defaulted, the lender could then foreclose and recover what it was owed. And because the banks had skin in the game, *i.e.,* wanted to avoid defaulting mortgage loans, and because people (who also had skin in the game) were terribly reluctant to lose their homes, mortgages led to lower losses than just about any other form of lending. Investment banks, like Lehman Brothers, did not engage in these activities. Mortgages were forbidden fruit, following the Depression-era legislation separating commercial banking and investment banking activities, through which investment banks could not lend to finance homes. In fact, the primary intent and result of the Depression's Glass-Steagall Act was to separate investment and commercial banking. With this legislation, the federal government ensured that the average Joe's deposits and mortgages would reside in the staid, quiet world of sleepy commercial banks that collected customer deposits and yawningly used them to fund loans at a somewhat higher interest rate. Investment banking was to be the world of speculation and big time capital markets. Unless average Joe was foolish, this was not a world in which he gambled his life's savings. So long as commercial banks were restricted from engaging in investment banking and other volatile speculative businesses, they would remain more stable than the banks that tanked or struggled during the Great Depression. And so long as the investment banks stayed out of retail deposit taking and lending, they would not easily devastate the nest eggs of prudent wage earners.

Along came mortgage-backed securities (MBS). Freddie Mac[37] and Fannie Mae[38] were the dominant players in this market. They would purchase large numbers of mortgages from the credit providers who had originated them, pool them together, and sell this package as a bond to

---

37. Federal Home Loan Guarantee Corporation, purchases mortgage loans from financial entities that extend the loans, packages large numbers of these loans together, *securitizing* them, *i.e.*, creating bonds that pay interest and principle from the interest and principle collected from homeowners on these mortgage loans.

38. Federal National Mortgage Association. Similar to Freddie Mac.

investors. Investors holding these bonds would indirectly receive interest and principal repayment from the large group of borrowers who reliably paid their monthly mortgage installments. Freddie and Fannie ensured the quality of these bonds by establishing a set of minimum guidelines for mortgages they would accept. These mortgages were called *conforming*. They garnered high ratings from the major rating agencies, Moody's, Standard & Poor's and Fitch. Institutional investors snapped up the low-risk MBS paper. These bonds, issued by the two quasi-government mortgage giants, became major fixed-income securities in capital markets. Naturally, a leading fixed-income house like Lehman became active, but only as a final conduit for Freddie and Fannie, not as a lender itself. We also traded these securities in the market. But, certainly, Lehman and our peers played no role in determining what mortgages to package in an MBS. That was prudently determined by Fannie and Freddie.

This system worked well for all. Standards for conforming mortgages were high so defaults were low. Lenders who originated the loans soon originated more than ever. Rather than funding mortgage borrowings for say, fifteen or thirty years, primarily off a relatively stable deposit base, they could now simply sell the loans off to Freddie and Fannie and earn a fee. At this point, the mortgage loans on the banks' balance sheets were replaced with cash, as settlement from Fannie and Freddie for the mortgages acquired from the banks. As deposits and other funding remained in place, the banks could then use the cash to originate another round of loans to replace those sold to Fannie and Freddie. Only if depositors withdrew their funds from the bank would the cash have to be used to repay deposits. But retail consumer deposits are largely stable. And so, in this way, mortgage lenders could originate loans that over time amounted to a multiple of their deposits and other funding. Fannie and Freddie got a cut too, and their volumes got so large that early investors in Fannie and Freddie stock did very well, so long as they disposed of the shares ahead of the current meltdown. (In fact, I used to own some Fannie and Freddie shares, but I sold all those holdings well before they got into trouble, the opposite of what I did with most of my Lehman stock. And my Lehman holdings dwarfed what I invested in Freddie.) The lenders originating loans sold to Freddie and Fannie no longer had any particular incentive to maintain their traditional high credit risk standards, since the risk was no longer on their books but had been passed to Fannie and Freddie. The two mortgage securitizers, in turn, packaged them and sold them to investors, but their adherence to a very specific definition of conforming ensured that the quality of new mortgage lending remained high.

During the mid 1990's, Bill Clinton pressured Fannie and Freddie to change their guidelines so that more mortgage loans would be considered conforming. He wanted more Americans to realize the great American dream of owning their own home. Fannie and Freddie, though considered quasi-government enterprises, were both profit-making ventures with their shares traded on the New York Stock Exchange. By defining a wider range of mortgage loans as conforming, they were able to package larger volumes of mortgages and thereby maintain the existing steep upward trajectory of both their profits and their share prices. But the risk inherent in the mortgage-backed securities they now created was by definition greater, as the mortgage pools securitized contained obligations that on average were originated with less creditworthy borrowers. Standards fell most dramatically during the later Bush years, when subprime ballooned and Fannie and Freddie initially quickly lost market share and further lowered standards to stay in the game.

During an interview aired on television in the autumn of 2008, Clinton was questioned about the wisdom of urging Freddie and Fannie to loosen their standards since this contributed to the subprime debacle. Clinton answered cheerily that his desire to make mortgages available to a wider range of folks was in the context of a very different, far stronger economic environment. What Clinton failed to address was that in contrast to, say, short-term loans to businesses to finance the purchase of inventory, mortgage loans generally mature over ten to thirty years, with the majority at the long-dated end of the spectrum. Had he thought this through? Did he expect that the economy would remain strong for an unprecedented thirty years? Also, many borrowers were signing up for floating-rate loans. Interest rates were low. Did he speculate as to how difficult it would be for borrowers to meet their mortgage payments if they were caught in an environment of rising interest rates and a weakening economy? This was not a scenario without multiple precedents. Finally,

Clinton indicated that low-income borrowers were unaware that they took on mortgages packaged into subprime securities, where default meant foreclosure rather than a restructuring. Should this not have concerned him? With the lender who originated the loan no longer involved, and the mortgage now part of a massive pool, workouts became impractical. While subprime securitization was a considerably smaller market during the Clinton years than it ultimately became, it did exist. Its attributes and practices were naked to those who took the time to examine them. Of course, like most politicians, Bill Clinton simply does not fully, if even meaningfully, grasp economics and finance. But where were his advisors, those who should logically have pointed out the defects in Clinton's thinking on mortgage lending? There is little question that Clinton is bright enough to have understood the potential for problems if expert advisors on finance and the economy walked him through the potential pitfalls. Where was Robert Rubin, Clinton's Secretary of the Treasury until 1999? How could he have missed the faulty reasoning underpinning Clinton's desire to put people who could barely make their home mortgage payments inside these ticking bombs? And what about Lawrence Summers? During the mid-1990's, as a senior official in Treasury, he was deeply involved in the Mexico bailout (inadvertently to Lehman's benefit) and other international matters. But he took over Rubin's post as Secretary in 1999. Shouldn't he have scheduled an appointment with his president to respectfully shout in his boss' face that the administrations meddling in the home mortgage market was an accident waiting to happen? Or did Clinton hear all about the pitfalls and ignore them, ever the smiling populist? Additionally, Summers, as Secretary, championed the Clinton-Gramm partnership on deregulation. He publicly supported the administration's doomed policies, whether he recognized flaws or not. Indeed, it is troubling that he now sits as Obama's director of the National Economic Council. It is only common sense that the administration appoint those who have a track record of getting it right, not those who played a key role in the economic policies which are in large part responsible for where our country is today.

In any case, Clinton may have been well-intentioned, but we will never know what his closest advisors did or did not tell him. What we do know is that Clinton's mortgage meddling was ill-conceived. Today, with the benefit of hindsight, he must realize how calamitous a misstep it was to encourage lower lending standards. Clinton's excuse that he encouraged these less stringent standards during a boom economy thus leads to one of two conclusions: either he simply refuses to take any accountability and deflects all blame, or he remains ignorant of facts long hidden behind the sheerest of veils. Bill Clinton is no idiot. He is a consummate politician.

In addition to the ill-fated, naïve presidential pressure to loosen mortgage lending standards, Clinton was apparently equally well intentioned and in the dark as he pursued, as a moderate Democrat, a policy of deregulation—a policy more frequently associated with his White House successor. In truth "W" essentially continued the deregulation trend started by Clinton with Phil Gramm, his strangest of bedfellows. Still, Bush may have well gone further than what Clinton intended. Clinton, in near lockstep with Gramm, and even with support of New York Democratic Senator Charles Schumer (from the 1990's into the new millennium) favored deregulation, but the Bush administration and its appointees presided over an SEC and other bodies for which not only the rules, but even enforcement, grew lax. In fact, under Bush, enforcement became less vigorous by design.

Also during the nineties, new mortgage lenders and brokers began to proliferate to address an unmet need. While the advent of MBS efficiently put increasing numbers in their own homes, there were also many people whose credit profile prevented them from qualifying for mortgages because they were considered overly risky borrowers, often with little money to put down. Any mortgages for these riskiest of borrowers were still disqualified by Fannie or Freddie as *nonconforming*. As a result, these would-be borrowers saw their loan applications consistently rejected by all rational lenders as too risky. Credit providers logically declined to hold this risk *on their own books*. It was in the murky swamp of this unmet demand for mortgage credit from unqualified borrowers that subprime would breed and multiply, like a voracious, newly introduced species that destroys a previously balanced ecosystem.

Indeed, the creation and growth of the subprime mortgage market provided an illusory panacea for these weakest borrowers' woes, as well as skyrocketing revenues for mortgage brokers, lenders and securitizers. But the solution, from the get go, as must already be clear, was fundamentally unsound. In part, this was because many of the new homeowners borrowed from predatory lenders. Such lenders are not a new species. Just stroll into most any car dealership, ask for financing, and you will see these evildoers in action. As long as there have been borrowers unsophisticated or gullible enough to fall victim, the unscrupulous have exploited them. No doubt, predatory lenders will continue to evolve new forms of unethical lending, always endeavoring to stay one step ahead of regulation and enforcement. When we do nothing, and thereby fail to act against these injustices, we effectively send the predators a mass mailing, encouraging them to rampage. The absence of effective regulation and enforcement is a financial aphrodisiac for the liars and cheats who lend with abandon, so long as they do not hold the risk of those they have at every opportunity deceptively convinced to borrow amounts they simply cannot service.

In addition to predatory lenders, there were innumerable brokers and originators that simply grew lax. Why? Because a market that securitized mortgages no longer required them to hold the damned risk. It is the prospect of losses on extension of credit that maintains discipline among lenders. This was gone, opening the door to dishonest borrowers who would not receive loans unless they submitted mortgage applications riddled with manufactured information that deceptively portrayed them as sound. Or just sound enough in this era of lax standards. There was also no shortage of cases in which mortgage brokers and others, paid on the volume of loans they originated, conspired with unsound borrowers to falsify loan applications and thereby increase their own paydays. Thus was the new system for unsound borrowers to obtain mortgage loans they could never hope to service perfected in its most elegant incarnation ever.

While mortgage lenders who lent to nonconforming borrowers at high rates had existed for some time, until the mid-1990's they long represented a relatively slender portion of the market. First Alliance Mortgage (FAM) was one such animal. It was founded in the early 1970's. In 1995, sadly, Lehman Brothers initiated a relationship with FAM, and sent a Vice President, Eric Hibbert, to meet with and vet the potential new client.

President Clinton

Tuesday, December 16, 1997. Among topics covered at the press conference, in which Clinton reflected on his fifth year in office, he revealed the name of his 3-month old Labrador as "Buddy." (photo by Chuck Kennedy)

White House National Economic Council Director Larry Summers

WASHINGTON - APRIL 23, 2009: (Photo by Chip Somodevilla/Getty Images)

Alan Greenspan

WASHINGTON - October 23, 2008 "Those of us who have looked to the self-interest of lending institutions to protect shareholder's equity (myself especially) are in a state of shocked disbelief."

-Greenspan, Testimony to House Oversight Committee

Internal Lehman memos, that have since become entirely public, indicated that FAM "had been accused of fraudulent lending practices since 1994 and was the subject of more litigation than any other non-bankrupt firm in the sector."[xvi] Moreover, internal Lehman documents indicated that FAM was a "financial sweatshop,"[xvii] where you only found employment if you checked your "ethics at the door;"[xviii] that much of the mortgage debt the company originated was the work product of "high pressure sales for people . . . in a weak state;"[xix] and that certain of FAM's borrowers had "no real capacity for repayment."[xx] Despite all this, Lehman, by now a firm on the up, hyper-concerned about its advancing reputation, moved ahead and by 1996 provided funding to first Alliance to the tune of $500 million, utilized to finance new subprime mortgages. With this funding in place, the Brothers went a step further and packaged $700 million of First Alliance mortgages extended to their subprime, nonconforming borrowers as newly emergent subprime mortgage-backed securities. This was not a deal that passed through Lehman's security checkpoints without coaxing from powerful figures within the firm.

My God, is this the Lehman I thought I knew? *Say it ain't so.* The endgame was always money, and as much of it as possible, but not at any fucking cost. We were not choir boys, but I always thought we were far more scrupulous whores than those who filled the ranks of other investment banks. How could it be that we had financed such a sleazy, low-life organization, securitized their loans, and sold them off to our trusting, investing clients? Could we really be buttressing our profits by screwing everyone involved in this obvious, systemic scam, *i.e.,* everyone other than our tacit co-conspirators who profited as we did? I long thought I lived in a community where good Samaritans conducted a vigilant, largely unblemished neighborhood watch.

Tossing my mask out the window, I cannot pretend that every deal in which I was involved as an investment banker was driven by altruism. Not even close. Such a contention by any investment banker is pure oxymoron. I could argue that I worked on countless transactions through which Lehman, and indirectly, I, profited while many, as a direct consequence, lost jobs, but that all of this contributed to a more a efficient, evolved and thereby a more competitive U.S. economy. Actually, this is technically true, though not everyone would admire or thank me for my role in these transactions—particularly those who my deals sent to the unemployment line. Still, nothing I did amounted to the unadulterated racket of the subprime mortgage contagion.

From a structural standpoint, there is little difference between a subprime mortgage-backed security and a traditional ABS (asset-backed security). Yet common sense alone informs us that a security based on loans to a pool of weaker borrowers, by definition, has to be riskier. Still, the rating agencies rated the new subprime mortgages at very high levels. Many have accused the rating agencies of a conflict of interest. After all, the ratings of both the various entities' obligations on the corporate and public sector side of the business, and the subprime MBS's packaged by the investment banks and others, are paid for by those who benefit most from a highly favorable rating agency assessment, *i.e.,* high ratings. Yet based on intermittent personal experience with rating agencies over the years, I find it hard to believe that this frequent accusation of conflict is fully grounded in reality.

I experienced the rating agencies wholly on the corporate side of investment banking. I know little other than the basic principles of structured finance, a category that includes all MBS's. At both Lehman and the agencies, structured finance was a galaxy away from all typical corporate finance deals. There are entirely separate groups that specialize in these securities. Having said this, I have never had the slightest inkling that a client received a high rating because it paid the agency fee. On the contrary, more often, clients have exited the agency buildings foaming at the mouth (on a good day) about what they regard as the absurd caution, and even lack of competence, of those rating their securities. Further, once the ratings emerged from the agency black box, clients at times expressed boundless frustration and pure rage at ratings they considered absurdly low, an outcome that tangibly raised their funding costs above what they have believed was proper and deserved. Indeed, the voices of clients decrying defective ratings, justifiably or not—and I personally believe the complaints were often reasonable—completely drown out voices expressing full ratings satisfaction. Moreover, Lehman had a group composed of former rating agency professionals on whom we relied to navigate the consistently puzzling rating process. Over the years, they repeatedly pounded the table that the agencies are the most conservative measurers of credit quality our clients are likely to confront when they issue debt securities. More than once, I received lectures from these internal Lehman ratings advisors, in which they vehemently insisted that the profit and analytical sides of the agencies are as separate as church and state. They have also consistently said that the agency analysts overwhelmingly are subject to greater internal criticism if they rate too high as opposed to the reverse, even if it means collecting less revenues (as a low rating at times prevents a borrower from accessing the market, with the agencies in turn earning less as they are paid incrementally for each debt security they rate). And so, as far as corporate ratings are concerned, I believe the charges that the agencies have been influenced by a conflict of interest are, at least in my long experience, groundless.

What our ratings oracles did admit was that while there were analysts at the agencies whom they considered to be Top Guns, there was no short-age of less-than-experienced analysts. These less-seasoned professionals at Moody's and S&P represent a sufficiently large number of highly influen-tial financial world professionals. Errors and inconsistencies abound. I, myself, have attended a handful of rating agency meetings and come across an analyst or two who fit this profile.

As for ratings on subprime mortgages, I am less certain as to whether there was conflict. On the one hand, the now obviously, absurdly high rat-ings on subprime securities that defaulted or, since the meltdown, were massively downgraded, have indelibly tarnished the agencies' reputations. Unless they had a death wish, it is nonsense to contend that they know-ingly erred. Still, to an objective observer, largely unschooled in structured finance, it is immediately self-evident that ratings on subprime mortgages were defective. Who in their right mind believes that a group of borrow-ers who do not qualify for conforming mortgages; who may in many cases live from paycheck to paycheck; who are victims of teaser rates and other predatory lending tactics; who borrow at floating rates, and who will have extremely limited capacity to service these obligations in a weak economy with rising interest rates; together possess low risk characteristics simply because there are lots of them? In fact, many had little capacity to service these very same mortgages, even in a strong economy, if rates moved materially higher. How is it that the rating agencies assigned such high ratings to the subprime securities backed by pools of loans to these borrowers? The question resonates louder when one considers that many subprime mortgages were financed at 100 percent or more of a property's value; that, as noted, there was widespread fraud in mortgage loan documentation; and that this fraud was perpetrated not just by borrowers, but also by mortgage brokers and others whose compensation was tied to volume. What a brilliant recipe for disaster. To boot, none of these attributes of the subprime market were well-kept secrets among any who followed the industry. Did Moody's, S&P, and Fitch turn a blind eye? Did Lehman, Bear, and the other investment banks have a tragic flaw in their financial acumen, a diseased blind spot in their minds-eye views of mortgage lending? Or was it all about generating revenues, while selling off the risk to guileless investors?

Investors have long relied on the judgment of the rating agencies in assessing risk. And in contrast to corporate ratings, where a company meets with the agencies to review its performance and any planned financings, in the world of structured finance, the rating agencies dictated the parameters that earned securities specific ratings in a highly iterative process with those packaging these instruments. The popular belief that the subprime rating debacle resulted from a conflict of interest never made sense to me. A *New York Times* front page article published on Sunday, December 7, 2008, quotes a Moody's managing director's anonymous response to an internal survey: "These errors make us look either incompetent at credit analysis or like we sold our soul to the devil for revenue, or a little bit of both."[xxi] The obvious distress conveyed in this quote buttressed my belief that the massive revenues generated on subprime ratings could not possibly justify the hits to the agency reputations and the fallout that followed, both internally and externally.

I initially concluded that due to the huge revenues, the agencies drank their own Kool-Aid, blinding themselves to the true risk. For the agencies, I supposed, this was a first misstep, a first gulp of the cyanide-laced mix that has long been a financial markets tradition.

Over time, I have learned what I believe to be the absolute truth—a truth not previously published. For some time, there were whispers that both Moody's and S&P blindly applied the same models to subprime that they had long-applied to the higher quality, traditional mortgage-backed securities. But these were mere murmurs in the wind and provided no explanation as to why the agencies would proceed so foolishly. What I have learned over time, however, is that the subprime ratings assigned by at least one of the two leading agencies resulted from tragic internal process dysfunction. The math geeks, who calculate the structure for a mortgage-backed security, operating in a vacuum, used the same mathematical construct for subprime that they used for far less risky mortgage-backed securities. Agency attorneys and others who designed the legal and other documentary requirements to achieve certain ratings for high quality mortgage-backed securities also operated in a vacuum, using their tried and true template. Everyone robotically did what they always did, punched out and jumped on public transit home. Incredible as it may seem, when the first of these securities were rated, there was no one in the center who looked at the whole. Had anyone done this, the gaping flaw in this poorly integrated rating fiasco would have been immediately clear.

It is entirely possible that before subprime cratered, some at the two major agencies spotted the horrendous error. If this light bulb finally brightened after billions of dollars of these securities were already rated, this moment would have been horrifying. The newly enlightened would have two choices: One, massively downgrade these frighteningly high-rated securities, ravaging the agency reputation and causing huge market disruption, or two, pray. If, as I speculate, some at the major agencies, in time, saw the gaping mistake, their prayers were not answered. The flawed, ticking bomb exploded in their faces.

The ratings on CDOs (collateralized debt obligations) underscore, in the extreme, mistakes made by the agencies. Many of these amalgamated the weakest tranches of the subprime securities, and in so doing, the whole received a higher rating than the parts. Again, it is so utterly self-evident that the obligations of the underlying borrowers, pooled in these securities, are likely to come under pressure in tandem during a difficult macroeconomic or simply rising interest rate environment, that one pulls hair out wondering how the CDO construct consistently passed muster.

Former Treasury Secretary Paulson's blueprint for regulatory reform (released in March 2008), without mentioning the rating agencies, states that "[F]or whatever reason, investors may not have fully evaluated the credit risk and liquidity risk with certain CDO obligations." The blueprint goes on to suggest that the Federal Reserve, in an expanded role, could publish its own take on risk of various securities to alert the markets. Not a lot of teeth in this proposal, but it would certainly undercut the role of the rating agencies.

By the end of 1998, a number of investment banks cut their lines of credit to First Alliance, but I reluctantly acknowledge that Lehman was undeterred. LB recognized it was exposing itself to negative publicity, an exposure that climaxed in Technicolor with the airing of an ABC network piece on its prime time news magazine, "20/20." The story was watched by millions of Americans, dragging Lehman's name through the muck, along with the unrepentant, slimy profiteers at First Alliance. Yes, these were our clients. Were we any better? Fast-forwarding, by early 2000, FAM shut its doors under the weight of lawsuits and investigations, and in 2003, a federal court assigned liability for 10 percent (about $5 million) to Lehman in a $50 million class-action judgment against FAM. How did the court determine that our role amounted to a 10 percent transgression? Apparently because it deemed 10 percent just penalty for doing business with a mortgage factory that we evidently knew was unclean, but where Lehman, itself, did not directly carry out the misdeeds that hurt FAM's borrowers. Like some spouses of destructive alcoholics, we were enablers. We supplied the damned whiskey to those who abused it just outside Alcoholics Anonymous meetings.

Still, the subprime debacle did not come home to roost during the 1990's. At this time, volumes were fairly small. By the late 1990's, Lehman and Bear, the two subprime pioneers, as well as other investment banks, raked in much heftier fees on securities issuance and M&A by facil-

---

39. A hedge fund that collapsed in 1998, leading to a $3.75 billion bailout, supervised by the Federal Reserve, but paid for by 14 major financial institutions to prevent chaos in financial markets. Lehman Brothers contributed $100 million. Bear Stearns declined to participate.

itating the bubble that was building in the dot-com sector and the larger technology industry. Additionally, subprime contracted from 1999-2001, due to an investor flight to quality following the Russian debt crisis and the collapse of Long-Term Capital Management.[39] This shift implies that investors' assessment of the risk of subprime mortgage securitization risk was not aligned with the high agency ratings on these securities. However, before the tech/dot-com bubble burst around 2001/2002, much was afoot in Washington that would pave the way for the Armageddon of 2007 and 2008.

Phil Gramm, the veteran U.S. Senator and chairman of the Senate Banking Committee, long crusaded against regulation. Unlike nearly all members of Congress (in fact, all known to me), Gramm possessed a background and diploma in economics—credentials that served as a potent strategic asset in arguing financial and economic issues. Other senators and congressional representatives, with few if any exceptions, like the voting public, were and are simply unschooled in these disciplines. Armed with this background, Gramm could rhetorically take down sober colleagues one by one. Between 1999 and 2001, he successfully fought legislation that would block predatory lending, despite the indisputable fact that foreclosures and personal bankruptcy were both on the rise. He also paved the way for other legislation that would hobble regulation of Wall Street; he was indeed the lead name on the bill that did away with the Depression-era legislation that segregated the activities of investment banks, commercial banks and insurers. Much of this was accomplished with Clinton's support and executive signature.

A byproduct of the deregulating legislation was that financial institutions that began to emerge in multiple subsectors of finance were now regulated by multiple government entities, each responsible for oversight of different aspects of their activities, an arrangement in which effective coordination and comprehensive control would prove difficult, at best. The various regulators, even forgetting about their various failures, were never constructed to function as an amalgamated regime. Additionally, the Clinton administration itself recommended legislation that entirely exempted many off-balance sheet financial instruments (*e.g.*, letters of credit and guarantees) including many forms of derivatives,[40] from federal regulation. The unregulated instrument that would ultimately become most infamous was the credit derivative[41] (discussed later).

Both Gramm and Greenspan believed that regulation of financial institutions was best left to the enterprises themselves. Former Treasury Secretary Paulson's blueprint to overhaul the country's regulatory system specifically identifies the lack of regulation of many mortgage brokers and lenders as a key factor that led to the subprime meltdown. The blueprint notes that more than half of all subprime mortgages were originated by mortgage brokers and lenders with no federal oversight and indicates that for the most part state regulation was moribund. The blueprint is unambiguous in stating, "Brokers and lenders not subject to federal oversight have repeatedly been cited as the source of abusive subprime loans with adverse and profound consequences for consumers, the mortgage markets, and the financial system as a whole."[xxii] Former SEC Chairman William H. Donaldson, a George W. Bush appointee, while still on the job, introduced a program under which investment banks could opt in and out of substantial oversight at will. This was an

---

40. It would be hopeless to attempt in a footnote to make clear to anyone not steeped in finance exactly what a derivative is. In reading this book, it is only important that you understand that financial firms use derivatives to hedge, *i.e.,* offset risk positions to avoid potential losses or take on risk positions to potentially profit. It also important that one knows that derivatives are generally not reflected in published financial statements, may be included in some form in notes to the financial statements, but are often so complex that only specialists within a financial organization understand certain of them. As a result, it is difficult for most outsiders to gauge the inherent risk of a financial enterprise involved in derivatives. A simple example of an off-balance sheet obligation is a guarantee.

41. Not really a derivative in the classic sense of the word and much easier to explain. In short, a credit default swap is one party insuring another against the default of a security held by the latter. The holder of the security pays the counterparty, guaranteeing or insuring the security a fee to cover loss, just as a homeowner pays an insurer to cover loss. If the security defaults, the party insuring must make the holder whole. AIG was active as a credit default risk-taker, a significant component of its difficulties, as many of these off-balance sheet credit default swaps they contracted insured against loss on today's so-called *toxic assets*.

obvious recipe for a collapsed financial soufflé, as capitalist greed often, if not invariably, clouds judgment. Of course, a framework for government regulation does not guarantee sound control and ethical behavior. An extreme case in point: the Swiss banks, historically highly intimate with and scrutinized by their national banking regulators, laundered a mother lode of Nazi gold. Until the late 1990's, when they were outed, they vehemently denied that at the end of World War II, and for decades hence, they held the deposits of Holocaust survivors (or the legitimate heirs of the murdered Jews) who entrusted them with life savings. Of course, this is a singularly nefarious example of regulation gone awry. If oversight is both ethical and sufficiently comprehensive, this reduces the likelihood of problems that can undermine us all.

In the United States, forces minimizing oversight and enforcement were only one part of the problem. The other was that regulation in our country has developed over about seventy-five years on a more or less ad hoc basis, with oversight bodies and practices created as needed. As a result, there are a fractured group of regulators with overlapping missions and many areas where unsound financial activity simply falls through the cracks. There are five federal depository regulators, supplemented by the many state-based financial supervisors. There is but one federal securities regulator that unfortunately has traditionally focused more on police work than maintenance of financial soundness. This body, the SEC, is supplemented by various state regulators as well as self-regulatory organizations for various subsectors within the broader financial industry. There is a single financial futures regulator whose duties have evolved to overlap substantially with those of the SEC. Insurance regulation is highly variable, as there are more than fifty, mostly individual, state regulators.

Greenspan also set the table for a significant ramp-up in mortgage lending and an unsustainable rise in real estate prices through an easy money policy that kept interest rates at historically low levels. The protracted low-rate environment led to elevated borrowing for mortgages and subprime ones, in particular, and also to a free-for-all in consumer consumption on easy credit terms. The impossible house of cards thusly constructed now lies flat on the table of what became a high-stakes economic casino.

Under Bush, the trend toward both less and increasingly impotent regulation exceeded anything Clinton had in mind. In 2003, "W's" administration obtained a Supreme Court ruling that regulation of national bank subsidiaries in individual states was a job for the federal government. But the federal government was heading down a road of minimizing regulation and enforcement (discussed further below). Essentially all of the States' attorneys general protested, understanding Bush's "do not enforce" credo would hobble oversight. Indeed, the most meaningful enforcement over the last decade has largely been at the state level. Eliot Spitzer, New York's attorney general, in 2001, well before his recent resignation from New York's governorship in disgrace (when exposed as a customer of prostitutes), as part of his anti-corruption crusade, investigated subprime giant Household International. He successfully obtained a judgment of $484 million to penalize the company for predatory lending.

In effect, the Bush administration abandoned regulation of the financial sector, leaving the task to a disinterested Fed. The SEC's investment banking oversight under Donaldson weakened, consistent with the Bush White House's preference for a hands-off regime. Donaldson, a former investment banker, only favored lax regulation for others of his species. In 2005, when he pushed for tougher regulation of mutual funds and hedge funds,[42] the White House pulled the plug on Donaldson. A long-time Bush family friend, he obediently resigned. He was replaced by Christopher Cox, a nineteen-year *business-friendly* congressman.

Early on, Cox was uncharacteristically quick to point out that the Donaldson program, under which Wall Street firms voluntarily opted in and out of supervision, was unsound. Indeed, this program was insanity in the extreme and Cox shut it down. This one action in no way foreshadowed his ideology in running the SEC. In nearly every other respect, Cox

---

42. A fund, usually used by wealthy individuals and institutions, which is allowed to use aggressive strategies that are unavailable to mutual funds and more highly regulated financial entities. Hedge funds have grown to become a potent, influential force in financial markets, but remain exempt from many of the rules that govern others in financial markets.

marched in lockstep with his boss, Bush and former Fed Chairman Greenspan, believing that for the most part financial institutions could best police themselves.

Under Cox, by design, SEC enforcement activities were decimated. Enforcement staff were stripped of their long-standing authority to determine penalties. These powers transferred to the SEC's five commissioners. As a direct consequence, after ticking up initially between 2005 and 2007, penalties and fines assessed plunged from $1.5 billion to just over a third that amount. In fact, between 2004 and 2007, broker-dealer cases accounted for only 3 percent of enforcement investigations.

In Cox's SEC, the commissioners, three Republicans and two Democrats, most often voted unanimously on petty, uncontroversial matters. When graver cases came before them, the three Republicans generally voted as a block. On the whole, the Republican commissioners, especially Paul Atkins, consistently pushed for relaxation of enforcement. Atkins even expressed the opinion that the agency in which he was a senior figure was not constitutionally authorized to exist. Former high level enforcement staffers have reported that Cox delayed major cases. When the commissioners split a vote, Cox might simply shut down the case. When the two Democratic commissioners vacated their seats, "W" left them empty for seven months, enabling the Republican commissioners, even more pro-business and anti-enforcement than Cox, to outvote his veto.

In addition to all this, even approval to begin an investigation, a quick, standard procedure under Donaldson and his predecessors, mired in glue. Cox reduced the role of a new risk assessment office Donaldson established to anticipate and then act to prevent or minimize future market troubles and crises. Donaldson's intention was to staff it with eight full-timers, but Cox only filled the positions with part-timers who, in aggregate, worked the hours of two full-time staff. Later, Cox endorsed Bush's proposed slight increase in the SEC budget, one so small that it could actually lead to the loss of staff.

Enforcement staff, finding themselves increasingly neutered, became demoralized. This led to an ongoing exodus of leading enforcement professionals. I have heard secondhand about the departure of individual ethical enforcement staff. Given the many efforts to declaw SEC enforcement, Cox and the Bush administration may have welcomed the loss of these best enforcers.

With oversight out the window, in the years that followed the dot-com meltdown, Lehman, Bear and others, entirely unchecked by government watchdogs, would fully embrace subprime securitization as a vehicle to drive profits. Lehman actually began laying the groundwork for its ramp-up of subprime securitization as early as 1999 by establishing a subprime unit with joint venture partners. However, it was during the Bush years that volumes accelerated enormously. In 2001, Lehman bought out its subprime unit partner. That same year, LB bought a stake in another subprime mortgage lender. In 2004, LB bought the rest and merged the two subprime units into one. The beauty, for Lehman, in owning this consolidated subprime unit was that the firm could harvest fees at all stages of the subprime process. The subprime subsidiary generated fees for extending the mortgage loans. Lehman then bought the mortgages from its subsidiary, as well as other subprime lenders, and generated fees by packaging them into securities—the sale of which was facilitated by the ratings assigned at erroneously high levels by the major bond raters, Moody's, Standard & Poor's, and Fitch.

Between 1994 and 2005, subprime market size would increase from about $40 billion to a number around a dozen times that size. In 2005 and 2006, Lehman led Wall Street in subprime mortgage-backed security issuance, pumping more than $50 billion of the securities into the market in each of those two years. It is particularly shocking that my firm continued down this path at breakneck speed as defaults on subprime had ticked up by 2006. But we were not alone. Subprime peaked as a percentage of total mortgage originations, reaching 20 percent in each of these two years.

* * *

With the market beginning to sour, Lehman became the defendant in numerous lawsuits. Comments by former Lehman subprime subsidiary employees are contradictory. Some characterize the Lehman-owned ventures as utilizing tactics similar to those used by a typical predatory lender, while others say they witnessed no improprieties. The precise truth is difficult to assess. But with many former employees reporting unsavory tactics at the Lehman subprime origination units, these subsidiaries could not have been squeaky clean.

Regardless, the bottom line is that Lehman was a leader among many players that profited from a market in which numerous red flags had been visible over a number of years. Knowing all this, it is befuddling that we acted without the moral compass I believed was central to Lehman's global culture. It is equally confounding as evidence mounted that the market was softening, and seasoned internal professionals shouted that we were headed down a treacherous path, that we continued to both sell massive amounts to investors and loaded our own balance sheet with a heavy real estate concentration.

Disaster struck in the summer of 2007 when subprime mortgages began to default, and two Bear Stearns hedge funds that invested heavily in the securities went bust. Each major rating agency received its worst black eye ever, with numerous defaults of highly rated subprime issues, as well as massive downgrades of many others now considered fundamentally more risky than when initially assessed. Moody's, for example, in July and August alone slashed ratings on nearly a thousand securities with a combined value of $25 billion. This substantially undermined market confidence in the three major agencies, which are now subject to increasing SEC oversight. This supervision became official through the Credit Rating Agency Act of 2006 that authorized the SEC to both license and oversee rating agencies as "nationally recognized statistical rating organizations." (Though it remains to be seen how effective this will be.) However, until the subprime meltdown it seemed the Bush/Cox SEC did little, actually, to perform this oversight, if indeed the function was even meaningfully staffed. The SEC has at least established new rules governing agency activities that target the perceived conflicts of interest and agency behavior in rating structured finance transactions, a category that includes mortgage securitizations. Most specifically, the aim of these new regulations is to prevent rating agencies from dictating to issuers of securities rather specific constructs to elicit desired rating outcomes.

* * *

In hindsight, it is crystal clear that neither Congress nor the Executive branch did anything to prevent the crisis, and unwittingly did much that contributed to the disaster.

Capping Cox's reign, he reassured the American public as to Bear Stearns financial solidity just days before its collapse. This is particularly disturbing as the SEC's independent Inspector General, David Kolz, criticized the commission's handling of a Bear Stearns investigation that might have served as an actionable early warning if it was handled appropriately. The investigation related to improper activities in the sale of CDO's to Latin American investors. But the case was handled by the SEC's Miami office, whose director is reported to have had a cozy, twenty year friendship with a Bear Stearns attorney. Incredibly, in 2007, this Miami SEC director dropped the case, letting Bear off the hook on a $500 thousand settlement the investment bank had already agreed to pay. It reeked of favoritism and conflict of interest, with ramifications that extended well beyond this particular investigation. Kolz said, "A significant opportunity to . . . uncover evidence of a systemic problem at Bear Stearns was . . . lost through neglect."[xxiii] Kolz has further criticized other aspects of the SEC's oversight of Bear Stearns, indicating that the agency ignored multiple warning signs.

Another recent SEC embarrassment that played out publicly was an allegation that roughly three years ago, when John Mack was about to step into the CEO post at Morgan Stanley, he was given special treatment in an insider trading case due to political connections. An SEC lawyer who persisted in efforts to take Mack's testimony was fired allegedly because he would not back down. Again, the SEC's Inspector General, Kolz, found fault with the agency's conduct and recommended disciplinary action for the enforcement chief, Linda Thomson. Unsurprisingly, again consistent with the "W" era trashing of oversight and enforcement, Kolz's recommendation was effectively ignored.

Kolz also received an anonymous tip that Thomson improperly provided J.P. Morgan Chase with information about Bear Stearns while the two firms were negotiating J.P.'s takeover of Bear. Nothing has come of this.

Though unproven, the prevailing climate provided latitude for such abuse.

The SEC's reputation has been further sullied by the Bernard Madoff fiasco. Cox concedes that the agency failed to act on "credible, specific"[xxiv] allegations dating back to 1999. As Cox led the SEC only since 2005, others were also responsible for the blunder. The fundamental take-away from the growing heap of SEC slipups is that as currently constituted, the agency is incapable of competent oversight. Because the SEC operated within a black box from the moment it was founded, many core practices are known only by current and former employees, and to a lesser extent, by those it has investigated. This renders clear-eyed assessment of its activities and effectiveness challenging, at best. Only recently, in 2008, did the agency make public its enforcement manual.

Around March/April 2008, Treasury Secretary Paulson recommended the previously mentioned overhaul of the nation's entire financial sector oversight apparatus. Not a bad idea and this is underway, driven by 2009's changes in the executive and legislative branches of our government. Unfortunately, Paulson's suggested initiative came too late to salvage Bear Stearns or Lehman. And once Lehman was directed by Paulson to file for bankruptcy—a decision hailed by many as the worst lapse in judgment during the continuing nuclear winter in financial markets—Paulson's tactics shifted and lurched by the hour. The once respected CEO of Goldman Sachs, it became clear, was just another Bush administration soldier acting independently, while lacking a clear, well-mapped plan.

The fallout in subprime, the primary source of financial dislocation covered in this chapter, spread across credit markets generally. But it was more a catalyst than a singular cause of the disintegration. Wherever one turned, our capital markets embraced imprudence and excess. Because the Fed had under Greenspan long maintained low interest rates, many institutional investors were in recent years increasingly willing to buy riskier securities than they had bought in the past to increase average yields in their portfolios. This, in turn, enabled many companies to take on

---

43. Leverage is synonymous with borrowing or debt. A highly leveraged company has a debt burden that is far higher than that of the average company.

unprecedented levels of debt, as markets of the past would have shunned such highly leveraged[43] borrowers. As investors increasingly craved the yield on securities of the weakest, most highly leveraged companies, private equity houses jumped into the fray, buying up companies with massive leverage to increase returns on investment.[44] However, when Bear Stearns' hedge fund collapse sparked the subprime implosion, investors rapidly reversed course, and the market for these highly levered[45] securities dried up.

Other casualties of the subprime debacle were those who took the risk in credit default swaps. In the simplest of terms, as described earlier in footnote 43, this is insurance that a holder of a security buys to cover any losses if the paper defaults. Many investors covered their investments in subprime mortgage-backed securities with these so-called swaps. AIG, as also earlier noted, was a heavy player, so that when the subprime market melted, losses for the massive insurer quickly mounted. Had the government not bailed out AIG, its failure to make good on its credit default or insurance obligations could well have caused a domino effect, where holders of the swaps, depending on AIG to make good on its obligations, might in turn have defaulted. The fallout, given AIG's tentacles, would have been even more destructive than that caused by Lehman's failure, given AIG's size and the nature of its obligations.

Highly leveraged loans, as well as the price multiples[46] paid and the degree of leverage, all peaked in 2007. Once subprime crashed, the market remained sullen for the remainder of 2007 into 2008. It was difficult to close on most new financings that would have been slam-dunk deals before the mortgage debacle. In M&A, private equity had displaced strate-

44. The return on equity invested. More explicitly, net profit divided by invested equity.

45. Same as highly leveraged, *i.e.*, with a high debt burden

46. Price multiples are the value paid for a company relative to some multiple such as the company's book value, market value (if publicly traded), or some measure of cash flow or earnings. The currency for the acquisition is generally cash (on the acquirer's balance sheet or raised through a debt offering) or the acquirer's stock, or some combination of the two. When a private equity house raises funds through a debt security offering to fund an acquisition, the debt obligation generally resides on the target company's balance sheet, to be serviced and repaid with the company's cash flow.

gic buyers, as these aggressive enterprise buyers were willing to pay far higher prices. Investor interest in the debt that funded these corporate finance adventures now plummeted. Indeed, the defaults in subprime prompted all investors to reassess the risk-reward dynamics in their portfolios.

But Lehman still, by all appearances both internal and external, while suffering along with other investment banks due to conservative risk management, appeared clearly less vulnerable to the harsh market than most. I cannot even begin to count the number of times I told friends and family not to worry. Sure, I expected a lower bonus for 2008, but Lehman would be fine. I was not concerned. In fact, in Investment Banking there was a silver lining. As usual in a down market, it looked like once again we were gaining market share. I was confident that once the current cycle played out, Lehman would emerge nipping at Goldman's heels, with everyone else a distant third or worse, and that all our stock would rebound to its highest level ever. I had experienced crappy years before. I worked in a cyclical industry. But each time the market fell, like Lehman, I too later rebounded with larger bonuses than ever, and a share price-driven net worth that would fund a relatively early retirement. Over the long-term, no doubt, these lean years would ultimately position me for an earlier retirement, and not an involuntary one.

CHAPTER 4

The Music Stops—2007

*"Of all human ills, greatest is
fortune's wayward tyranny."*
—SOPHOCLES

2007 was an odd year for all of Wall Street. It began with robust markets in which Lehman and others raked in profits, then tanked in the summer. Of course, I never counted my chickens, my bonus possibilities, before the end of November when our financial year ended. Difficult years generally do not begin and end with the financial calendar. Lehman was on track to smash the record profits of the previous year, 2006, but I have seen multiple reversals of fortune end a record-breaking run in the past. So no, it was not a complete surprise that the thunderous crescendo that accompanied Lehman's surging fortunes in the new millennium stopped on a dime during the summer of 2007. This was a moment I knew would inevitably arrive, the only question was when. I had my answer. However, I did not know that, this time, the reversal of fortune would be patently different. Indeed, the abrupt downturn in market conditions marked the beginning of a fall that stood a veteran LB investment banker's belief about the firm on its head. Before 2007, the up years far outnumbered the down ones. Our firm was pure. We had ethics. Sure we were greedy, but not in a bad way. You cannot be an effective investment banker unless you are constantly in motion with your eyes steadfast on potential revenues.

I took comfort that at Lehman we were extraordinarily risk averse, guarding our profitability and our reputation with equal vigilance. It was, in fact, a point of pride that when other firms suffered from major exposures to risks gone bad, Lehman emerged as the nimblist of firms. With minimal pain, we repeatedly managed hazards that rocked others' worlds. Certainly, our fortunes rose and fell with the market environment, just as all ships rise and fall with the tide. Yet, we did better than most in the good years, and impressively outperformed in the down ones. Until mid-2007 and the subprime debacle, Lehman had been on a tear, especially after 9/11, outperforming most of Wall Street during both good and bad market environments. My bonus would be constrained for 2007. Nonetheless, I was fully confident that the setback would be more than offset by later firm-wide and personal earnings, reflecting gains in market position that would bear fruit as we emerged from just another downturn. The lower share price that I would receive on the stock portion of my bonus would result in subsequent outsized gains on Lehman stock, when the substantial portion of my compensation vested.

I, like most, observed with envy Goldman's singular success in placing a significant bet against subprime. Uniquely among investment banks, the devastation of subprime MBS values substantially benefitted Goldman's 2007 bottom line. The newspapers were replete with stories about the massive 2007 bonuses for Goldman's ranks, in stark contrast to what investment bankers at other firms, including Lehman, were earning in that difficult year.

At the same time, I was perfectly satisfied that LB had not placed a similar bet. In fact, I told many people that Lehman would never risk a Goldman-style position. Its track record on these bets was impressive, truly defied the odds. But Lehman, I told everyone, was far too risk averse to take a position that, if right, could massively boost earnings, but if wrong, could sharply reduce them. Our downside was the industry downside. Unlike in the Glucksman era, and even in the 1990s, we would never bet the firm. And in the worst of times, market share would slip through our competitors' fingers into our fast grip. Indeed, since becoming a public company, even in the most horrendous of downturns, we had never registered even a quarterly loss.

Moreover, no other firm's shares rose as Lehman's did. And while all public companies' stock prices are a measure of success, in investment banking the sense of this is particularly keen. It is in this industry that money and share price are most singularly revered as evidence of triumph. A surging share price in an investment bank with substantial employee ownership creates both vast wealth and pride among its troops. At Lehman, where employees owned nearly a third of the firm, the share price performance was our religion. Many in our ranks, with the ascent of Lehman's shares, on that book value alone, became quick multi-millionaires. For a number of bankers who had been at Lehman from the time the firm went public, if they had held onto most of their Lehman holdings, this alone put their net worth at eight figures, numbers similar to what Peterson and Glucksman had pocketed years earlier. At least one Investment Banking industry group head regularly bragged that he never sold a single Lehman share. He wore this statement like a badge of honor. The top handful of Lehman executives had nine figures of net worth, and in Dick Fuld's case, probably surpassed the $1 billion mark. This was an unjustifiable golden age for corporate chiefs: top executives received bonuses (most of their compensation) that even on an inflation-adjusted basis amounted to multiples of what senior executives received years earlier.

The portion of bonus one received in shares was based on both title and total compensation. The higher one's title and total pay, the larger the percentage of shares and options in one's bonus. For anyone in core revenue generating functions, *i.e.,* those most highly paid, the shares represented a particularly large portion of bonuses. This is typical of most investment banks. But there was a certain magic in the Lehman bonus equation. First, employees received these shares at a discount of 20–25 percent to market value, and for a number of years, these shares were priced on a date when the stock had lulled. Based on the price upon which one's stock bonus was pegged, the value in shares often already reflected a substantial gain upon delivery, albeit as restricted stock units (*i.e.,* stock one couldn't touch for as much as five years until they fully vested or unless you retired). Second, the shares delivered an incredible long-term return. All professionals who remained at LB long enough grew wealthy on the share price appreciation alone. Those who got more of their bonus in shares than others saw their wealth rise at a breathtaking pace. In round numbers, from the 1994 initial public offering to the stock's peak, the shares returned an average of 25 percent per year, or about twenty times their value.

Ironically, in 1994, the year of Lehman's IPO, not everyone was thrilled to see their bonuses partially and later increasingly allotted in shares. Lehman was an underperformer, and upon its spin-off from American Express, many wondered if we would even survive. Early losses, remember, had left capital at a flimsy two percent of assets. Cash was looking pretty good compared to Lehman shares. Personally, I felt I had enough exposure to Lehman simply because it was my employer. Did I really want to hold this dicey, second rate firm's shares as well? It is fair to say that none of us for a moment imagined we would see the roughly twenty-fold increase in the share price between the initial public offering and the stock's peak. Of course, the double irony, for those of us who held onto most of our shares, was that this wealth was paper or electronic, and disappeared with Lehman.

This legendary ascent of the Lehman share price, naturally, reflected Lehman's performance. But, yet another irony: it was because the firm was such an underperformer when we went public that we were able to increase our earnings so singularly. Had we already been a top Wall Street firm on the date of our IPO, we could not have seen the gains that accrued before our final decline. We were initially valued as the laggard we were. The fact that we so totally sucked but rose to become a top performer is what led to such massive returns. Prior to 2007, while I had the greatest confidence that The Brothers would continue to prosper, and the share price continue to climb, the returns of the past were now clearly obsolete. We had gotten too good. The gains would be in increments rather than multiples.

Lehman overcame many hurdles between its spin-off from American Express and 9/11. For starters, the firm successfully weathered ongoing rumors that it would again be acquired or would likely fail. This was most notable during the Long-Term Capital Management hedge fund crisis, when the banter in the markets was that Lehman's exposure to LTCM would bring it down, causing the share price to crater. Rumors also circulated during the "Russia Crisis." On each occasion, senior management sprang into action to dispel rumors. In an encounter that became Lehman folklore, Dick Fuld, who suspected Goldman was part of the LTCM rumor mill, told that firm's then CFO, John Thain, while glaring at him menacingly, "When I find out who it is, I'm going to reach down his throat and tear out his heart."[xxv]

Obviously, winning friends among the elite at other Wall Street firms was not the top item on Dick Fuld's agenda. In fact, he often resented his blue-blooded counterparts at other firms. Despite a reasonably affluent upbringing and the mega-wealth he amassed as Lehman's CEO, Fuld continued to harbor the bitter class resentments that had agitated his mentor, Lew Glucksman, and was not interested in mixing with the moneyed Wall Street powerbrokers. To many, he seemed paranoid, as if it were Lehman against the world, with the world insidiously determined to squash Lehman. The anger that often flared and the hostile reaction this engendered would come back to bite him. Still, when news of Dick's comment to Goldman's CFO spread throughout Lehman, we applauded his pluck. We were so accustomed to the role of underdog that moments like these were a twisted source of pride.

And so, Fuld's view of Lehman's place in the world was one he managed to spread to a surprising degree throughout the Lehman culture—and not just in the U.S., but globally. Lehman's former head of corporate communications in London, Andrew Gowers, in an article for the Sunday *Times* of London wrote, "I lost count of the number of times I had to listen to senior executives explaining that there was no point in engaging with the press because the press actively wanted Lehman to fail."[xxvi]

In time, the recurrent rumors each dissipated, with Lehman regaining the market's full confidence. During these same years, Lehman also began to diversify its business with mixed, but increasing success, reducing its longstanding reliance on fixed income.

It was after 9/11, however, that Lehman truly ascended anew to the upper ranks of Wall Street firms. "9/11" exacerbated the inevitable broad market sell-off and recession that had to follow the years of Internet bubble excess and a generally overcharged, overconfident economy. For investment bankers, this meant reduced deal flow and a couple of years of falling bonuses. Many firms on Wall Street went through several rounds of layoffs. Lehman, however, held off, looking beyond the immediate, subdued period to the inevitable recovery ahead.

Lehman's strategy to maintain strength during this down market was distinct. It was also clear that this was Dick Fuld's vision. This was not a time to shrink. It was a time to hold together the franchise we were so painstakingly building. In fact, instead of off-loading employees, Lehman actually went on a spending spree during this period, picking off teams of big producers from other firms, with the lure of guaranteed fatter year-end bonuses than they would receive if they stayed at their current firms. As a result, Lehman was able not only to preserve its franchise—a work in progress—but actually strengthened it during a down market when we outperformed most other Wall Street firms. Sure profits fell, as did our compensation, but we picked up market share and received Lehman stock in our bonuses at valuations that reflected the market lull, so that once the market recovered, our stock price and individual wealth again soared. It was only after these doldrums extended for a couple of years that Lehman culled some from its headcount. Still, there was far greater stability than at other firms, and as the economy and markets turned, Lehman was able to flex its way to the podium on an increasing number of high profile mega-financings and advisory assignments.

In 2003, Lehman, a non-entity in M&A advisory only a few years earlier, was involved in deals amounting to nearly $100 billion, or about 20 percent of total mergers and acquisitions. Toward the end of the same year, Lehman bought Neuberger Berman, substantially beefing up asset management, a stable source of revenues in both up and down markets. This source of revenues is a must for a broadly successful investment bank, as it partially offsets earnings softness that occurs when market access for issuers of securities becomes difficult There was initially some criticism of the price Lehman paid for Neuberger, but over a relatively short period, revenue growth in this asset management business proved the critics wrong.

From 2005 to mid-2007, Lehman compiled an uninterrupted string of record quarters, with bonuses matching the firm's improved prosperity. Moreover, while Fixed Income had accounted for 66 percent of revenues in 1998, in 2007 it contributed 31 percent. Fixed income remained as strong as ever. But its contribution was a smaller slice of the pie because Lehman had built other robust businesses. The diversification was even greater when one considers that we sourced an increasing share of Lehman's profits overseas. In fact, in 2007, for the first time, Lehman generated a majority of its revenues in non-U.S. markets.

Within the Investment Banking Division, our success was broad. Certainly, our climb up the league tables (lists measuring issuance of a variety of securities by financial houses) was a chief, highly visible marker of Lehman's growing success. Internally, Skip McGee, the current head of investment banking, introduced a new ritual, the "Big Deal" award. This would become iconic of all that we ultimately accomplished.

Skip, along with Dick Fuld, recognized that for IBD to join the ranks of the leading firms, the division would have to hit a lot more home runs. For some time we had been hitting only singles and an occasional double—more and more of them—but not enough extra-base hits. Even in abundance, singles would never be sufficient for us to realize our aspirations. And so Skip made it starkly clear that in IBD the Holy Grail was winning not just deal mandates, but "Big Deal" mandates. These were and continue to be defined, in the new BarCap incarnation, as deals earning the firm fees above a specific eight-figure threshold.

At Monday Morning Meetings for all investment bankers, "Big Deal" awards (identically engraved Lucite blocks) are ceremoniously distributed to all team members. During the year, these special Lucite "deal toys" were introduced, only a few such awards were earned. But as Lehman hit its stride, these awards were handed out at virtually every Monday Morning Investment Banking Division (IBD) meeting, often for more than one deal, and frequently with fees earned surpassing the revenue threshold by a wide margin, if not by a large multiple. We were succeeding as never before or at least to an extent not seen in decades.

Having initially, in a tortured decision, joined a laggard firm characterized by divisive infighting, a one-dimensional fixed income business, with third-rate positions in virtually all other broker-dealer activities, this new reality felt amazing. I marveled at my dumb luck in joining a firm that turned from a crippled toad into a celebrated prince.

The inverse of the feel good "Big Deal" rituals were dreaded calls from

Skip McGee when we failed to win a key deal mandate. Invariably we would be held accountable: "Why weren't we leading the deal? Why was this 'Big Deal' a trophy for another firm?" And these calls, or similar emails, or even meetings, were effective. Money and fear are both primal motivators.

The latter part of 2007 severely cut into the surging, robust profits earned in the first half of the year. Subprime, as discussed in the last chapter, was the spark. And Lehman, as noted, led the charge into subprime in the mid-1990s, and upped its devotion to this extremely lucrative pursuit as the subprime bubble grew larger. Moreover, from 2004 forward, Lehman with near total abandon, increased its exposure to mortgages generally, most notably commercial real estate and Alt-A loans.[47] But what was going on behind the scenes at Lehman that allowed this to happen? After all, were we not the once sloppy firm, now a born-again conservative risk manager? The answers to these simple enough questions are all the more puzzling when one considers that Dick Fuld, on several occasions, voiced concerns that would logically have motivated him to direct his minions to reduce, not increase, Lehman's real estate risk.

As early as November of 2004, Dick told people around him that he was concerned the continued low interest rate environment might be creating a bubble. During a meeting with colleagues around that time, he said of the easy money, "It's paving the road with cheap tar. When the weather changes, the potholes that were there will be deeper and uglier."[xxvii] And yet, we continued to pile on real estate risk, this cosmetically winning, but ultimately defeating tar.

In January of 2007, when Fuld attended the annual World Economic Forum at Davos, he told lunch guests that he was concerned about the U.S. housing market, the huge amount of debt that many companies had put on their balance sheets through leveraged finance transactions and the run-up in crude oil prices. As a result, he said, Lehman, always keen to limit risk, had "taken a bit of money off the table."[xxviii] He impressed his guests with this sage caution. Internally at Lehman, it was the sort of

---

47. Mortgage loans to homeowners who lack documentary proof of their income.

prudence we now expected. What Fuld had said, however, was complete fiction. Lehman was not reducing its exposure. Even in early 2007 with visible fissures in the housing market, Lehman was increasing its real estate holdings.

Fuld seemed to read the tea leaves correctly. In his bones, a trader, one would have expected him to cut his losses when he could. A good trader knows better than most that it is a bad idea to up the ante indefinitely. In fact, Dick, years earlier, grew nauseated as he watched a gambler in a casino double down again and again without a win. He recalled the reckless foolishness as the most cautionary of remembrances. But there are those who claim Dick was increasingly out of touch with many of his firm's activities, and this was true to a meaningful extent. Still, he was fully aware of Lehman's overall real estate strategy. Just a few months earlier, Fuld conducted his annual review of Mike Gelband, global head of Fixed Income. Gelband, with good reason, become bearish on the real estate market. Commenting on Lehman's exposure, he told Fuld, "The world is changing. We have to rethink our business model."

Fuld responded. "You're too conservative. You don't want to take risk." In trader lingo this was an obvious, belittling dig. He was in Gelband's face, like a small-minded playground bully taunting another kid as a complete pansy. Gelband was not intimidated, and more importantly, as would become clear, his caution was well-grounded. Had his advice been followed, Lehman may well have survived and even rebounded from the then harsh market, still a leader, still admired for its ability to dodge risks that crushed others, perhaps with an even stronger market position.

The only conceivable basis for Fuld to be unaware of Lehman's full real estate exposure was if he believed the firm's hedges limited the visible risk. Even so, hedges generally reduce the profitability of a risk position, and Lehman, despite its diversification away from fixed income, was making big dollars on its real estate book. In fact, Lehman was bigger into real estate than any other investment bank, with the possible exception of Bear Stearns, if one tallied all Bear's credit default swaps on mortgage securities. Still, I cannot entirely rule out the hedge excuse, if only because there are no CEO's on Wall Street who, in today's world, understand the complexities of all aspects of their firms' businesses. It simply is not possible.

Richard Fuld had started his long Lehman career in trading and so probably had a better feel for fixed income risk than many other Wall Street
CEO's, but trading has evolved into a far more complex endeavor of exot-
ic hedges and derivatives that simply did not exist when Fuld was actively on a trading floor. Fuld still operated with a trader's mentality, relying
on his core instincts. This would not serve him well. He could not possibly have fully grasped all aspects of Lehman risk, let alone relied on pure
instinct to navigate today's complex waters. Like his counterparts at other
firms, he relied on teams of highly specialized risk managers to protect the
firm in its wide-ranging activities. He was not up to speed on the intrica-
cies of our risk positions. But let us not forget, *he had taunted Gelband for
the latter's well-founded caution.* He was aware that Lehman was placing a
huge real estate bet. It was the elephant in the room.

Against this backdrop, in 2007, Lehman added $12 billion of commer-
cial real estate exposure. The largest chunk of this came in late May when,
together with joint-venture partners, LB, at the absolute top of the market, bought Archstone Smith Trust, a property investment company.
When commercial real estate values soon fell, this investment became one
of Lehman's most toxic assets. An investment of this size had to gain the
approval of the executive committee, chaired by Fuld. How did he go
along with such an investment, given the misgivings that I have cited
above? It had to have his sanction. And no one dared contradict him. If
this committee meeting was like many others, Joe Gregory, Lehman's
president, primed Fuld to approve this transaction before the committee
convened. Yes, Gregory had an insatiable appetite for real estate profits.
Unfortunately his hunger would outlast the feast.

In March 2007, Gelband, had lunch with Joe Gregory, Fuld's long-
trusted number two, the firm's president. Gelband again voiced grave concerns about Lehman's real estate exposure at this lunch, just as he had with
Fuld. Like Gregory and Fuld, Gelband spent his entire career at Lehman,
and so was disturbed, as only a lifer could be, about the irresponsible concentration in real estate. Surely he agonized that, in effect, Gregory was
willing to bet the firm and said so, though perhaps not in so many words.
Nonetheless, the message from Lehman's powerful president was clear.
From his seat opposite Gelband, Gregory told the highly regarded head of

Fixed Income, "Either you make a change or I'm going to."[xxix] In May of
2007, Gelband was gone. A revolving door of Gelband successors,
between his departure and Lehman's bankruptcy, all lacked real estate
experience. Gregory, by now a junkie, hooked on the real estate returns
realized to date, recklessly pushed forward.

Even in the best of times, any competent risk manager avoids too large
a concentration in any one sector, in any one form of risk. Indeed, this
practice is what one learns in Credit Risk 101. Risk concentration is so
obvious that many far-less finance savvy individual investors make certain
that their nest egg portfolios are diverse. Too large a concentration, these
average investors know, can quickly sink you if the area of concentration
takes a major hit. And indeed, this is precisely what happened to Lehman.
Concentrations in real estate, both direct and indirect also played a role in
the troubles of Bear Stearns (as noted), as well as Merrill Lynch, AIG, Fannie Mae, Freddie Mac, Washington Mutual (WaMu), Wachovia, Citigroup, and Union Bank of Switzerland (UBS), to name just a few. All
received government support (in UBS' case, a Swiss government bailout[48])
or salvaged themselves through mergers with other financial institutions.

While Gregory was the self-anointed "feeler" among senior management, pioneering Lehman's sharp focus on such issues as diversity and
employee philanthropy, and spouted liberal politics, he was also a pit bull,
famous for his rage, and tolerated no dissent, as seen in his conflict with
Gelband. In short, if you stood in his way, you were a goner, not even a
speed bump. And in slight contrast to Fuld, who at least occasionally
voiced some concern about Lehman's real estate position, Gregory's real
estate addiction was unwavering as he was determined to amass increasingly vast positions, with the ill-fated view that the real estate market had
bottomed. In this conviction, he had company, but certainly not among
those whose job it was to be coolly objective.

I rarely saw the ugly side of Joe Gregory. In my dealings with him, he
always appeared gregarious and anything but mean-spirited. The few
times I saw him admonish a banker he seemed justified and his reaction,

---

48. The terms of the Swiss government bailout of UBS are so severe that they hobble the
institution's ability to maintain its global investment banking franchise.

if stern and tinged with anger, was appropriate to the situation, even restrained. And while he generally stood just outside the limelight in the adjacent shadows, when he did speak to a group, he immersed himself in the role of a supreme commander with the gentlest of souls. Others I know saw the harsh, intolerant side. Alex Kirk, for example, who had worked with Gelband and shared Gelband's concern that Lehman's real estate exposure was a ticking bomb, was equally vocal, though knowing Alex, probably louder about his misgivings. Gregory soon made it clear to Kirk that he had no future at Lehman, leading Kirk to resign in February of 2008.

So who was running Lehman anyway? Was Dick still in charge? Glucksman's bloodless coup, when he wrested total control of Lehman from Peterson was a history through which Dick Fuld had lived. Based on his senior staffing decisions over the years, it is clear he never wanted a strong number two who could do to him what Glucksman had done to Peterson. After ousting Pettit in 1996, it would be six years before Dick appointed a new COO. In 2000, Mike McKeever, one of two co-heads of investment banking, left the firm after Dick gradually stripped him of most of his responsibilities. Rumors circulated that his fall from grace occurred when he differed with or opposed Dick. (Originally, McKeever had been one of three heads of Investment Banking. Shared leadership is rarely a condition that endures long on Wall Street. I have seen it several times at Lehman, always short-lived, leading one to wonder whether such appointments are more a contest than a long-term leadership plan.) By the time Dick elevated Gregory to president, who triumphed over Co-COO Brad Jack in securing the spot, Fuld had known him for decades. (Brad, previously sole head of Investment Banking after McKeever left, when promoted to Co-COO, ceded Investment Banking Division leadership to Skip McGee. He would ultimately outshine Brad in the role.) After losing out on the president spot, Jack languished for a while in a senior client relationship role, *i.e.,* a bullshit job, and then retired with the usual "Dear Colleague" email announcement from Fuld thanking Brad for his years of invaluable service, noting the retiring executive planned, of course, to spend more time with his family.

In any case, while there was regular talk that Gregory could succeed

GLSEN's 2005 Respect Awards New York Gala

Joe Gregory, Chairman of and representing Lehman Brothers, and guest (Photo by Desiree Navarro/FilmMagic) 16 May 2005

Fuld as CEO, Joe made it clear that he did not covet Dick's throne. Indeed, in 2008, at a small internal function I attended, Gregory flat out said as much. In fact, he indicated that he would likely retire within the next few years. Others heard the same in other venues and in conversations. For this reason, Fuld was comfortable delegating much of the day-to-day business of the firm to Gregory. Indeed, for Fuld, after years of running Lehman, it seemed a relief to cede the day-in-day-out management drudgery to one who would never seek to unseat him, while continuing to be credited for Lehman's unparalleled turnaround and success. Perpetuating this, Fuld focused on the highly visible big picture, core strategies, and high-profile clients. And so, more than any other Lehman executive, his reputation continued to flourish. He may not have been a favorite of many Wall Street leaders, but he garnered grudging praise from many among them and certainly innumerable others for Lehman's seemingly unstoppable rise. As noted, Dick did not typically impress when he talked. But his reputation as the architect of Lehman's relentless climb from the sewer of the industry granted him the luxury of basking in the accolades. Gregory meanwhile, as noted, maintained a much lower public profile. Outside Lehman, he was largely a faceless name with a title. It is remarkable how few hits one receives when Googling so prominent a Wall Street executive. (At least until he became synonymous with Wall Street corporate greed.) Within Lehman, when Gregory sneezed, we all heard it. But outside Lehman's walls he received scant attention. Lehman, in the public eye, was Dick Fuld. In fact, there was no firm on Wall Street in recent years so singularly identified with its CEO, almost to the point of personality cult. It would have barely surprised me to see Fuld's face unfurled on a banner above our Times Square headquarters, much as Mao's visage dominates the entrance to the Forbidden City in Beijing.

Getting back to the question of who was running Lehman, at least in its final years, it really was not just one executive. Still, I have got to go with Gregory as the most active senior leader. Fuld was not a non-entity—not yet, anyway. But he had delegated the day-to-day running of the firm to Joe. And while Gregory may not have coveted Fuld's title, it appears he wanted to exercise maximum authority while he remained at Lehman. For Dick, this was a satisfactory arrangement. He remained a rock star CEO, without getting mired in detail. And unlike Peterson with Glucksman running day-to-day operations, Fuld, as noted, was fully comfortable that he could trust his longtime friend. There would be no palace coup. He would have his cake and eat it too.

Despite his diminished day-to-day role in Lehman's last years, Dick's vision in turning Lehman into a broad-based investment banking power-house was anything but baseless, even if this platinum achievement proved fleeting. It was his clear-sighted vision that broke down the barri-ers between traders and bankers. Certainly, 9/11 was a transformational event for Lehman. Yet it took more than this alone to unify the firm, as one where we thrived in a culture of teamwork. The initiatives to achieve this are too numerous to list and describe, and frankly would not make for scintillating reading, so I will permit myself just one example: While rev-enues that involved more than one unit of the firm were traditionally divvied up, new policies gave each unit 100 percent credit for such trans-actions. This was a highly successful change. Instead of battling for rev-enue credit that would figure into each deal participant's year-end bonus, with the introduction of the new rule, these battles immediately ended. This was a true win-win. Rather than expend time and energy on an inter-nal contest for the spoils, a process that often left all parties feeling slight-ed, everyone now worked together for the greater good. In a heartbeat, there was nothing over which to squabble. Instead, we could refocus on Lehman conquering the world. I also credit Fuld with the massive upgrade of Lehman's human capital and brick by brick build of a broadly powerful broker-dealer franchise, both by deliberately culling the underachievers from Lehman's ranks, as well as investing significant dollars in luring tal-ent to the firm. It was painful to see good people who were not up to the job become unemployed, but the decision, in the late 1990's, to shed those who underachieved was good for business. While from an ethical stand-point I abhor Dick's nod to dive headlong into the subprime business, it certainly generated substantial profits for a number of years. And Lehman exited subprime quickly enough to avoid most associated outright losses. The subprime meltdown nonetheless reduced revenues as it did for all of Lehman's peers who were of scale in this business. Had Lehman not accu-mulated massive other real estate risk, I am sure that instead of writing this book, Lehman would have been one of the survivors and I would be in my old office at 745 Seventh Avenue.

Despite all this, Fuld shares in much of the blame for Lehman's deterioration. He was not just a perfunctory captain who officially goes down with his ship. He took his eye off the ball. With Gregory in place, he became at least out of touch with much that was important. Part of what made this possible was that over time, more and more, Fuld believed the accolades awarded to him in the press. He believed he was that good, a superman CEO who would be denied nothing. The wolves might howl at the walls of his fortress, but he would stare them down. His will had been tested, but never broken. His stalwart conviction that he could maintain his footing as a tsunami washed over him was indelibly stored on the hard drive in his head. So pathological was this belief, that the immortality of Lehman's skin had become his own calloused flesh.

And so, Fuld gradually transferred even most high level staffing decisions to Joe Gregory. As Dick became less involved, Gregory inhaled Fuld's discarded power. In Lehman's last years, Joe's low profile in accumulating power was so profound that it was easily missed by the masses. He maintained a close, informal relationship with his chief. Many times during the day, one of the two would wander into the other's office on the executive thirty-first floor to talk business, or to talk about their families. They had dinner together with their wives. Dick trusted his friend Joe entirely.

At the same time, Dick's isolation was not solely of his own making, though in some ways he both incited it and acquiesced. Gregory, undiscouraged by Dick, did much to insulate, even separate the chief from what was happening in the firm. At an executive committee meeting in 2007, one of the senior executives erred by questioning a unit's performance in front of Fuld. Fuld responded, "You've got some balls to say that knowing how much I hate the topic."[xxx] Gregory further humiliated the recipient of Dick's ire by pelting him with another dose of criticism, and went so far as to follow-up by admonishing him again after the meeting. Joe also made it clear that such issues should be discussed directly with him before executive committee meetings, not in Dick's presence.

This arrangement had a profound impact on Lehman. Fuld had long been a dominant character, somewhat in the mold of the totalitarian Bobbie Lehman. No one in the firm wanted to deliver bad news to Dick, fearing he would shoot the messenger, perhaps after disemboweling the poor soul. Nor did anyone consider it career enhancing to question his judgment. On such occasions, his deadly, cold-blooded stare would drill through the offender, ensuring that the transgression, to Lehman's ultimate detriment, did not repeat. On top of this, with Gregory patrolling access to Dick, like a Doberman watching a perimeter, the CEO heard little bad news. To an important extent, it is clear, what reached his ears was often that which passed through Gregory's personal filter.

In recent years when Dick would put in a rare appearance at an Investment Banking Monday Morning Meeting, maximum attendance was prearranged, and questions from the bankers filling the auditorium were scripted, ensuring that Dick's visit was a pleasant non-event. Everyone in the auditorium except Fuld seemed to be in on the ploy. Similarly, Fuld held quarterly internal webcasts at the end of which employees were free to ask questions. Few ever did.

As Lehman entered 2007, the year when the markets began to implode so severely that Wall Street would change forever, beneath the surface, we were vulnerable to the approaching storm in ways that very few of us saw, though there is no shortage of those who now claim they saw it coming. The CEO's authority was still widely regarded as absolute, but Dick continued to leave most senior management responsibilities to Joe Gregory. And by now Gregory had dispensed with the rule book that spelled out the basic relationship between risk and reward, lunging headlong into a real estate maelstrom from which the firm would never recover. To some extent this is reminiscent of the unsound positions Dick had taken to prop up Glucksman decades earlier. Of course, Fuld, unlike Glucksman, was not under fire. Indeed, his stellar reputation and certainly his position in the firm were secure. But in a market that was tough for everyone, Gregory, with Fuld's unquestioning nod, accumulated large unsound positions, with the doomed hope of Lehman bucking the trend. He drank his own Kool-Aid, hallucinating that Lehman would sensationally outperform. Indeed, Goldman pulled off just such a trick in 2007, placing a bet the directional opposite of Gregory's, generating profits that were the envy of every investment banker on Wall Street. LB's real estate executives were perhaps too close to the business to be objective, but Lehman like all financial institutions had checks to prevent exactly what went wrong. One by one, these checks were methodically dismantled.

Gelband and Kirk were cut loose. The executive committee was entirely flaccid. The Board of Directors was light on members with a finance background. And also, just beneath the veneer of cuddly teamwork, a new rivalry developed, the spirit of which Lehman had not seen since the Peterson-Glucksman days, though the scope was far more limited. With Gregory indicating his retirement was approaching, two key players, like ghosts from Lehman's past, began to position for his spot, if not outright control of the firm. Did Gregory stoke this rivalry? Like Bobbie Lehman, he pitted rivals against one another, though not quite as poisonously or pervasively. In this case, one of the two players was Bart McDade, a long-time Lehman executive who held numerous posts, most recently heading equities. His rival was Jeremy Isaacs, International chief, with both Europe and Asia under his rule. In light of the increased contribution of International to earnings, Isaacs, like Glucksman, felt he deserved greater power in the firm. But McDade was not easy to displace. Having held various senior posts over his long Lehman career, he had deep roots and support in New York, both among legions of Lehman veterans as well as top management.

In early 2007, while teamwork remained acutely embedded in the Lehman culture, a rivalry reminiscent of the old days of infighting was quietly, but actively brewing among a few—but these few were among Lehman's most important players. Still, as indicated, unlike the Glucksman-Peterson days, there was no large-scale pitched battle, or even animosity, between opposing spheres of the firm.

Around this time, HSBC became the first major financial institution to announce multi-billion dollar subprime mortgage losses. In February, with Lehman's share price beginning to slip, Chris O'Meara, Lehman's CFO, during an earnings conference call, plainly indicated that Lehman's subprime exposure was fully under control, that the firm had actively hedged its exposure. I certainly believed this contention (and in the end, subprime had little to do with Lehman's defeat). After all, Lehman's cred-it culture was conservative and our risk management over the years improved so greatly, that as already detailed, we seemed immune to the massive losses from time to time registered by other firms. The degree to which hedges covered not just our subprime positions, but in the end, and far more importantly, those in other real estate assets was either exagger-ated or our risk management staff was hallucinating. Given the track record our risk management team had compiled, it is hard to believe we could have gotten this so wrong.

Madelyn Antoncic joined Lehman in 1999, hired as head of Risk Poli-cy. In 2002, she ascended to the post of global head of Risk Management, reporting to Tom Russo, a vice-chairman, chief legal officer, and very much a core, but low-profile member of Lehman's inner circle on the thir-ty-first floor. Prior to Madelyn's arrival, Lehman, at best, had an inconsis-tent risk management track-record, with troubling shortcomings over the years only partially public. Even internally, the true capability of risk management was far outside most Lehman bankers' fields of vision. Traders may have had a better sense of the inadequacies, if only because they bought and sold the assets and, at times, interfaced with risk man-agement staff. Indeed, since they were savvier than those controlling their trading positions, some may have used this to their advantage, accumulat-ing positions poorly understood by the internal credit exposure police. To the limited extent that over the years I have personally interfaced with risk management, my sense is that their capacity for sound analysis, at least through the 1990s, was highly variable. Madelyn, however, ran a spick-and-span ship. She had no tolerance for underlings whose capacity to do their jobs amounted to what could be learned in an *Idiot's Guide to Invest-ment Banking Risk Management.* I have never seen her smile. *Never.* But that may actually be a desirable attribute in a risk management chief. Among the good ones I have known, if they have had a sense of humor, it was gen-erally deadpan and sarcastic or cantankerous. And Madelyn was probably more capable than anyone who has held her position at Lehman before or since.

Madelyn is also, well, memorable. To describe her is to describe a char-acter in a Wall Street satire. Middle-aged, with dark hair stiffly quaffed, she always appears as if she just stepped out of a salon on Manhattan's posh Upper East Side where the final process is to coat her from head to toe in high-gloss acrylic. Precisely applied make-up fully coats her face, and yet she is odorless. Impeccable suits, both fashionable and trim, drape neatly over her form. Her weighty, gold accessories are both substantial and distracting. In sum, the ensemble screams money. Yet, somehow she glitters without appearing garrish. I do not know her true pedigree, but she drips old money. There is an odd decorum in her mien. As for her carriage, Madelyn is not a woman who strolls. No, she strides with a quick, purposeful, and exacting gait, as not a hair on her head, or even her arm, seems to quiver.

Based on the tidbits I heard, people found her a difficult manager. Certainly, I found her "no nonsense" in our limited discourse over the years she worked for Lehman. As a boss, she was demanding, exacting and intense. But then, she was not hired to be compromising any more than the primary focus of an investment banker is pure altruism. In the end, bankers and traders exist to make as much money as possible, and Madelyn's purpose, in her Lehman life, was to ensure that we did not do anything foolish enough to expose the firm to unacceptable risk, erasing all the profits raked in by those generating the revenues. And so, while she probably would be scary on a camping trip, she is exactly what one looks for in a risk manager. I took comfort that she occupied the risk management seat. Under her watch, we compiled many quarters of earnings unblemished by risk management-dropped balls. In large part, I attribute this to both her technical expertise and her steely discipline. And my impressions as to her abilities were confirmed when Risk Magazine awarded her its Bank Risk Manager of the Year award in 2006.

However, Madelyn eventually came up against an obstacle that also derailed others who stuck to their principles: Joe Gregory. As noted earlier, the costs associated with hedging cut into the profits of the positions they de-risk. Gregory was unwilling to permit Madelyn to cut the earnings heft of his real estate profit machine. Madelyn, in turn, is widely known to have insisted that Lehman more fully hedge worrying risk positions. I do not know how determined a political operative she is, but I do know this: for Joe Gregory to break Antoncic's discipline he would also have to break her spine. And Madelyn's spine is pure titanium. Her confidence in her own acumen is unwavering. And when I observed or interacted with her, it was evident her makers had omitted the humility gene. Diplomacy, for Madelyn, is also a needless bother. Bottom line: she would never quietly roll over if one more senior than her, in this case, the exalted Joe Gregory, was pushing her to go along with a risk strategy that she fundamentally opposed—even if this meant he would harm her professionally. No, it simply is not in Madelyn's DNA to hold her tongue in such a situation. Moreover, she must have calculated that she had more to lose personally if she folded and went along with a risk strategy that, as global risk manager, would attach itself to her name for years to come. Looking past her immediate fortunes, thinking like the true risk manager she was, her downside was greater if she consented to faulty risk-taking than if she suffered a demotion and then resumed her career elsewhere, reputation intact. And so, Gregory, for whom Madelyn was now a petty obstacle, unceremoniously pushed her aside around April 2007.

Ironically, the official announcement of Antoncic's meaningless new title, global head of Financial Market Policy Relations (an impotent government relations post), came in September, a month after Lehman shut down BNC, its subprime mortgage subsidiary and eliminated 2500 mortgage-related jobs. This of course came on the heels of the meltdown in subprime mortgages and the related securitizations discussed in the previous chapter. Yes, ironically, the Lehman real estate meltdown that Madelyn would have at least mitigated through better hedging and control was gaining momentum as the firm swapped its subprime exposure for other real estate demons. A few months later at a risk management conference in New York, Madelyn specifically stated that because hedging mortgage positions cut into profits this was not something top management wanted to utilize sufficiently to offset risk. And indeed, by the end of 2007 and early 2008, though Lehman generated a positive net profit, real estate-related write-downs of various stripes began to substantially offset revenues.

For me, one surprise was that Madelyn accepted the demotion. Since she was not a Lehman lifer, having worked as an economist at the Federal Reserve, as a bank treasurer, and in several other risk management jobs, I was surprised she did not immediately resign. Unless she was wearing all her wealth (and she wore more than the bullion in the treasury of a small country), she could surely cover the rent and keep the lights on at home for some time, until, with her reputation pristine, she landed a senior risk management position elsewhere. And yet, I am absolutely certain that Madelyn, of all people, had her reasons for staying put.

* * *

It is unnecessary to rehash the details of the subprime debacle, but the fallout was profound. You, of course, recall that the meltdown obliterated a business in which Wall Street, and Lehman, more than anyone else, had generated huge profits that are surely gone forever. (Without question, the financial world will devise other faulty financial structures that lift the bottom line unless we begin to devise mechanisms that truly wed effective regulation and free market enterprise.) But the subprime fallout quickly leached into other credit markets where excess and blindness to true risk had run rampant for at least several years. Some of the causes for this excessive risk-taking were the same as those that caused the subprime debacle, but there were also fundamental differences. A key common attribute was the breakdown of a sound assessment of the risk-reward relationship in investing, spurred by a low-rate interest environment. Subprime had flourished because high-risk borrowers could start with teaser and adjustable rates at historical lows. But the securities created from these mortgages paid relatively low returns, in large part due to their illogically low perceived risk, as endorsed by the high ratings assigned by the major rating agencies.

Low interest rates fundamentally altered the behavior of investors in high-yield securities as well. From a technical standpoint, high-yield securities are any with ratings below investment grade (below BBB- by S&P and Fitch, and below Baa3 on the Moody's scale). And their very name (alternatively they are called junk bonds) plainly enough indicates that these are securities for investors seeking a high return.

However, the risk of high yield securities spans a wide spectrum. The highest rated of these tend to be issued by companies with solid businesses and finances while the lowest rated securities may be debt obligations of companies on the verge of insolvency. Historically, investors avoided securities with ratings below a certain threshold, or demanded extremely high returns to invest in these, often at rates that would be uneconomic for the issuer of the debt, killing the debt underwriting.

Under an easy money Fed policy, as interest rates fell and remained low for some years, high yield investors found that securities with risk they long deemed acceptable were generating returns falling to undesirably low levels. Since one increases yield on investment in debt instruments by acquiring riskier ones, this is exactly what high yield investors did, in an ill-fated attempt to pump up returns. In short, they chased yield. And they chased it big time. As a result, over time, in a virtual feeding frenzy, investors placed huge sums in increasingly risky securities. This helped inflate the yield on their portfolios, but these portfolios now held securities that on average were generally far riskier than historical holdings. Moreover, because investor demand was so voracious, this drove down the risk premium (*i.e.,* the additional interest a riskier security must pay versus a comparable less risky one), so that the yields on these securities became irrationally low. The only rational economic laws reflected by this unhealthy activity were the basic rules of supply and demand. While the supply of highly risky securities surged, there seemed no limit to investor appetite. Demand was great enough to actually put the highest risk issuers in the driver's seat, able not only to issue massive amounts of debt at attractive interest rates, but able to dictate looser terms than those accepted by lenders and credit providers in the past. Investors still earned more on risky securities than safe ones, but not nearly enough relative to the risk they held. Moreover, not only had average portfolio risk increased, but many institutional high-yield investors now held huge sums in extremely risky securities that in the past would not even warrant a close look. Indeed, all rating agencies, in their various statistical reports, cited declines in the average rating of all securities and an enormous increase in those within their lowest rating bands.

Why would a portfolio manager venture down this path? The answer is tragically, unsurprisingly simple. Once investing in lower rated, higher risk securities gained a foothold, it became impossible for individual risk managers to stick to their usual knitting. For any individual fund manager, abstinence would mean lagging performance versus peers—not a recipe for strong annual compensation. Not even a recipe for job retention. Investors in funds, many blind to risk, would flee the underperforming ones. Vindication, several years after losing a job due to deficient returns, no matter how prudently driven, would be small, intangible reward for the financial compensation foregone. Again, it was all about immediate returns.

And so, over a period of years starting in the early part of the current century, market practice became increasingly unsound. Irrational risk-taking was the only way to generate returns, a fix, to sate the high-yield fund junkies. Because of what I have noted above, until the subprime meltdown, I was deeply concerned that investors seemed so shockingly unconcerned about the risk they assumed in portfolios of highly risky, high-yield corporate debt instruments. I knew a day of reckoning would come. We all knew this, even if some never said so out loud. But for some years, interest rates were low, the economy was humming, and losses were minimal. The riskiest of companies were able to refinance maturing debt they could not repay—even in part. Companies that went years without positive cash flow to reduce debt easily accessed markets, avoiding the defaults that would have unquestionably occurred if investors were more cautious about where they placed their bets.

Not all of this highly risky investment in debt led to problems, and indeed the back half of the story is still being written—if, in fact we are even halfway through the financial and economic bust. Nonetheless, there are success stories. There are innumerable companies that in a more normal environment, as amply noted, would have failed to get off the ground. Investors would have shunned their debt offerings due to low ratings and high intrinsic risk. In the easy money times, however, there were some low rated "junk" companies that funded operations, delivered on cash flow and paid down debt sufficiently to diminish the risk of their remaining obligations. But the majority piled on so much leverage that even as underlying businesses prospered, once they serviced their high interest expense burden, there was little, if any cash left to pay down debt. In fact, as alluded to above, many companies had to borrow incremental new dollars in the bond or loan capital markets just to pay the interest on existing debt—an insidious cycle in which few companies gain sound footing.

Who profited from all this massive funding of high risk debt? For some time, investors profited. Few companies defaulted, as is normally the case when a financial bubble is inflating. Certainly, Lehman and the other investment banks that underwrote and sold this debt profited mightily, spurred by both the surge in high yield volume as well as the higher fees this business generated versus underwritings for high-grade issuers. Historically, issues by high-grade companies were substantially larger, and so while fee percentages were smaller than those on high yield deals, the absolute amount of the fees were normally more significant. This changed in recent years with the return of the private equity-financed leveraged buyout, providing enormous paydays for underwriters of the debt, as they charged fees at a higher rate on much larger debt issuance than was typical of low rated companies in a more normal financing time. Indeed, many of the LBOs involved large companies with strong enough businesses to warrant investment grade ratings at more moderate leverage levels. Many LBOs, in fact, involved investment grade companies with ample cash flow to cover their obligations, even in an adverse operating environment, prior to the buyouts. But the leveraging of these companies was irresistible, as the private equity shops behind the new wave of leveraged buyouts realized unheard of returns.

As an investment banker whose thoughts rarely included the word *subprime,* I long believed the profits on private equity LBO's would continue until our economy inevitably skidded into the sluggish part of the economic cycle. At that point, I expected, many of these highly leveraged companies would default and restructure. This by itself would bring pain, but not Armageddon. But as is now obvious, there was excess wherever you turned, and the collapse of subprime in the Summer of 2007 was more than enough to cause investors to slam on the brakes and retreat like turtles contracting into their shells. Suddenly, even many healthy companies found it difficult to tap both debt and equity markets. No one was investing. The pendulum that lingered irrationally at one extreme, now swung irrationally to the other. And indeed, once-steady investment grade companies levered up by private equity deals began to stumble with finances tightening, and bankruptcy filings soon mounting.

* * *

It was on September 20, 2007 that a particularly surprising internal announcement of key management changes blasted throughout Lehman by firm-wide email. As always, the missive from Dick was highly complementary of all the named executives, including Madelyn whose new title and function, as noted earlier, were a perfunctory gesture that hardly saved face. The even bigger news was that then-CFO, Chris O'Meara, apparently destined to support Joe Gregory, wherever that led, replaced Madelyn as global head of Risk Management. Even more startling was the elevation of Erin Callan to the job O'Meara was vacating, CFO.

Erin Callan, the Harvard-educated daughter of a New York police officer, joined Lehman in 1995 from Simpson Thacher & Bartlett, the prestigious Wall Street law firm where she was a tax attorney. Simpson was one of Lehman's core law firms, and given the LB revenue hours they logged, like any firm in a similar position, would never complain when a client such as Lehman poached one of their best and brightest. Initially, Erin worked with our clients on issuance of preferred stock. At the time, due to a tax change making preferred a particularly attractive funding instrument, its issuance was surging. Within three years she moved into the Investment Banking Division, was promoted to managing director in 2000—a quickly rising star—and headed two units, the Global Financial Solutions Group and Global Financial Analytics Group. While leading these two groups, her reputation blossomed, as she was the brains behind innovative new funding instruments that brought high ticket business to Lehman and enhanced the firm's reputation. The security that quickly became the jewel in her crown was one called an enhanced trust-preferred,[48a] concocted by Erin in the first quarter of 2006. Of course, the securities she invented were copied by competitors, but Lehman got a

---

48a. Part of a class of securities known as hybrids that have characteristics of both debt and equity. It would require pages of text to fully describe these. The bottom line is that companies could issue this security to fund their balance sheets, deduct interest on these securities for tax purposes, but get high equity credit from the rating agencies. The benefit of getting high equity credit from the rating agencies is that they only count a small portion of the security as debt, so that when they calculate a company's leverage, i.e., debt burden, the level is lower than if the company issued a plain vanilla bond. All things being equal, lower debt levels earn companies higher ratings.

head start, and certainly the kudos for having impressive creativity that met previously unsatisfied clients needs and desires. Erin began to show up in the financial media, and plainly enjoyed the sport. A blind man would miss the preening vision, but not the relish in her newly amplified voice. She would, also, at times stand at the Investment Banking Division's Monday Morning Meeting podium, profiling her new financial technology, so that the troops would fan out and sell her wizardry to our clients. Erin's next move came in early 2006, when she became head of Global Hedge Fund Coverage, where again she developed a stellar reputation. Then the surprising announcement in September of 2007, that she would join the inner circle as CFO, effective December 1, the beginning of Lehman's next and final fiscal year. With her office now on the dream-team thirty-first floor, she reported directly to Dick Fuld and Joe Gregory, with a more or less dotted reporting line, for day-to-day matters, to Ian Lowitt, co-chief administrative officer.

Given Erin's smarts and vertical career trajectory, one might ask why her elevation to CFO came as such a surprise to nearly everyone in the firm. In short, despite her intelligence, financial acumen, and superbly articulate delivery, she lacked the critical experience one looks for in a CFO. Unlike the two previous CFO's, Erin had never worked as an accountant. Moreover, she lacked experience in treasury or internal financial management, the typical and most relevant training realms for future chief financial officers. Still, Erin was so very impressive, that although we were already, as an industry, up to our thighs in the percolating financial quagmire, most felt she would rise to the occasion.

Why Erin? Joe Gregory was her champion, and in easy hindsight, plucked her with precise purpose for CFO. Fuld, all agree, easily went along with the choice because he deeply trusted Gregory, and by this time was less involved in executive staffing, even at this level. In a smallish gathering, not long after she had assumed her new role, Gregory in a rambling speech, mentioning Erin said, "I'm loooooving her." Erin was at this time in a CFO honeymoon period. But this would not be a carefree passage. She would have to hit the ground scrambling. In 2008, Erin was to be a key member of the team that jumped into action after the fall of Bear Stearns. Indeed, Gregory spoke of her key public role. And unquestionably, as was consistently noted by the media, Erin instantly became the face of Lehman. For someone with her presence, taking this particular center stage was the one aspect of her new job that made perfect objective sense. Joe Gregory, who always kept an extremely low public profile, was positioning Erin to become the Lehman media darling in effect picking the lowest-of-hanging fruit. And while Dick Fuld was by this time a living legend, considered among the best CEOs in America, the man was short on personality. He had improved as a public speaker, but this was neither his strong suit (other than on that one shining moment after 9/11) nor a realm where he typically appeared comfortable.

But not Erin. She reveled in her enhanced public persona. Youthful, 40-something, fair-haired and haute couture, she was a Wall Street phenomenon who an Oppenheimer analyst referred to as the "best accessorized"[xxxi] CFO on Wall Street. For the Wall Street press corps, she was an irresistible magnet as well. It was a match made in heaven. The camera loved Erin and the feeling was mutual. An insatiable media hound, she had waltzed with the press in the past. But as CFO she stood in the spotlight on a far larger stage and was an overnight on-screen sensation. In a heartbeat, the financial media crowned her The-Most-Powerful-Woman-On-Wall-Street.

At the same time, back at her desk on the thirty-first floor at 745 Seventh Avenue, Erin, though precise and insightful, apparently viewed Lehman finances from thirty-thousand feet, scanning briefer, more terse reports than the CFO's who preceded her. She appeared to pay more attention to what she gleaned from exchanges with her friends and old contacts from her product days on the trading floors. Not surprising—that was her comfort zone. With Madelyn out of the picture, Erin would have relied on Chris O'Meara, Madelyn's replacement as global head of Risk Management, and Erin's CFO predecessor, to alert her to troubling exposures. She was not a risk manager, had never been a treasurer, but she was the CFO. And under Erin's novice watch, with naysayers swept aside, Lehman, as Joe Gregory wished, was adding to its real estate exposure. By all accounts, internal and public, my firm was well-hedged. But through internal scuttlebutt, and later in the public post mortem, we learned that Madelyn, as earlier noted, was not satisfied that our hedging was adequate. She had been shoved aside and the many thousands inside Lehman had been hoodwinked. Ian Lowitt, then co-chief operating officer, to whom Erin reported day-to-day, was a former Lehman treasurer, but management of the firm's balance sheet was no longer in his primary portfolio. A pity.

On various floors below the thirty-first, we in investment banking were more perturbed about a 2007 fiscal year that seemed certain to deliver bonuses far lower than what we expected ahead of the recent summer's credit market dislocation than we were about Lehman's financial solidity. Our greatest concern, at this point, was that 2008 would be an even worse year. Clearly, the LBO party was over and would not return any time soon. But markets always recover. The question on everyone's mind was not if, but how long, before the environment improved. Few contemplated the meltdown that devastated our party. Bear was not yet forced into J.P. Morgan Chase's arms. And those of us who had decades under our belts had experienced ups and downs at least several times before. Since becoming a public company, we endured lean years along with the rest of Wall Street. But unlike so many others, since our IPO, we never had registered even a quarterly loss. On December 13, 2007, in Lehman's official earnings announcement, Dick Fuld stated, "Our global franchise and brand have never been stronger, and our record results for the year reflect the continued diversified growth of our businesses. As always, our people remain committed to managing risk."[xxxii] And so we were complacent. Dick had made such statements amidst past trials. Each time, we weathered the storm better than most peers, despite repeated rumors of our imminent demise. Frankly, no one was worried about losing their job. Our stock price was off, but we were sure it would rebound to an even higher level than our previous peak. After all, we were Lehman. We were incredibly well managed. Sure, Fuld was not exactly Mr. Personality, but he was an awesome CEO. He did not make the rounds much, but then the proof was in our numbers. We were not immune to market conditions, but always kick-ass outperformed. And we did not take the kinds of risks that sink firms—at least not any more. That was the old Lehman. 2008 would surely not be a good year, but our long-term prognosis was as bright as ever. We were Lehman. We were fucking awesome. We would continue to outmaneuver and humble competition. This was the game of life. And we would win.

CHAPTER 5

Kool-Aid

"How hard it is, sometimes, to trust the evidence of one's senses! How reluctantly the mind consents to reality."
—Norman Douglas

In November 1978, Jim Jones, the founder and leader of the People's Temple in Jonestown, Guyana, after seeing to the murder of a visiting Congressman and certain others in the legislator's delegation, told his followers that they would soon be attacked by paratroopers. Jones and most of his followers believed this absurd fantasy, as he and 908 of the other inhabitants, in an act Jones rationalized as revolutionary suicide, drank cyanide-laced *Kool-Aid* and died. (In actuality, they drank grape *Flavor Ade,* but the makers of Kool-Aid have had to live with misplaced notoriety for the last thirty years.)

They were full-blown believers, half-crazed sheep following a completely crazed shepherd. And so, like the finance professionals at Lehman who followed Joe Gregory's real estate stratagem, *they drank the Kool-Aid.* As for Jones, he seems to have believed *his own* bullshit. He *drank his own tonic.*

It is unseemly to commingle the story of a greedy financial institution with that of a tragedy like Jonestown. But in the context of these pages it is apt. This is the culture of Wall Street. Indeed there is a longstanding tradition on *The Street* that in the immediate aftermath of horrific breaking news, cynical, brazen jokes or one-liners *must* be created. This brazen humor is typically born on a trading floor, generally within minutes of ini-

107

tial reports. The jokes and one-liners spread like wildfire among traders everywhere and then filter through the ranks of all their organizations. Within the finance industry, the more cleverly offensive the punch line, the louder and more admiring the laughs. I, myself, find these jokes hilarious. But then my sense of humor is dark, and sometimes it is easier to laugh than to cry. Perhaps others laugh for different reasons.

As to the precise genesis of the "drinking the Kool-Aid" metaphor, I have minimally researched it, and the former Mayor of Washington D.C., Marion Barry, is credited as the first person publicly invoking the expression. While he may have been the first to whom the expression is attributed in print, in a darkly romantic corner of my heart I feel that the cynical phrase absolutely reeks of the trading floors. Certainly, soon after the Jonestown tragedy, it entered the popular vernacular of this stratum of American society. Since then, it has spread among a broader populace, so much so, that among those who use the term, its association with Jonestown has, over what is now many years, dissipated. It is no longer edgy. It just means one has rationalized bullshit.

The Lehman Brothers meltdown is by no means the first instance of financial ruin in which a herd of very smart people drank the Kool-Aid, rationalizing away risks that a good sanity check would have brought into sharp focus. Wall Street and the financial markets in general, driven by healthy capitalist desire, have a long history of derailment when all reason goes out the window, with dealmakers then raging at full speed, like a locomotive at full throttle, with disabled brakes. There is an unfortunate tradition of delusional financiers indulging in the Kool-Aid. This is fundamental to what brought down Lehman, and so many before it. Eventually there will be a new Kool-Aid flavor, when sufficient time has passed for lessons both grudgingly and painfully learned to be forgotten and stowed out of sight in the attic of Wall Street's collective mind. Think of a motorcycle daredevil who has broken multiple bones but continues to push the limits.

How can I be so sure that once we emerge from the current financial and economic nightmare we will repeat our mistakes? Simply because over a long career I have seen financial enterprises stumble or fail due to this Kool-Aid phenomenon at almost predictable intervals. The tendency to rationalize away risk is innate to the capitalist beast that hungers to maximize both his employer's and his own personal wealth. Indeed, the failings of the past return as surely as upchuck of dicey peyote jettisons from the mouth of a hallucinating user who is convinced that his thinking and visual errors are reality. Moreover, once the herd instinct takes over, anyone who is not printing deals on the new money machine feels like the school outcast stuffed into his locker by bullies. The non-participant is labeled an underperformer because his revenue production now lags. In reality, on Wall Street, no one ever holds back. If there is a profit-making party to which you have not received an invitation, you definitely crash it, clutching the newfangled financing architecture in a deep and meaningful embrace, perhaps even groping its ass. We also malign those both internally (*e.g.*, credit geeks) and externally (*e.g.*, rating agencies) who with well-measured sobriety opine that the money machine is defective. The name Madelyn Antoncic comes to mind.

Lloyd Blankfein, CEO of Goldman Sachs, in the early aftermath of the meltdown, wrote that "self regulation has its limits. We rationalized and justified the downward pricing of risk on the grounds that it was different. We did so because our self-interest in preserving and expanding market share, as competitors, sometimes blinds us—especially when exuberance is at its peak."[xxxiii] At last, the voice of a sane Goldman Sachs high priest.

In each of the many ill-fated financial stampedes, there have been a series of regrettably predictable steps:

Step One—A clever finance professional conceives a new financing vehicle capable of delivering a juicy revenue windfall. While one of the basics he learned in business school Finance 101 is that there is an unvarying risk-reward relationship (*i.e.,* more reward always means more risk), he skips that chapter.

Step Two—If asked about risk, the "genius" with the new idea convinces himself and ultimately a phalanx of illustriously educated and pedigreed colleagues that they have found the Holy Grail; drool-inducing returns with *de minimis*[49] risk. More often than not, the guy with dollar signs for pupils is derisively thrown in a cold shower by colleagues who

---

49. Legal term for negligible.

instantly identify the risk to the firm and unceremoniously flat-line his pipedream. Indeed, I have seen many an unfortunate soul laughed out of meetings in exactly these circumstances.

Step Three—If, however, the new idea makes it past Step Two, the new financing hits the market and initially succeeds, exactly in line with, or perhaps even giddily surpassing the originators' wildest dreams. Profits rise, and the new alchemy becomes a financial sector cult. We investment bankers are beside ourselves with glee. The client calls are incoming. The pitch books write themselves. And the bluest of the chips[50] line up to ride the magic carpet.

Step Four—Other firms, in a nanosecond, lock their gaze on this Holy Grail. They ponder the surging revenues accruing in their competitor's accounts. Soon, very soon, they figure out how to clone this newfangled profit stream. It is at this precise point that the herd mentality has the market (the institutions, the dollars, and the people) in its hypnotic thrall.

Step Five—The herd of bulls, having grown drunk on the spiked Kool-Aid they have lapped up at the collective trough, break into a no-holds-barred stampede toward the pot of gold that is now theirs for the taking. Why, it almost feels too good to be true.

Step Six—well . . . this is the mess that later reveals itself. It is the quicksand in which our financial system and economy has sunk, except that, in most of our lifetimes, it has never been this bad.

The current subprime mortgage crisis is merely one of a long history of crises resulting from such crazed behavior. But—and this is a huge 'but'—what differentiates the financial meltdown of 2007, 2008 and now 2009 from crises that preceded it is the utter complexity, the hopelessly tangled tentacles, of today's financial markets. In contrast to our current travails, so long as a reversal in financial markets is well defined, containable, and discreet in breadth, the damage can be managed, with perhaps a few hiccups. Not the present case.

* * *

---

50. A blue chip is one of a select group of large companies considered well established and highly sound.

Still, while there are multiple causes of our current troubles, the Kool-Aid factor is a prerequisite. Without irrational risk-taking, there would be no meltdown. For example, the root causes of the Great Depression, like today's financial/economic dislocation, took hold well before the stock market and the banking system went into the trash can. The Federal Reserve, then, as under Greenspan more recently, employed an easy money policy[51] throughout the 1920's. This encouraged both industry and consumers to over-borrow. Their pockets stuffed with cheap cash, Americans and their banks became drunken optimists, driving up housing and stock markets' valuations to nonsensical levels. Banks lent to depositors on margin who invested in the very same overvalued stock to which these banks themselves were both lenders and equity investors. This is why the twenties fucking roared. *Sound familiar?* Completely wasted on spiked Kool-Aid, before the Great Depression erupted, our society frenetically danced a Charleston that it seemed would never lose its verve. Few saw the bubble that would, whether by the laws of physics or the laws of economics, stretch to the nth degree and inevitably burst.

By 1925, though real estate had peaked at unsustainable values and begun the inevitable decline that would eventually become a full-blown collapse, banks welcomed customers who mortgaged their homes to fund investments in the still-surging stock market. *What drugs were the bankers on? Were they auditioning for roles in Reefer Madness?* Yes, where was the sanity check? And where was our sanity check more recently, when for more than a decade, we put people in homes funded by subprime mortgages they would so predictably one day be unable to service or repay?

* * *

The most serious crisis to hit the financial sector after the Great Depression was one that, again, had been years in the making, but came into focus when, in August of 1982, Mexico's Minister of Finance announced the country lacked the financial resources to meet a payment on an $80 billion debt obligation. This sparked the start of the first major lesser

---

51. A policy whereby the Federal Reserve, or any other country's central bank, seeks to increase the amount of money in the economy, in part through low interest rates which encourage borrowing.

Before the Crash of 1929

WALL STREET - AUGUST 23, 1929: Every investor believed the market had no where to go but up—leading to the Great Depression. (United Press International)

developed country (LDC) debt crisis. Within fourteen months, along with Mexico, twenty-six other LDC's were in discussions with the major money center banks[52] to restructure loans they could no longer service per existing terms. Particularly troubling was the naked fact that the exposures of these eight money center banks averaged more than 200 percent of their equity capital.[53] How in the world did we allow ourselves to become so exposed to countries whose economies and finances teetered, with this instability threatening the solvency of our entire financial system? I suppose it all began with an unsound mantra: *Countries do not default.* Dang, in the current global crisis, Iceland has gone bankrupt and Ireland is lurching.

* * *

LBO's, or leveraged[54] buyouts, are the ultimate example of the financial industry drinking the Kool-Aid. Why? Because we ingested the stuff with abandon not once, but twice, with a breather of little more than a decade in between. Have our memories really become so incredibly short? While more than just LBO's killed Drexel, the mass meltdown of these leveraged deals was a key factor.

---

52. A virtual anachronism in today's world, these traditionally were the large commercial (*i.e.,* not investment) banks with the financial muscle to lend to governments, major corporations, other financial institutions, and if they were in the mood to consumers, as well. With deregulation, the lines dividing the activities of these institutions and investment banks have substantially disappeared.

53. Put simply, equity capital is the value on a company's balance sheet that belongs to its owners or shareholders. When losses arise, equity capital takes the first hit. Once losses consume the equity capital, a company or bank becomes insolvent. All additional losses are taken by debtholders, vendors, and other third parties holding obligations of the loss-making enterprise, placing the company in default.

54. Leverage, or financial leverage, is the extent to which a company uses debt obligations; *i.e.,* money borrowed from other people. Most of a company's assets are financed through a combination of debt and equity. Shareholders' equity represents the funds contributed by shareholders, plus the cumulative amount of retained earnings that has not been distributed to shareholders through dividends or by other means.

Most recently, Lehman and the other investment banks profited immensely from these financings, at least until the credit markets fell apart in the summer of 2007, and as previously noted, underwriters got stuck with debt they could only sell at a loss. Still, these losses are a mere fraction of the LBO profits generated in preceding years.

But what makes an LBO potentially so bad? Very simply, it is way too much debt. LBO borrowers are typically like consumers who have maxed out on all their credit cards, with incomes that often constrain them from paying little more than the high interest on their debt, if in fact they can even manage that. The basic idea behind an LBO is that an owner/investor buys a company with a relatively small portion of their own investment dollars and finances the rest of the purchase price with a mountain of borrowed funds, *i.e.,* other people's money. By doing this, they increase the percentage return on their own minimized investment. The owner is typically a private equity shop, a financial enterprise that sources funds from both high-net-worth and institutional investors and then uses the funds to buy companies. The heavy debt load leaves little cushion for a setback. With our economy now in a deep recession, the companies that Lehman and others financed as LBO's are under stress. Some have defaulted and filed for bankruptcy protection. This will not be a banner year for the private equity houses and their investors that stand to lose their entire investment in companies that file and restructure. And it is still early days, with new developments, as of this writing, rarely very encouraging.

* * *

Following both the money center banks' LDC debacle and the first LBO meltdown, Lehman and other investment banks boldly proceeded into the nineties. We had never underwritten or even held LDC obligations. These governments had borrowed directly from the major commercial banks. Now these countries were healthier. At least, at Lehman, this is what we told ourselves, as we saw other investment banks generating sizable profits through their Latin American activities. We had to jump in. Even after the many internal meetings where we debated the conspicuous risk that sat like a large, stinking, decomposing rat on the center of a conference table around which we gathered, we took the plunge.

And so, during the 1990's, investment banks foolhardily stepped up activities with LDC's, now called emerging market countries. Lehman and others issued securities for many of the very same nations that had previously defaulted on their loans from commercial banks. This go-round, the borrowing in capital markets was not as concentrated in Latin America as it had been during the earlier LDC crisis. Asian emerging market countries were growing full throttle, and increasingly entered the capital markets. However, Lehman's growing success in the U.S. was not matched by its efforts in most emerging markets. Our emerging market bankers, particularly those active in Latin America, were largely recycled, fallen commercial bankers, now wearing far more expensive suits than they could afford in their retail commercial banking incarnations.

While neither as long-lasting nor as widely impactful as the 1980's LDC crisis, emerging market crises in the 1990's did shock financial markets. At Lehman, we loaded up our own balance sheet with select emerging markets securities to enhance profitability. Not unlike the Lehman concentration in real estate securities that recently sank the firm, a deliberate strategy of betting on short-term, dollar-denominated Mexican government issued debt, called *tesobonos,* nearly sank us in 1995, thirteen years earlier than LB's eventual downfall. Within Lehman, as in the days before our bankruptcy, management did not acknowledge we were vulnerable. As employees bought up shares on weakness, Dick Fuld met with the head of trading floor credit approval. How exposed are we, Fuld wanted to know? He learned then what is now known by some inside Lehman/BarCap but not known publicly. We held a huge position in *tesobonos,*[55] one that approximated our total equity capital, at a time when the Mexican government edged toward default. Fuld was shocked. He actually did not know. And so, had Mexico defaulted, I might have

---

55. These are Mexican government debt securities, like U.S. government treasury bonds or treasury bills. However, the tesobonos interest payments were indexed to the U.S. dollar. This meant that when the Mexican peso fell against the dollar, an increasing number of pesos were required to satisfy the interest and principle payments. This led to a total destabilization of the currency and rampant inflation, as the government had to effectively print more and more pesos to satisfy its obligation. In a vicious cycle, the more the government printed pesos, the more their value fell.

written a book much like this one thirteen years ago. But the International Monetary Fund (IMF) and U.S. government came to the aid of Mexico, seeking to avert a new LDC meltdown by leading the provision of an emergency international loan to Mexico, with the proceeds used to pay off the tesobonos. Mexico recovered and Lehman soon began an effort to modernize its technology for measuring credit risk. The firm was behind the times. While many commercial banks already had long-developed systems to measure daily if not real-time risk exposures, Lehman was aggregating its risk exposures to individual and related counterparties and borrowers by manually adding figures on disparate reports. In any case, in the aftermath of the tesobonos crisis, one chief risk manager's career at Lehman ended when our CEO, who until the eleventh hour was clueless as to the severity of our risk position, discovered we had bet the firm. This near-death experience of poor risk management (it is but one example) sobered up Lehman management, compelling it to assemble a sturdy credit capability and culture, only to toss it down the drain some years later, along with the most competent professionals responsible for maintaining the firm's solidity.

* * *

Another crisis was the dot-com bubble. This was another example of the world drinking the Kool-Aid. The Internet was a new frontier and most could only speculate as to its impact on the economy and traditional brick-and-mortar retailers. At Lehman, as across Wall Street, while we could not answer that question, we all recognized that an unsustainable bubble was forming. With low interest rates and lots of speculative money looking for a home, it seemed all one needed to tap feverishly willing venture capitalist pools was a half-baked idea that was Internet-related. If a business was named "4idiotsOnly.com," it could launch a highly successful IPO. The Kool-Aid all the entrepreneurs were drinking instructed them to grow as rapidly as possible, despite mounting losses. The universal dot-com business plan was to spend and expand and worry about generating positive earnings later. Who needed profits, the illogic instructed, when one could dip into a bottomless sack of investor dollars for dot-com initial public offerings, watch the stock price surge starting on the day it priced,[56] sell a portion of holdings, and become an instant multi-millionaire. If cash in the business waned, one could do a follow-on offering[57] to again stuff the coffers that paid salaries and electric bills. At Lehman, as everywhere on the Street, we all knew this was a party that would one day abruptly stop. There was no question many of the new ventures were fly-by-night businesses grounded in lighter than air, wistful ideas. Indeed, in many cases these companies' business plans amounted to little more than virtual pipedreams. But we underwrote countless Internet and Internet-related technology IPOs anyway, and sold the shares to investors. The only alternative was to lose market share and forego easy revenues. Bonuses soared, even for those in the firm whose business was far from the Internet epicenter; that is, until the bubble burst. For the entrepreneurs who founded the dot-coms what did it matter? Unless, like many at Lehman that were foolish enough to hold onto most of their shares, they stuffed their pockets with the proceeds of capital markets' sourced fool's gold. The inevitable Internet implosion and 9/11 made for some rather anticlimactic bonuses on the heels of some spectacular years. But there was little regret to be found on the Street. Underwriters had for the most part passed the Internet risk to investors, so direct losses in our own books were insignificant. Nonetheless, it was with melancholy and a tearful goodbye wave that we saw the gears of the Internet IPO machine totally stripped, no longer cranking out revenues. In the least-damaging Kool-Aid busts, bittersweet final curtains, not global meltdowns, are what we endure.

---

56. When an investment bank underwrites an IPO, or initial public offering, on the first day the shares trade, the underwriter prices, *i.e.*, determines the price at which the new stock will trade, based on the range it has previously estimated and the demand, or amount of orders for the new shares from institutional investors to whom the underwriter has presold the stock.

57. If a company is already public, that is, has shares already trading in public markets, public offerings of additional shares, typically underwritten by an investment bank, are called follow-on offerings, as opposed to initial public offerings when a company floats its shares in public markets for the first time.

* * *

In the next chapter I jump into 2008 and Lehman's undoing. But only if you understand the Kool-Aid mentality is it possible to fathom any financial disaster, including the one described throughout the pages of this book. One has to understand how extremely intelligent, money-hungry people, consciously or not, decide to fool not only others but, often, themselves. Of course this is avoidable. But one would have to be as naïve as Greenspan to assume that raging financial capitalists would rein in their most profitable activities. Only adequate oversight can ever save them from themselves, from self-inflicted wounds. More importantly, this effective regulation can prevent them from hurting us all—which inevitably occurs when our financial sector hemorrhages. The justified current public outrage and mob-like rumblings for retribution will neither right our economic and financial malaise nor prevent future implosions.

Despite all this, I remain a rampant capitalist. In fact I think capitalism totally rocks, big time. But free markets devoid of adequate checks leaves us doomed to repeat the mistakes of the past, to descend into crises, for, well, the rest of time.

CHAPTER 6

Lehman Isn't Bear . . .
The First Half of 2008

"Surprises kill you."[xxxiv]
—DICK FULD

2008 began much as 2007 ended. The market was semi-comatose and we prepared ourselves for the worst: the steep bonus cut that always come in a down market. Having lived through the inevitable ups and downs in the past, most veterans could simply grit teeth and remain dispassionate. We had been here before.

Erin Callan, still capable of only baby steps in these early days as CFO, optimistically predicted Lehman's ROE (return on equity) for 2008 would be in the lofty mid to high teens. I scratched my head at this optimistic forecast, wondering out of whose ass she pulled that number. In this I was not alone. As early as January, we cut 140 MBS traders, around 4 percent of the fixed income division. Of course, given the distressed state of the MBS market, spurred by the subprime meltdown, a rising body count in these operations was by no means a shocker. In fact, it was, for those not directly affected, a non-event. Subprime was dead and would not return anytime soon, if ever. If subprime would somehow mount an eventual comeback, clearly it would be done differently and would no longer be rubber stamped with high debt ratings. So the headcount reductions were necessary. *This* was business as usual.

Lehman had already, as noted, shut down its subprime origination operations. Still, though it had pioneered that market, with many investors in LB subprime underwritings taking hits, Lehman successfully reduced its own subprime exposure to a very manageable, low level. This was not very different from what we had done during the dotcom-bubble, when investors embraced the notion that *if we build it they will come.* We raked in the profits while ultimately retaining little of the risk embraced by irrational legions of fervid investors.

More recently, at the 2008 World Economic Forum in Davos, Vice-Chairman Tom Russo, said as clear as a bell that the interest rate reset on $550 billion of subprime mortgages would lead to defaults. He added that Lehman would ably cope. So it was situation normal. Business changed. We took a surgeon's scalpel to areas that were no longer viable, a superb display of risk mitigation, while investors took losses on what we created. In the meantime, we waited in our seats, perhaps impatiently, but poised to furiously crank away at the new money machine that would inevitably debut. In the meantime we did our damnedest to generate what revenues we could off the good old plain-vanilla activities that had always been our mainstay. There were no bells and whistles. And as ever we methodically turned over all stones to locate profits. A fundamental difficulty, however, was that these regular-way financings were themselves difficult in uncertain markets and could never make up for the revenues lost once the easy credit boom sputtered. Nonetheless, when the profit machine would ramp up, and our fortunes return with a vengeance, Lehman and others would easily hire and recycle staff from the legions of brilliant, yet unemployed investment bankers that were put out with the cat during the current downturn.

However, I get way ahead of myself, if only because the above cycle is a drill I slogged through for years. Indeed, we now know that this time, at least for Lehman and some others, the routine changed. We thought we had been here before. We had not.

Early in 2008, The Brothers began to load up on other real estate assets, most especially Alt-A mortgage[58] and commercial real estate investments. Joe Gregory, forever Joe-the-trader, believed these were oversold. As in

---

58. These are generally not as dicey as subprime, but by no means the cream of the crop. Borrowers are people with solid credit histories and scores, but with unverified income. Yes, lending standards were at least a bit fast and loose.

the past, we would boldly act at the bottom of the market, and emerge in the recovery stronger than ever. In fact, he clung so tightly to this belief, that as you have read, he found the presence of naysayers intolerable and showed them the door. That Lehman always emerged from a downturn stronger than ever was, by now, a full-blown Lehman tradition. To believe or say otherwise was blasphemy. But avoidance of huge risk concentrations was also a new-millennium Lehman tradition. Unfortunately, there was no one capable of stopping Gregory and his yes-men as he broke with tradition and backed the massive build-up of real estate risk. Anyone with a spine who disagreed was no longer on the scene.

Mark Walsh, who headed global commercial real estate, was a deft and skilled real estate dealmaker who led a business that generated huge Lehman paydays. He is also probably a special case. In line with Fuld and Gregory's desire to perpetuate the real estate money machine, he continued printing deals. Many have criticized and vilified Walsh as the individual most to blame for Lehman's collapse. Sure, he might have better anticipated the extremely precarious financial condition in which his deals placed his firm. Like many in similar situations, he may have been too close to the business to see the cliff not far ahead. He was given substantial autonomy to continue to plow, full throttle, as he saw fit, with no checks to stop him. Interestingly, no one questioned his integrity. Still, if he favored a pull-back in real estate risk, he might have been pushed aside like others who voiced concerns about LB's real estate exposure. Recall, Mike Gelband, who was concerned about the real estate exposure, like others, brought his concerns to Fuld and Gregory. And it was the previously noted confrontations with Gregory and Fuld that drove Gelband from the firm. Walsh cannot have been completely in the dark as to the concerns of some, but more senior executives who favored the aggressive real estate strategy consistently silenced those who believed Lehman was dancing with the devil. (Ironically, around the summer of 2009 Walsh would be hired to manage the toxic real estate assets on the books of the now-bankrupt Lehman holding company.) History repeats itself. You will recall that when many Lehman partners, decades ago, wanted to oust Glucksman due to weighty trading losses, Peterson retained him, figuring that the person most involved in creating Lehman's problems was exactly the person best placed to resolve them.

In any case, as noted, Gelband, the Fixed Income chief who worried about our real estate exposure, was by now long gone. Antoncic, who wanted to hedge risky positions, was wearing a dunce cap in a meaningless government relations job, stripped entirely of her God-given role overseeing risk. O'Meara, the former CFO who replaced Antoncic as global head of Risk Management (a lateral move) had to be in Gregory's court, given the simple fact that Gregory wanted him in Antoncic's old spot. And poor Erin Callan, the rising star, was a quick study, but could not possibly come up to speed fast enough to challenge anything O'Meara's risk management group told her. Moreover, newly in her job, and beholden to Gregory for being elevated to this highly senior and visible pedestal, she could not realistically be counted on to challenge Gregory's Glucksman-era trading mentality, his ill-fated real estate push. Both anatomically and emotionally, she lacked the balls of a Gelband, at least while she was a newborn CFO, struggling to remain upright on her young legs. Behind the confident couture image was a fledgling capable of greatness, but for now taking its first CFO steps. Erin, brilliant Erin, was in the end a patsy in Joe Gregory's grand scheme to bet the bank on real estate. Under the circumstances, she became an easily managed "talking head," both beholden and new to the job. I could readily make the case that she was seduced by her own vanity. But, of course, many very good, even ethical people are easily seduced when they are singled out for an elevated role. Erin, I know with absolute certainty, was talented, but was mesmerized and perhaps blinded by her rapid rise from tax attorney to CFO. This is only human. This daughter of a cop (reputedly dating a cop as I write this) was living the dream. She was not evil. And I also do not believe she was dishonest. But it now appears painfully clear that her singular communication skills and love affair with the financial media hardly qualified her to be CFO. Still, smart as a whip, had she come to the job at a less challenging time, she may well have grown into it.

Before January ended, all investment banks had reported full year 2007 results. As noted, Lehman registered record profits, driven by our robust performance prior to the summer subprime downer. Goldman had placed a risky, but correct bet that subprime would fall, so that they bucked the directional trend, with not only a strong year, but with fixed income up 13 percent. Morgan Stanley, on the other hand, was down 93 percent. So while not registering results at Goldman's level, there was no red flag based on Lehman's posted numbers. On the contrary, based on the information available to me, I could boast that Lehman had not only outperformed all but Goldman, but had taken more stringent mark-downs than others on the LBO debt we got stuck holding when the credit markets shut down. We were so conservative, based on the information disseminated, that just after Labor Day 2007, when we sold off a piece of lingering LBO debt, unsellable when the subprime disaster initially led to a full-blown credit crunch, we actually took write-ups, *i.e.,* showed a profit on the sale of this paper. It seemed we had been so conservative in our original markdowns, that the actual sale prices allowed us to recapture some profit. (Essentially, what this means is that we had expensed an estimated loss in the value of the securities and when we sold them for a higher-than-expected price, could show the positive difference as revenue.) Yes indeed, these were tough times, but I was glad to be at Lehman, a firm all of us believed was conservative in its risk-taking and loss recognition.[59] We were outperforming. Other firms were taking additional losses on the very same paper we were now able to write-up. Moreover, most had taken bigger profit hits despite taking less conservative write-downs than Lehman. Surely sounding like a broken record by now, I was certain we would again emerge from the downturn like a boxer in his prime. I anticipated secretly smirking at many of our competitors, with their boxing trunks fallen from waist to ankles, lagging behind The Brothers, stumbling awkwardly back from an elusive prosperity that would already be generating "Big Deal" awards at Lehman. I suppose I must acknowledge that my attitude was not entirely uncharacteristic of the arrogant investment banker prototype.

---

59. To be conservative in risk recognition means a company doesn't skimp on expensing expected losses, but instead expenses an amount that will easily cover potential losses. Companies that are not conservative may take additional losses when they actually sell a partially written down security, while those that have been conservative may recapture some of the previous loss/expense as revenue.

* * *

Toward the end of January 2008, the FBI opened investigations into fourteen subprime lenders, including Countrywide Financial. But we were now out of that business. Bank of America offered $44 billion for the troubled mortgage lender. I hardly took notice. Not my world. I thought it was entirely irrelevant to my future and that of Lehman.

* * *

In February, there were still no red flags marking Lehman, or for that matter, any other bulge bracket investment bank, as vulnerable. In fact, Christopher Cox, SEC head, told the European American Business Council that the five institutions forming this group were all rock solid. Oversight? Regulation? On what information was the head of the SEC basing these offhanded assurances?

* * *

The Fixed Income chief position left vacant when Gelband departed was filled by Roger Nagioff, a London equities trader. Nagioff quit in early February 2008. He left primarily because he could not get his arms around the real estate portfolio. Of course, this was probably a key reason he was tapped to head Fixed Income. This basis for Nagioff's appointment was a factor in subsequent choices for Fixed Income chief. Gregory and Fuld would not select a fixed income head who well understood real estate for what remained of Lehman's life. And so, Nagioff was replaced by Andrew Morton, another Fixed Income chief lacking real estate expertise.

It was also around this time that Alex Kirk (who you will recall agreed with former Fixed Income chief, Mike Gelband, as to concerns about Lehman's real estate exposure) departed. Why? Joe Gregory had told him that his position on the real estate portfolio, if he stuck to it, would mean he had no future at Lehman. Alex has a spine.

Still no widely apparent red flags. The removal of those who opposed the aggressive real estate push occurred quietly. There were firm-wide announcements, but the true reasons for the changes were not widely disseminated and conjecture was fleeting. Yes, there was no shortage of

Kool-Aid. By the end of February 2008, Lehman and its subsidiaries were down about 6400 jobs, while about 28,100 people remained employed by Lehman Brothers globally. More cuts would follow. In March, the body count climbed by another 1400, around 5 percent of the end of February total employment number.

Within investment banking, there were no announcements—just colleagues cleaning out their offices, farewell emails trickling into inboxes, and survivors' guilt. Not everyone sent an email. One would hear about a redundancy when trying to reach those who had unceremoniously vanished, like bodies snatched in the night. Depressing. We thought we had been here before.

What distinguished Lehman when we had come together as One Firm on 9/11, and in the dismal period that followed, was both the limited headcount reduction and an aggressive stratagem of hiring the best talent away from other firms. Why in the world did we now place our firm on the bleeding edge of job eliminations? This was not the collegial Lehman I thought I knew. The conventional wisdom, well Kool-Aid, was that we had matured as a firm; that after 9/11 we still had ground to make up if we were to play in the big league. Now that we were there, we would deliver bullets to the heads of our faithful as harshly as the rest of sociopathic corporate America.

Yes, this is the capitalism I have embraced and defended. And honestly, I cannot find fault in downturn driven lay-offs, not even my own. But of course, when people you care about, even those who barely qualify as a footnote in your life get hurt, it becomes personal. Still, we expeditiously move on. It is only because we have, by absolute necessity, become desensitized, that rather than experience wrenching despair we allow ourselves only brief, muted sadness. We choose to pack the latest round of life-changing displacement that surrounds us into a closeted box filled with a career's worth of such trauma, reacting on the surface as if these people with whom we have often worked for years are the most casual of acquaintances. Of course, casual acquaintances rarely collapse on our doorsteps. Sure, capitalism rocks—especially if you know when to close your eyes.

As I tap out these words, I grow weary. I do truly believe that survival-of-the-fittest capitalism is the only economic order that works. At the same time, I also wish Karl Marx's vision had been a sound blueprint for world economic order (sacrilegious words for an investment banker), but at the end of the day, Adam Smith's *The Wealth of Nations* as embraced by Alexander Hamilton trumps the *Communist Manifesto*.

* * *

All this touchy-feely mush is not what you would typically hear from an investment banker. During a Lehman leadership offsite during which I checked boxes on a questionnaire intended to define personality types, the results placed me in one of four corners of the room. There were several others in my corner. But one corner was empty—the "feeler" corner. My self-assessment should have placed me there, certainly not together with the aggressive types with whom the assessment indicated I supposedly had much in common. I was not like them. As far as investment banking goes, I was a square peg jammed into a round hole. My best client relationships were not with the self-aggrandizing corporate barbarians. They were with people with whom I connected, who found me refreshingly unlike most other investment bankers. These very same traits left some clients unimpressed. I was an *unbanker*. Much of my success over the years I attribute to one piece of advice received from a veteran banker when I was still green. He suggested I focus most on clients whom I liked on a personal level. This, he predicted, would make for a fruitful career, as well as one I would enjoy. The suggestion was sage advice. I am comfortable working with senior executives of just about any disposition—and some have been major head cases. But there are those whose company I enjoy as much as that of a good friend. And friends are exactly what some of these clients have become. Yup, the narcissistic executives with matching egos and attitudes, even surpassing those of say, the most powerful, bulldozing investment bankers at the top of some firms, Lehman included, are not my favorites.

So why was I not in the "feeler" corner, I wondered, gazing at the clusters of more brazen personality types in the other three, including my own. It is only in hindsight that I have discarded the test as meaningless, having learned that the only Lehman leader to occupy the "feeler" corner was Joe Gregory. In a book filled with countless ironies, I smile about this now. It is a wrinkly smile. Clearly, the definition of "feeler" during that offsite was one which I now rejoice excluded me from the category. At the same time, until I knew better, I too would have stuck him in the feeler group, even before I placed myself there. Just as Alan Kaplan had been the "conscience of Lehman," Joe Gregory was the "feeler" responsible for so much that made Lehman a kinder, gentler investment bank. In the end, we are all complex. No one is simply a greedy villain (well, maybe Madoff and Thain). So kudos to Joe Gregory for the initiatives he spawned that made Lehman a great place to work. Maybe, in part, he is a "feeler." Maybe.

* * *

So right, March 2008. While the recent headcount reductions at Lehman were a source of personal upset, the largest financial headlines of that month all concerned the collapse of Bear Stearns. It was on March 16th that the deal with J.P. Morgan Chase was announced. Shareholders were to receive a paltry $2 per share. Apparently J.P. Morgan was prepared to offer $4 a share for Bear, but Paulson interceded and insisted on the lower number. Ideologically a believer in fully free markets, like his boss, George W. Bush, Paulson constantly rattled a sword engraved with the words "moral hazard."[60] Charles Duhigg of the *New York Times* recounted, perhaps paraphrasing, what Paulson said, "I want it to be so, so, so painful for any Bear Stearns shareholder, that it is almost as if they went out of business."[xxxv]

Erin Callan, bless her heart, was among the very few Wall Street executives who expressed shock at the low purchase price. Later the price was raised to about $10, valuing Bear Stearns at $236 million, a similar price to that paid by Barclays for Lehman, *i.e.,* once you subtract from the sum the portion of the purchase price related to the Lehman Brothers headquarters building.

Of course, there were significant differences between the two meltdowns. Though the ultimate price Bear Stearns employees and other Bear shareholders received fluctuated with the stock price of J.P. Morgan Chase, they all got something. Certainly the amounts were a fraction of Bear's

---

60. Risky behavior taken when one believes that they will not suffer the consequences of a bad outcome.

peak market value, but, nonetheless, something. And, far more importantly, and of distinctly greater import to the rest of the world, Bear's debtholders and other creditors were kept whole, as its obligations transferred to J.P. Also, potential losses on the Bear Stearns book were offset by multi-billion dollar U.S. government backing, arranged primarily by Fed Chairman, Ben Bernanke, with Treasury Secretary Paulson's grudging nod. Bear was clearly deemed too big to fail. Great Depression scholar, Bernanke, firmly believed that the global systemic risk was too great if Bear simply went under. Bernanke's underling, Tim Geithner, then New York Fed chairman, was initially prepared to let Bear go under. But once he examined Bear's books and saw the extent of its entanglement with other institutions globally, he believed its failure was a highly dangerous option. Only at this point did it dawn on Geithner that the failure of Bear would likely trigger a meltdown, much like the one that ensued when Lehman filed for bankruptcy.

Both Bernanke and Paulsen were subject to criticism for their role in what many in Congress and others called a bailout. *Bailout.* The word was used as if it were a four-letter pejorative, tinged with accusation that Bernanke and Paulson saved a lot of the greedy bastards on Wall Street who deserved to pay an even more meaningful price for their ill deeds.

This almost certainly was one factor that caused Paulson to cross his arms and disastrously sneer at any mention of government support to keep Lehman afloat or ease it into the arms of an acquirer. In the scheme of things, though we number in the thousands, our cumulative loss is a pimple compared to the swollen financial and economic boil on the butt of our nation and our world. Why? Not because Lehman shares are worth zilch, but because our massive web of obligations, unlike Bear's, froze in bankruptcy court, spurring the larger panic and meltdown. Paulson must have tuned out or dismissed the words of the J.P. Morgan Chase executive who around the time of the Bear Stearns salvage operation lucidly pronounced that a going-out-of-business-sale of Bear Stearns assets and unraveling of its obligations had been averted so that its balance sheet could be cleansed in an orderly manner. Sure, the markets reacted. How could they not? The loss of Bear as an independent firm was profound. Yet abject chaos that would spread like a rabid cancer was arrested. Paulson must have also missed or dismissed the Reuters article that speculated that an unmitigated Bear collapse could have created mass havoc in the global financial system.

So much for Bear Stearns: it disappeared in an orderly fashion. As of the middle of March, banks globally had taken write-downs of $150 billion on "toxic assets." Bernanke and the Fed, and certainly Paulson, were surely acutely aware of this number. And so, just one day after Bear Stearns disappeared from the landscape, the Federal Reserve established short-term collateralized lending for investment banks, similar to the "Fed window" that had long existed for commercial banks, to forestall a larger, liquidity-driven crisis.

There are those who have said that the Fed's liquidity mechanism would have saved Bear. Certainly many of the vanished firm's employees bristled that the government extended this lifeline for all Bear's peers immediately after, rather than just before, it fell. It could have saved Bear, so many said, with immeasurable frustration. But the truth is that "the window" alone would have only delayed the inevitable. There was still the problem of Bear's real estate exposure. On the other hand, government liquidity, along with the very same support provided to J.P. Morgan Chase to facilitate the Bear acquisition, might well have kept Bear in one piece and independent. It *may,* I cannot say for sure, have been enough to prevent the epic spread of financial sector damage. Of course, this is all conjecture and Monday morning quarterbacking. We will never know.

Incongruously, and even grudgingly, I have to give Henry Paulson props where props are due. The Bear Stearns debacle at least prompted him to comment that investment banks were under-regulated and required the same sort of oversight that has long protected commercial banks from themselves, *i.e.,* from Kool-Aid-driven folly. *No shit.* Of course this oversight has not always worked for commercial banks, but at least Paulson's comment and intent to provide a map that would better match the regulation necessary for today's markets, versus the creaking, rusted apparatus that has long been out-dated, was directionally sound. As noted earlier, this was too little too late. And Paulson, in managing the crisis that would deepen, schizophrenically changed course by the day, like a navigator sailing through uncharted waters with an unbalanced compass.

Once Bear Stearns was history, this naturally ignited concerns that other investment banks might all be overvalued and even in danger of a similar fate. Recall, thanks to Paulson, Bear had been valued as low as $2 per share. Had he thought only of causing shareholder pain, of teaching all who held Bear stock a lesson? Had he not considered the wider consequences of this government directed valuation? Stocks of the remaining four independent investment banking firms, Goldman Sachs, Merrill Lynch, Morgan Stanley, and Lehman Brothers all sank on the Monday after Bear's death, reacting to the oppressively brokered acquisition. Financials on the whole had rather frightening share price movements. But at Lehman we told ourselves, once again, we were here before, and goddammit, will rise again from the depths like a powerful serpent piercing the ocean's surface with a roar. We would not be denied.

Most, however, were not aware of our own vulnerabilities. Bear Stearns, the firm that ran at our flank in subprime volume, was the only financial enterprise in our country to originate more mortgage-backed securities than Lehman from 2004 through 2006. Sure, Lehman moved quickly and effectively in minimizing our subprime exposure. But this wasn't the whole story. As noted, we were growing other risky real estate exposures. Subprime was the weakest, though ultimately not the fatal link. When Bear Stearns effectively failed, its commitments taken on by J.P., with Paulson's reluctantly proffered government support, its total balance sheet mortgage exposure consisted of $15 billion of Alt-A mortgage risk, $16 billion of commercial real estate, and only $2 billion of subprime mortgage risk. This does not take into account Bear's many billions of off-balance sheet credit default swaps, much of which represented massive mortgage risk. It was this risk, in fact, that led Geithner, more than anything else, to conclude that Bear could not file for bankruptcy without causing systemic disruption. That Lehman had minimized our own subprime exposure was only part of The Brothers' story, the part we would stress publicly.

Unfortunately for Lehman, Alt-A and commercial real estate were precisely the goddamn crap that Gregory, primarily through Mark Walsh, had been loading onto our balance sheet. He had Fuld's nod, and his puppets and true believers in place. Moreover, Gregory and Fuld's Lehman had not grown these assets at the bottom of the market. And the market continued what was by now a steep decline. Gelband was gone. Kirk was also history. Antoncic was gathering mold in a purposeless job. We thought we had been here before. But in truth, we were starting to slip into new territory. Still, on March 17, Fuld denounced as pure fancy that Lehman Brothers was having problems that remotely resembled Bear's. Times were tough for all investment banks. But Lehman was not Bear.

While no one at Lehman was particularly concerned that we stood in the same wingtips as Bear, it was always comforting to hear "our big swinging Dick" dispel as unfounded the mostly untrue rumors that we had long accepted would always dog us. *Shit,* Bear was, well . . . Bear. They were aggressive, messy bankers without any sort of standard. All investment bankers are whores. But these were the cheapest of streetwalkers you would find late at night on the abandoned streets of the Meatpacking District alongside the Hudson River. Just roll down your window and they would hop in to service you for any sort of fee. Hardly surprising that in a down market a firm like Bear had tanked. There was sympathy for the people, though the firm itself would not exactly be missed. And over the years, in the world of corporate investment banking, they were a weak competitor. I have attended innumerable meetings at other finance houses with which we partnered on transactions. But Bear: I had been there a mere handful of times. Its offices were pretty. But I figured that was just Botox. And when we poached Bear bankers, well, we had to bring them to heel like junkyard dogs that did not know how to behave in even moderately civilized company. Sure, Lehman was a sort of melting pot. But at least in the context of investment banking, we wanted, at a minimum, to behave with a meaningful semblance of ethics and good corporate citizenship.

Unsurprisingly, on March 18th, the day after Dick's pronouncement that Bear's problems were not to be found at Lehman, the rumor mill churned, in fact gained momentum. Lehman's shares were down 48 percent at one point. Fuld circulated an internal email pointing out that the new Federal Reserve liquidity mechanism for investment banks "from my perspective, takes the liquidity position for the entire industry off the table."[xxxvi] In fact, many have said that Fuld, who was on the Board of the New York Federal Reserve Bank until being booted when Lehman was in its death throes, was a key figure, maybe *the* key figure urging that this

Fed liquidity source be made available to investment banks. There were a number of investment bankers at other firms who referred to this Fed liquidity lifeline as "The Save Lehman Act of 2008."

I recall, weeks after the initial melee had subsided, Joe Gregory telling me and a group of others how Lehman's most senior management had sprung into action. He contrasted this with the Bear Stearns' lackadaisical response. Like Nero, their CEO had famously fiddled while Bear Stearns burned. Without question, we all knew that Lehman management was hustling, as in times past, to arrest the falling share price. Our sense of this was palpable. In my mind's eye, our titans seemed to be thunderously pounding the table like a group of executives in a Coen Brothers movie. And Erin's face-of-Lehman was on all the business channels and tele-magazines that were voyeuristically eager for the photogenic, stylish, most-powerful-woman-on-Wall-Street to talk the talk.

At 745 Seventh Avenue, where we could go to the internal Lehman-live.com page and click on "Lehman TV," we carried on business as usual, but in the background kept our eye out for an Erin appearance on *CNBC*, or *MSNBC*, et al. Typically, we knew when and where to find her, either alerted by a firm-wide email, or because word had simply traveled through the building like a dry season brushfire. And we were uniformly impressed. I winced, just a little, at the even more fashionable incarnation of the all-business Erin I knew before she was, for every financial journalist in the country, a Lehman icon. Still, there was no denying that she was armed and confident.

All of the nervousness around the Lehman name climaxed, at least for the moment, with the first quarter earnings call in March. (Since Lehman's fiscal year began on December 1st, the first quarter ended on the last day of February, with the earnings call occurring within the next several weeks.) Erin was under considerable pressure. This could make or break her career, not to mention Lehman's fortunes, for when confidence evaporates, any financial house is soon yesterday's news. Henry Kaufman, a former Lehman Brothers director and chairman of the Board's finance and risk committee has said, "When there are rumors spread, or uncertainty about the sanctity of financial institutions . . . liquidity can dry up very quickly."[xxxvii]

The earnings call was long and felt even longer. Erin, as usual, was articulate and her tone crisp and forthright. Results for the quarter had dipped substantially. Yet, in a difficult environment, we still logged a half billion dollar profit. Still, there could be little joy; this was our lowest quarterly profit in five years. Erin was peppered with questions. In the end, she was able to convince a consensus of the call's participants, all laser-focused on Lehman risk, that hedges would protect the firm from losses, and firmly put forth that Lehman had "the leadership, the experience, the capital strength, and certainly the liquidity to ride out this period."[xxxviii] The proof that she had soothed the market was in a 46 percent surge in our now crazily volatile share price. Internally, all were impressed. She had pulled it off spectacularly, with extra points for style. Those who had wondered aloud whether she was in over her head were temporarily silenced. Dick's absence from the call was conspicuous. But then Erin was the new face of Lehman, and Dick, by now, was a serial delegator. After the call, when Erin later appeared on a Lehman trading floor, she received a standing ovation. With Joe Gregory so conspicuously disseminating that he had no designs on Dick's chairmanship and would likely retire before his boss, many began to conjecture that Erin could eventually be Lehman's next chief executive. But Lehman's real estate time bomb was ticking off-stage.

Following this successful earnings call, Erin appeared on *CNBC*. They audaciously, as far as we were concerned, still asked her if Lehman would be the next Bear Stearns. Erin Callan's response: "Categorically no." We ate it up, a Kool-Aid candy bar. And because I believe Erin to be categorically honest, at least most of the time, and surely when it truly counts, she may have nibbled on the same sugarcoated treat. She added, in a tone that emanated candor and seriousness, that Lehman, by policy, at all times maintained adequate liquidity, on a rolling basis, for the next twelve months. *Cool,* there were not many around the firm outside of Finance who knew that. Bear's crisis had been liquidity. (At the time I had not the benefit of 20:20 hindsight.) We knew it all along, but this sealed the deal. Lehman would endure. If I have not yet shouted it from the rooftops, I am doing it now. *LEHMAN WOULD BOUNCE BACK STRONGER THAN EVER!*

There is an added subtext to all this bravado. Lehman's profits, as noted, fell, as did all investment banks'. Yet, if you scanned the line items of our profit and loss statement for the quarter, you would see that IBD's profits were up a whopping 2 percent. To be clear, I do not choose the word *whopping* cynically or sarcastically. In what at that point was the most difficult industry environment in which Lehman had operated since its IPO, the Investment Banking Division managed to not only turn a profit, but register a slight increase, largely due to our growing success in M&A. And investment management, the business that naysayers smirked we overpaid to acquire, had emerged as an important revenue driver, with profits up 39 percent, a whopping increase by any measure, in any environment. And so, believing the worst was behind us, at least in terms of Lehman writedowns, we saluted those who spackled Lehman with a Bear Stearns brush, with our raised middle fingers.

Yet here I sit, a number of months later, with Lehman gone. On the one hand, does it really matter why Lehman went down? Does it matter who was at fault? It happened. Move on. But after traveling the road that was my career and writing just this much of my Lehman book, if I did not come out and say I am angry and incredibly disappointed I would spontaneously burst into a ball of flame. We were *so* One Firm. We had risen from the ashes of 9/11 as one enormous family that we all felt had carved out a special, unified place in the brutal world of investment banking. We loved Lehman. This was not a place where we medievally drew and quartered people who disagreed. (Maybe a few of our leaders occasionally did this, but had the discretion to inflict this in a remote dungeon from which we could not hear the screams.) The truth is that years ago during the leadership offsite, when I stared at the "feeler" corner of the room in which I felt I should have stood, I quietly rejoiced that Lehman was a place that embraced *diversity,* not only in the current ethnic sense of the word (which was one part of the recipe), but also in the personality types that collaborated in our growing organization. There was strength in this pooling of quants,[61] gregariously smart talkers, obsessive generalist nose-to-the-

---

61. On Wall Street, quants are the people who excel in the most quantitative aspects of finance, typically found creating innovative new structures for all aspects of the business through skillful, creative, complex math.

Richard S. Fuld Jr., chief executive officer of Lehman Brothers, testifies before the U.S. House Oversight and Government Reform Committee October 6, 2008 on Capitol Hill in Washington, D.C. Fuld told the committee, "I take full responsibility for the decisions that I made and for the actions that I took." He defended his actions as "prudent and appropriate" based on information he had at the time. 'I feel horrible about what happened," he said. Committee chairman Rep.Henry Waxman D-CA,questioned Fuld on whether it was true he took home some $480 million in compensation since 2000, and asked: "Is that fair?"
KAREN BLEIER/AFP/Getty Images), October 6, 2008

grindstone overachievers, and more true feelers than the single one identified during leadership off-sites.

* * *

Goldman, in the first quarter of 2008 experienced a profit decline, but
fared better than Lehman, again in large part due to a bet against subprime. But the favorable impact of that bet had dimmed. It clearly had a
certain shelf life and would not offset the onslaught of crumbling financial markets indefinitely. Other firms, ones that were not captive to
rumors, actually did far worse in 2008's first quarter than either Goldman
or Lehman. Merrill Lynch posted a loss of close to $2 billion. Citigroup's
number was a negative $5 billion. Behind these numbers were more trou-
bling figures. Together, Merrill and Citi had taken $45 billion in write-
downs.

Meanwhile, Lehman's titans continued to wield their swords to slay the
dragons that were actively working to consume us in their fire-breathing
rumors and short-selling.[62] Erin, whose name by now was hard-wired to
the phrase "most-powerful-woman-on-Wall-Street," made the rounds,
arranging numerous meetings and calls to reassure important investors
and business counterparties that Lehman was not the next Bear Stearns. To
her credit, I have heard she pushed the few above her for more disclosure
of financial information. It is now apparent that she was only mildly successful. Still, many found her straight talk (at least that is what they
believed it to be, and in all likelihood, so did Erin) refreshing. But at
times, in her fervor, her efforts back-fired, and she found herself holding
the tail of a tiger that was snapping at her head. Lehman was in deeper
muck than it likely understood, but there were lucid minds outside the
firm that on occasion solidly challenged her contentions.

There was little we could do to quiet the rumors, other than brandish
even greater bravado. In late March, Lehman successfully launched and

---

62. Put as simply as possible, when one shorts a stock, one places a bet that the stock will
decline in value. If it does, the short-seller makes a profit. If it doesn't, the short-seller
loses money. If there is substantial short-selling of a stock, this alone places downward
pressure on the share price.

funded a $4 billion preferred stock issue. Our management disingenuously told the world that we did not need the money, that the only reason we undertook so substantial an offering was to show everyone that we could. That was it. We fucking could. So put that in your pipe and smoke it, we told the world. And when I say "we," this time, I do mean many of us. I, personally, repeated this explanation to all outside Lehman who asked about the capital raise. (Unfortunately, it turned out, what we were peddling was not the absolute truth. Its substance was closer to snake oil.) Still, like drones, with a middle finger still raised, but now behind our backs, we demanded that the world chill out on Lehman. The rumors plaguing us were utter nonsense. The 2008 calendar year's first quarter closed with talk of a Lehman collapse dissipating to a deceptively faint murmur.

Unknown to almost all was the fact that Dick Fuld had earlier, before issuing the preferred, quietly tapped IBD chief, Skip McGee, to call Warren Buffet and investigate whether his Berkshire Hathaway fund was interested in making a meaningful investment in Lehman. *Right, we did not need the cash.* In a dance that would repeat itself with other parties, an offer came in, but Fuld judged it too low. At this point LB turned to the market for the $4 billion. This reinforces the adage that no matter what you think you know—in this case the reason why we had issued the preferred stock—in reality you may know nothing. Our most senior management would for some time continue to manage the internal dialogue and preserve calm, preventing an exodus of our most productive rainmakers. We were hard-nosed, foul-mouthed cynical bankers who took little at face value. And yet management was able to keep most of us as ignorant as baboons.

* * *

In late March, the Office of Federal Housing Enterprise Oversight (OFHEO) reduced the capital requirements for Freddie Mac and Fannie Mae. This did not make for major headlines. In fact, if one misinterpreted the change, it could easily be understood as a signal that the two companies' loan portfolios were sounder than ever, that they required less capital to maintain a prudent financial position. But of course, given market realities, one would have to be legally blind to reach that conclusion. On the contrary, the change was an early warning sign that both mortgage giants' capital cushion had thinned due to growing losses. OFHEO was loosening standards for each of these companies so that they could far more easily comply with regulatory standards.

Red flag.

* * *

Noted primarily in the U.K. press, but not making major headlines even there, was a strategic initiative afoot at Barclays PLC.[63] Bob Diamond, the massive U.K. commercial bank's London-based president and chief executive officer of Investment Banking and Investment Management, was to split his time between London and New York. Diamond, the number two Barclays executive, believed the upheaval in U.S. financial markets was far from over and that in the period ahead he might well find an opportunity to substantially strengthen the U.S. position of Barclays Capital (BarCap), the investment banking arm of Barclays PLC. BarCap to date had developed strong businesses in several areas, but was anything but a major player in the U.S. It was certainly outclassed by the U.S. bulge bracket firms. Even foreign-based upstarts, such as Union Bank of Switzerland, went head-to-head with firms such as Lehman far more often than BarCap. BarCap was not even on the radar for most of us. But at this juncture, Diamond, dreaming of growing BarCap's North American presence in a stroke, had the support of John Varley, Barclays PLC's CEO, when he stated that "the biggest opportunity in investment banking is in the U.S."[xxxix] By the time this quote appeared in the British press, the President of BarCap, Jerry del Missier, had without fanfare moved to New York.

* * *

It was on the last day of March that Paulson's Treasury unveiled its new blueprint for reform of financial sector regulation and oversight. The announcement noted that the blueprint had been in the works for a year; the document was over two hundred pages. It suggested an objective-

---

63. Private Limited Company. Like "Inc." in the U.S.A.

based model for regulation, presumably because objectives would ideally evolve with the market. In short, the blueprint proposed a market stability regulator, essentially to take form by expanding the Federal Reserve's duties, a prudent regulator to deal with poor market practices enabled by government guarantees,[64] and a business conduct regulator to protect individuals and small businesses.

The blueprint envisioned an expanded Federal Reserve role to place oversight under one organization. This makes good sense. But as far as the securities industry is concerned, the blueprint stops short of suggesting that this oversight and enforcement be focused on individual institutions. The report states, "[C]orrective actions would also influence market behavior, which likely (and hopefully) would limit the need to take formal corrective actions. If corrective actions are necessary, they should, wherever possible, be focused broadly across particular types of institutions or asset classes. Such actions should generally not focus on specific individual institutions."[xl]

Does our current crisis afford us the luxury of a regulatory framework that "hopefully" works? Incredibly, the word "hopefully" is a direct quote from the blueprint. It is unfathomable that a mechanism Paulson considered so uncertain would be recommended and further, that the blueprint would be so clumsy and tentative in its wording at a time of crisis and aimless market chaos. For any plan to gain support a certain confidence and resolve is needed. A forceful approach does not automatically limit flexibility.

Moreover, suggesting that we avoid steps that prevent the dissolution of individual institutions, and instead take measures aimed at the broader market, given the experience of Bear Stearns before this blueprint was released, is incredibly clumsy. The further example of Lehman's bankruptcy only serves to underline my point. Given the Bear example, it would

---

64. This reflected Paulson's reasonable view that those protected by guarantees would have less incentive than others to curb risk, and in fact might ignore grave risk to generate high returns, as government guarantees would cover potential losses. Essentially, he worried that those with far more upside than downside required regulation as the lack of downside eliminated the consequences of faulty business practices; in fact, eliminated the "moral hazard" that was a cornerstone of his philosophy on how markets function best.

have been rational for Lehman to seek a solution to its growing problems while it was still entirely feasible to avoid a Chapter 7 or 11 filing. But Lehman's top executives "hoped," and rejected the reality that we were in a downward spiral. Do we really want to rely on individuals who run single institutions to use sound judgment? Do we want to chance another meltdown, causing widespread misery, if instead of reasonable, objective judgment these Wall Street leaders flounder, or worse, deliberately take on enormously imprudent risk?

While the Treasury document has a number of sound suggestions, it fails to sketch out a framework that would ensure soundness of the institutions that have to date been inadequately regulated. Is it any wonder, in light of the foregoing, that Paulson schizophrenically switched tactics in the days and weeks after Lehman's damaging fall? But then, Paulson has lots of buddies at Goldman Sachs who might have considered him a turncoat, if he, in a truly meaningful way, suggested curbing their free market bets. Recall Goldman, through the first quarter, offset much of the negative environment's impact with a bet that subprime would suffer. But what if they had bet wrong? Are we really to believe they would moderate risk if the Fed suggested to the broad market that it should tread more prudently, but left it to Goldman to determine whether they wanted to follow this broad guidance? Have we not heard Greenspan admit he erred in believing financial institutions could best police themselves? And let us pretend for a moment that Goldman's bet against subprime had been ill-timed, that instead of Bear and Lehman on the ropes, it was Goldman registering heady losses. Who reading these pages believes Paulson would have permitted the firm he formerly headed to fail?

If I could foam at the mouth I would. If you are of my vintage, then you may recall the 1976 movie "Network" (William Holden, Faye Dunaway, and Peter Finch). I just watched a particular clip on YouTube that, for me, resonates today, when the renegade, unhinged anchorman portrayed by Finch goes on the air and rants, "Everybody knows things are bad . . . Everybody's out of work or scared of losing their job . . . Banks are going bust. Nobody anywhere seems to know what to do, and there's no end to it . . . I want you to get mad . . . I want all of you . . . to get up right now and go to the window, open it, stick your head out and yell, 'I'm as mad as hell and I'm not going to take this anymore!'" [xli]

* * *

At the beginning of April 2008, Lehman Brothers announced a $3 billion issue of convertible preferred stock. Again, we said we did not need the money. We only wanted to boost our capital and increase our already adequate financial flexibility. It was April Fool's Day. Erin Callan was predictably out front and center explaining that we were opportunistically taking advantage of a market window, with good demand from solid institutional investors. But, were we any different than other banks that had taken write-downs on mortgage assets similar to those Lehman had recently been accumulating? The funds raised, at least in part, would be consumed by offsetting real estate write-downs. At the time, most inside Lehman were at least uncertain as to why we continued to raise so much capital. Clearly, we were potentially diluting[65] the value of our already pummeled shares. Indeed, we would only fail to dilute them if our business failed to rebound, so that the common stock price remained low and the $3 billion of preferred did not convert into more common. All this dilution was disheartening. This was definitely not a place we had been before. During previous soft markets or rumor-driven share price drops (sometimes at least partly well-founded, other times not) Lehman had never sold shares, and absolutely not common shares or shares convertible into common, as this would reduce the value of employees and other investor holdings, as well as our employee's percentage of ownership of the company. And employee ownership was always a pillar of Dick Fuld's strategy for the independence of the firm, as well as a means to incentivize the troops as owners of the enterprise in which they worked. In

---

65. Dilution occurs when a company issues additional shares of common stock. Because the value of the business does not change, but its value is now divided among a larger number of shares, each share is, by definition, worth less. In this case, Lehman issued convertible preferred stock. This does not immediately dilute, or even definitely dilute common shareholders in the future. In general, conversion can occur at the preferred holder's option at a set price per share. If the common share price rises above the strike price (the set price), it becomes profitable for preferred shareholders to convert.

fact, Lehman over the years generally bought back shares to offset the dilution that resulted from the annual vesting of shares employees received as a substantial portion of their annual bonus and total compensation.[66] Been here before? Now we were in a new and increasingly shadowy world.

According to a Treasury spokeswoman, Fuld spoke to Paulson frequently. This was not widely known internally. There are reports that the sheer number of calls puzzled Paulson. Dick, on the other hand, saw the ongoing exchanges as cultivation of a relationship with an important figure whose advocacy would be important if Fuld's worst fears became reality. Any relationship Dick conceived he established, however, was out of all proportion with reality. Paulson, for his part, on many of these calls encouraged Fuld to find a buyer for Lehman, particularly in the summer of 2008, but these words left Paulson with the impression that he was speaking to a deaf man. Fuld would only consider a strategic partner, an arrangement that would leave him firmly in control. To take Lehman from him would be to cut off a hand or a foot. Yet, even within this limited framework, there was no offer that Fuld could ultimately stomach as adequately reflecting the value of a Lehman stake. Because Fuld's heartbeat had long ago aligned with Lehman's pulse, he inevitably felt that his own worth as a human being was rapidly declining, that these inadequate offers were personal. In light of Fuld's narcissism, in part a product of who he had always been, and also a byproduct of years as a virtual monarch, this was not devaluation he could accept. As he sought investors, Fuld was looking for validation, a premium, and what he instead found were skeptics who, particularly if they got a peek at the books, saw the malignancy

---

66. For all employees, bonuses constituted a portion of total compensation. In general, the higher an employee's pay, the higher that person's bonus both in nominal terms and as a percentage of their total compensation. The higher an employee's compensation, the higher the portion of it that they received in shares that once vested (*i.e.*, changed from restricted units—essentially shares earned, but not held by the employee—to fully owned common shares) over a set schedule of up to five years. Lehman bought shares in the open market, and, in layman's terms, retired these repurchased shares, reducing the total shares in the market, and thereby controlling the dilution of each share caused by the issuance of employee bonus-related shares.

just below Lehman's outer skin. Objectivity was not present when Fuld assessed offers he found personally demeaning.

* * *

Not yet tabulated and public was the fact that April 2008 foreclosure rates were up 65 percent versus April of 2007. But an IMF conclusion that the U.S. was moving headlong into a recession was public. Moreover, the IMF believed the sluggishness in the U.S. economy would pull the rest of the world in the same recessionary direction. One more data point: WaMu took a write-down in excess of $1 billion for the first quarter. Faced with bankruptcy, WaMu later succumbed to an acquisition.

* * *

As noted, there was a distinct sense among many within Lehman that Fuld was increasingly out of touch. Yet, with compensation every investment banker's raison d'être, the specifics of Dick's current role, at least for now, paled beside our more pressing concern. Without exception, every Lehman colleague I spoke with despaired that all of 2008 would undoubtedly be a difficult year, in part based on the way the year seemed to be developing for The Brothers specifically, as well as the overall negative market sentiment in which we were unrelentingly suffused. The question on most people's minds was whether by the end of the year, and the beginning of 2009, we might see the beginnings of a meaningful market recovery. Dick, on the other hand, in April told shareholders that the worst of the credit crunch was at last behind us. It is difficult to fathom how at this point anyone could feel optimistic, let alone fully confident, that the trough was history. So three takeaways: 1. Dick was out of touch; 2. Despite this, most of us were more focused on our compensation and net worth by year end 2008; 3. We should have worried more that Dick was out of touch.

As May rolled around, Lehman was not in crisis, but pressure on our stock continued to weigh heavily on not only everyone's electronic net worth, but also on morale. At this stage, no one was even thinking about bankruptcy or a Bear Stearns scenario. Yet, a building stuffed with financial professionals is one brimming with people who fully understood that the stock dilution was an irreversible setback that substantially altered retirement game plans, even the financing of a college education for many lesser paid bankers' and other employees' children.

* * *

A public stoning is probably just punishment for any mainstream investment banker claiming difficult markets created financial hardship. Of course, the high profile earners are only one component of any investment bank's employees. There are many who fall into the vast category of middle class-wage earners who have been forced to tighten their belts by more than a notch or two during the current malaise. And even among the average moneyed investment banker, each of us made a very specific choice. We would work harder and longer hours than almost everyone we knew who was not an investment banker. This commitment demanded that we often leave non-industry friends agape, when at social gatherings we would retreat to a corner, say at 10 P.M. on Saturday night, for a business call. Or when in similar situations, amid friends, we incessantly pecked away at our Blackberries. Or when we routinely canceled plans because an out of town business trip had, out of thin air, become imperative at the very last minute, sacrificing precious time with family and friends. Or even just a free moment. For all this we were well compensated. Of course, I know that there are people far worse off, even within investment banking; people working two or more jobs just to keep their heads above water, if even that. Still, I and others in investment banking made choices. And at Lehman, many of us ended up financially worse off, given the erasure of share price net worth, than we would have been if we had selected far less demanding careers. But we chose investment banking. For this, we and our families paid a steep price. Still, make no mistake. I am not sawing a violin. We chose high-risk, high-reward and in many cases we lost. Oh well. It was good while the party lasted. The world is now a very different place and the time we put in will never be reclaimed. But indeed, we went in with our eyes wide open. So, all the foregoing serves only to describe where people's minds and emotions were as Lehman got closer to unwinding. After years of working in an environment where no demand was so great as to be considered unreasonable, in many cases, those of us foolish enough to hold most or all of our stock felt we had wasted our working lives. I would always have been, despite my occupation, one to insist that money really does not buy happiness. Soon this contention would be tested.

* * *

Dick, for his part, ever the Rottweiler, resorted to pointing fingers at those he believed conspired to sink Lehman. As he had done during past sell-offs, he called CEO's of other Wall Street firms claiming their traders were spreading false rumors about his firm. David Einhorn, a hedge fund president, drew special Fuld attention for publicly questioning Lehman's valuation and shorting[67] the stock. Erin, who had overseen Lehman's hedge fund relationships and business before becoming CFO, had also publicly tussled with Einhorn. This was one of those occasions where her very direct approach backfired. On May 21, Einhorn publicly stated that in private conversations with him, Callan had changed her story on how Lehman valued a specific private equity investment. This fueled his basic contention that Lehman was not properly valuing impaired assets. In a May 26, 2009 email that was released to Congress, as it prepared for hearings on Lehman's failure and its interrogation of Dick Fuld, a long-time senior Lehman executive, David Goldfarb, suggested utilizing the capital that Lehman was planning to raise to buy back stock, "hurting Einhorn bad!!"[xlii] Fuld emailed back, "I agree with all of that."[xliii]

In a move that was incredibly imprudent, and now quite apparently driven by personal animosity—never a good basis for business decisions—Lehman did begin buying back shares. Sure we were not happy about the dilution, and this would to some extent reverse that damage. But the timing could not have been more wrong. We used precious capital to try to prop up our share price and also as a vendetta to deal Einhorn and the other short sellers a blow. We had a history of buying back shares in normal times, to reduce dilution related to issuance of shares to employees as part of their compensation. But this was not a normal time. This was money ultimately scattered in the wind.

---

67. Short-selling

At the time, within Lehman we remained tense but as always support- ive of our world class management, and largely believed what we were told. We did not know then what we came to learn later. And so, for the most part we believed that the share repurchases were a positive sign, that we really did not need all the cash we had raised, and were undoing some of the dilution that was such a blow to our long-term share values. This, at least, was the only logical explanation. To use necessary liquidity to buy in shares that were better left outstanding to absorb losses would not just be illogical, but irresponsible, even insane. We could not be that crazy. I was a true believer. We were okay, I told myself. The share buybacks were proof. I had never been here before, so gullible in the face of mounting evi- dence as to how bad things really were.

* * *

Business in May remained sluggish, as it had been since the summer of 2007, but by all accounts, in investment banking, we were at least gain- ing market share. Again this fueled our belief that with a shoulder to the wind, once we weathered the harsh environment we would emerge stronger than we had been before the subprime crash. We had no hopes that the private equity mega-LBO's would return in the foreseeable future, but we had the highest of hopes, if not a near certain belief, that eventu- ally the market would turn and we would continue to prosper. We, The Brothers, despite the rumors, had thus far maintained our brand's solid reputation among clients. Even within the industry we continued to be widely respected.

* * *

During May 2008, the Bush administration's SEC, in a by now unusual feat of active oversight and enforcement, began to investigate the "triple A" ratings assigned by the rating agencies to mortgage backed securities, including one in Europe that was rumored to have been mistakenly assigned due to an agency computer glitch.

* * *

Also during May, Fannie Mae and AIG both announced huge quarterly losses. But so far as we all knew, Lehman was well hedged, with ample liquidity. While revenues had slowed considerably, we were not an endangered species. Still, with losses mounting at many financial institutions, SEC Chairman Cox, a bit late in the game, called for better bank oversight, and AIG announced a $20 billion capital raise to offset losses. Given market doldrums and ongoing investor wariness, the AIG number was ambitious. But at least we closed out the end of our second quarter, free of any tangible negative news about Lehman.

We rolled into June expecting soon to hear Q2[68] results that were more or less as depressed as those for the first quarter. Since becoming a public company fourteen years earlier, as noted, we had never suffered a quarterly loss. We had no particular reason to believe the wheels had come off and that we would post one now. *Right.*

On June 9th, Erin Callan led the earnings call that stunned Wall Street, sending shockwaves up and down the ranks inside our building at 745 Seventh Avenue. Erin announced to the world Lehman's first quarterly loss during its fourteen-year public company history. But even more startling was the size of the figure. We netted a negative $2.8 billion due to massive write-downs of $4.7 billion. The size of this loss was more than four times the most pessimistic analyst forecast. After all, Lehman was the firm that always beat analyst expectations. The reason for the loss supplied to the stricken and the dumbstruck who listened to the call was that the hedges Lehman had prudently utilized to offset a fall in real estate values had back-fired. I have not seen the books, so I will not comment on the basis of this statement that spilled from Erin's never-more-poised mouth. Still, given the departures of senior Lehman executives who disagreed with the Gregory-Fuld real estate focused strategy, as well as the removal of a respected global head of Risk Management who was insisting on better hedging, are we really to believe that what was said on this earnings call was the full story? As I said earlier, I find it hard to believe that Erin

---

68. Second quarter of the financial year. For Lehman the financial year began on December 1 and ended on November 30.

would even consider uttering a bald-faced untruth, but while she was not a risk manager, upon learning of the losses she must have dug in and commanded those who brought her the figures to take her through the math in excruciating detail. Certainly, she had the smarts to understand if somewhere along the line she had been fed bogus information. It just does not add up, one of the handful of small mysteries around which, even now, I cannot get my arms. Of course, there are multiple rumors within Lehman, now Barclays. And certainly insiders have made both naked and anonymous statements to the press. Laying out the many sound bites creates a jigsaw puzzle where some of the pieces simply do not fit together.

Erin announced plans for yet another Lehman capital raise, this one larger than the last, amounting to $6 billion. Again we despaired at the long-term dilution of our employee holdings, but the figure seemed plenty large enough to offset the difficulties.

Much noted was the fact that Dick had not been on the call. Given his discomfort as a public speaker, it is unsurprising that he would have dreaded taking part. Still, this was far from Dick's finest hour. As CEO of a firm with so momentous an announcement it was incumbent upon him to be present and vocal. His absence only served to add froth to investor worries that were now fully engulfing the firm. According to Andrew Gowers, Lehman's London Corporate Communications head, who flew into New York to help craft the second quarter announcement, Fuld absolutely refused to be present on the call. Even more distressing, he was put off by the necessity that he devote time to developing the call's script, bluntly eager to be done with it, put the second quarter result behind, virtually before it was announced, and move forward. He expected the market would take the loss in its stride, and we would go into the third quarter with a clean slate.

This was a monumental miscalculation. Naturally, Dick's absence spooked outsiders who listened to the call. Internally, we were equally shocked. Erin was not a target on the inside. But, to the outside world, with Dick pulling the covers over his head and Joe Gregory scarcely in the public eye, the wrath of those who believed Lehman had strung them along for months all zeroed in on Erin, who became The Street's and the financial media's Lehman punching bag. And the $6 billion capital raise amounted to pissing in the wind, as even so large a capital augmentation did nothing to calm market nerves. Again Lehman's share price plunged, along with the wealth or financial well-being of all who worked at Lehman.

That same day, IBD head, Skip McGee, forwarded to Dick an email received from a former senior Lehman executive. The missive sensibly advised, "Senior managers have to be much less arrogant and internally admit that some major mistakes had been made."[xliv]

But, this suggestion ran counter to Fuld's disposition. Ever paranoid, he likely still felt this was another case of the world against Lehman, *i.e.,* the world against him. Indeed, Dick did not appreciate fully the difficulties in which Lehman was mired. Rather than genuinely move to sell Lehman while it still had some value, and accept a price that would be hard to swallow, Dick undoubtedly wasted a great deal of energy on his enemies list. Einhorn, the hedge fund president who had shorted Lehman, became Fuld's obsession. Because the *Wall Street Journal* caught wind of and pre-reported likely plans for the $6 billion capital raise that was formally announced on the earnings call, Fuld made it law that absolutely no one carrying a Lehman ID was to speak to that newspaper's reporters.

On the morning of June 12, as we read our email, we were shaken to learn that Joe Gregory and Erin Callan were history. Officially, neither was resigning from the firm; rather, they were moving to other senior positions within Lehman. But you did not have to read between the lines to know that Erin was essentially moving to an outplacement office and that Gregory was retiring. He would quietly slip out the back door a bit later. None of this should have surprised me. After a bombshell like the one that had exploded on the June 9 earnings call, followed by a huge sell-off of all things Lehman and the quickening beat of the short-seller drums, the senior management changes should have, in fact, been in my thoughts. But when it is personal, it is different. One loses objectivity. And even at this point, though we were nervous, most of us, at least in banking, believed Lehman would pull through.

As for the management changes, Dick Fuld and Joe Gregory had sat down the afternoon before, on June 11. Together they decided there would have to be a rather dramatic gesture to calm the market. Gregory, as I have said, made no secret of the fact that he planned to retire within a couple of years, anyway. Naturally, he hoped to leave under very different circumstances, in triumph, but resigning his post was undoubtedly less of a sacrifice for him than for Fuld. Gregory had spent his entire career at Lehman. Still, no matter what the firm meant to him, it could not be as anatomically tethered to his ego as it was to Fuld's. Since blood had to be spilt over the historic loss, why not that of the man who was most determined to place the doomed real estate bet?

There are few people who will ever know exactly what words passed between these two long-time colleagues and friends, but just before 4 P.M., the die was cast. Gregory would effectively (though not officially) resign, ending his long Lehman career.

The circumstances surrounding the decision for Erin to clean out her desk in the CFO's office are a bit sketchier. She has consistently stated that it was her decision to step down, a statement that has not been disputed. At the same time, once her champion, Gregory, resigned, no doubt she felt enormous pressure to do the same. Erin's telling in the press is a little different. She indicated that it became crystal clear to her within a day of the earnings call that she would be unable to continue as CFO. She points out that while internally it was clear that Gregory's resignation would send shockwaves through the firm, few on the outside knew him. On the other hand, Erin was the face of Lehman. She assumed no responsibility for the real estate mess. And indeed it was not of her making. She described her six months as CFO as a period consumed dousing fires and trying to dispel rumors that Lehman was another Bear. Erin, as CFO, played a six-month-long game of whack-a-mole. From her first earnings call until her second one, she had never wavered in insisting that Lehman was on solid ground. But she said she knew, with the reaction to the second quarter results call and the ensuing fire licking at the exterior walls of 745 Seventh Avenue, that her credibility was in pieces. She could no longer be effective. And as Lehman's now heavily rouged public face, her resignation would mean more in the media and the markets than Gregory's. I am sure she is sincere when she comments on her love of the firm and her expectation that she would spend her career there. (The thought of eventually becoming the first female CEO at a major Wall Street firm must have crossed her mind.) But, in the end, she says, she knew her resignation as CFO was the right thing to do for the firm. She has also noted that when she told Fuld she was resigning, he fell apart, and in fact wept. Dick bawling, at that moment, is hard to picture, unless Erin had triggered his undoubtedly vast fears and despair about the larger tableau of Lehman woes. This might have drawn a reluctant, self-pitying tear. While you've got to love Erin, I can't imagine that I would share so intimate a moment with the press. Egos, in different shapes and sizes, were now off the leash on the thirty-first floor.

Later, after the two *de facto* resignations were announced, Erin cleaned out her office on the thirty-first floor and retreated to a house in Long Island's Hamptons to rest, or maybe just slip away for a bit. She surely had no desire at this very moment, sapped of her power, to be any sort of public face. At least not for the time being. There would be press interviews later as her circumstances changed.

All of the foregoing is the juicy detail many like to ponder, but on the larger stage that Erin and Joe had just exited, debate about alleged CEO tears are of little consequence. Erin Callan and Joe Gregory, from this point forward were just names around Lehman, not factors. Yet just to tie up a few loose ends, Erin, within about a month, landed at Credit Suisse First Boston (CSFB) in a newly created position, heading their global hedge fund business in investment banking. This was her old stomping ground at Lehman. And within this realm she remained respected. Recently, however, she has taken an extended leave of absence, likely related to various government investigations and lawsuits, discussed later. When Erin started at her new CSFB job, lawsuits and investigations were not in her dossier. Lehman had not yet gone under, and her new employer probably did not anticipate the legal entanglements that would soon occupy and distract her.

Rumors and press reports about Gregory are fuzzier. There has been news that he put a lavish beachfront Long Island getaway up for sale. This castle is a second, rarely visited Long Island house owned by the former Lehman executive. The other one is the primary residence from which he commuted to 745 Seventh Avenue by helicopter. The beach house was listed for sale at $32.5 million. The official explanation for the liquidation of this asset is that the Gregory family rarely used the house over the couple of years that they have owned it. Now that Joe is retired, one would expect he would have greater use for it. The explanation for the sale reported by much of the press is that Gregory borrowed against his Lehman stock to refurbish the house and had to list it for sale to avoid bankruptcy. Honestly, I have no idea as to what is true and untrue about the Gregory family's finances. Perhaps one day there will be an item in the *Journal*[69] that will settle the inconsistencies. Certainly, rumors will circulate among former Lehman employees at BarCap. As far as the Lehman story is concerned, however, none of this much matters.

On June 13, following the dual resignations of the President and CFO posts, Lehman shares rose 14 percent. I suppose that was of import to a day trader, but for most of us it was a minor, brief rise on the roller coaster wobbling on the tracks. Even with this temporary lift, Lehman's shares were still the worst performing stock year-to-date on the AMEX Securities Broker/Dealer index. Employees had thus far lost about $10 billion since the '07 high, and the firm's market value was down $30 billion.

Of course, when your president and CFO resign amid market hysteria, it is always critical to fill the positions quickly. And so concurrent with the announcement of the two resignations, Bart McDade, a well-liked and respected Lehman career veteran who, as a younger man with rectangular glasses was something of a Buddy Holly lookalike, became The Brothers' new President and COO. He holds an undergraduate degree from Duke University and an MBA from the University of Michigan. Joining Lehman in 1983, he was appointed head of fixed income in 2000, and then moved laterally in 2005 to head the equity division. Ian Lowitt, the executive to whom Erin had reported on a day-to-day basis, replaced her as chief financial officer. Having served in finance, most especially as Treasurer, he was a logical, safe and intelligent choice.

McDade and Lowitt received a standing ovation when they appeared on the trading floor. Another standing ovation. Given Erin's precedent, this was not necessarily auspicious. Fuld, growing increasingly distant, addressed the firm over an internal speaker system. Jeremy Isaacs, LB's

---

69. Single word commonly used to refer to the *Wall Street Journal*.

international chief whose rumored rivalry with McDade I wrote about earlier, immediately called Fuld to resign. Dick convinced him to stay on for another three months, for appearances. Undoubtedly, Fuld was overwhelmed by the prospect of also filling the top spot in Lehman's overseas operations. He no longer had Gregory at his elbow to participate in the decision. The relationship with McDade, while not fractious, would never compare to the one that developed between Fuld and Gregory over decades of working closely together and even socializing during downtime. Needless to say, with McDade as President and Isaacs running International as a lame duck, the gulf between New York and London became, well, an ocean. And without question, McDade was a New York choice and certainly had the support of IBD. There may well have been an exodus of key producers if he had not gotten the spot.

That Dick was even less in control of matters than ever and had a different relationship with McDade than with Gregory is hardly debatable. For starters, McDade quickly brought back Mike Gelband and Alex Kirk, the two senior fixed-income executives who had opposed Gregory and Fuld's real estate strategy. The mere fact of their return was a signal that Dick's position had weakened. These were not his friends. To that point, Gelband is reported to have bluntly, in Fuld's face, told him that he had only returned because of McDade. And so, it was increasingly clear that Fuld was no longer the iron-fisted leader who would always have the last word. Other scuttlebutt strongly indicates that when McDade and his team poured over Lehman's internal accounts, the firm's weak financial situation stunned them. There is no indication whatsoever that McDade, seeing all this, openly criticized Fuld, but then he really had no reason to do so. Why bother? Bart was increasingly running the firm anyway.

The McDade team's surprise when Lehman's impaired financial condition was revealed to them flies in the face of claims by some who now insist they long saw the inevitability of Lehman's fall. Given that McDade, certainly a key management figure before becoming president, was shocked by what he found, are we to believe that others more junior and far more distant from the epicenter had better foresight?

Fuld, by now, was in denial and was of little use to those who were looking for practical solutions to Lehman's unacknowledged dire position.

Dick's instinctive, simplistic wish was to will Lehman back to the top ranks. As you will hear, he vacillated between the conviction that the Lehman ship would turn and the launch of desperate attempts to sell a stake in the firm or, too late, the whole kit and caboodle. For example, around late June, I learned that we were talking to private equity houses about a capital stake in our firm. How far these talks went was never clear. Also unclear, even now, was whether Fuld was looking for a minority investment or a full management buyout. In fact, he may well have vacillated. This would not be at odds with his behavior over the coming months, though at this stage, Dick was generally looking to shore up Lehman, not sell it. In any case, whatever the full substance of the discussions, they went nowhere.

* * *

June 2008 was not an easy month for others in the financial and business world. Citigroup cut 6500 heads from its investment banking unit. Debt defaults for the month rose 50 percent versus June of the previous year. All but one of the major defaults was by a U.S. company. Automobile sales hit a ten-year low. And you can be sure that the rating agencies, until now freewheeling, were unhappy when three SEC commissioners announced that new regulation on the debt raters was a critical priority.

Unfortunately, despite a horrific June, Lehman and many others had by no means hit rock bottom. Indeed, at Lehman, we were not yet even ready to sign ourselves in for clinical rehab. In hindsight, it is hard for me to believe that most of us were still just concerned or worried, but pleased to have Bart and Ian on the bridge of our ship, and largely confident that we would survive. With the massive share price dilution, no one had illusions about recouping their peak net worth, at least not for quite some time. But with no more sense than lemmings, we, and I include myself, were armed and ready to wage war to reclaim the spot we so long battled to reach. For me, what gave this notion traction was that despite an already appalling year for all of Wall Street, within investment banking, as incredible as it may seem against the ghastly canvas I have colored, by all accounts we were gaining market share.

CHAPTER 7

Rumors, Shorts,
& Other Misdemeanors

*"When I find a short-seller, I want to tear his heart out
and eat it before his eyes while he's still alive."*

—RICHARD FULD

The Brothers limped into July like Ashley Wilkes of *Gone With the Wind* returning to Tara from the Civil War on a crutch. We were badly wounded. But we still had our Tara, 745 Seventh Avenue. And in contrast to the 1939 movie's run-down plantation, a common site no doubt when the original Lehman Brothers aided a ravaged Alabama in its fundraising, there was nothing about our environment that, on the surface, appeared changed. Unlike McDade's new regime, by now effectively running the firm, few had seen the internal numbers. In fact, other than the second quarter loss, there was nothing tangible providing clues that the firm was under greater stress than we realized. The official internal and external word was that Lehman had cleansed its balance sheet with the second quarter write-downs. Business was not hopping, but this was a rough period for all of our peers, as well. Lehman was one of many who took write-downs. As one of the now leading firms on The Street, it seemed to most that the greatest pain was behind and that we would roll with the market.

Still, leveraged finance markets remained bolted shut. This was an area that had generated substantial revenues for all investment banks until the summer of 2007 subprime crunch. Most definitely, Lehman's leveraged finance group had been a favored destination of new junior bankers just joining the firm. Assignment here meant long hours, a good thing in investment banking, as you would work on large, high profile deals. In particular, you would be on deal teams for the headline-grabbing equity sponsor LBOs that were saddling some of the country's larger, sounder companies with mountains of debt. There would be little time for anything other than work, but the skill set developed was the best an aspiring investment banker could hope for in launching a career.

* * *

While it was obvious that the U.S. economy was badly faltering it was not yet 100 percent clear that we were mired in a full blown, extended recession. Our President, George W. Bush was apparently a contrarian.[70] During a July 15 White House press conference, with less eloquence than Dick Fuld, he said, "When will the economy turn around? I'm not an economist. But I do believe we're growing . . . I'm an optimist. I believe there's a lot of positive things for our economy."

* * *

There were differences between the current period and other periods when deal flows had slowed. It would be delusional to expect a quick rebound to the heady times before the credit crunch when we could leverage companies through the roof, issuing securities to investors who bought these debt instruments at nearly unprecedented low ratings and in unprecedented volume. You may recall that pre-crunch, borrowers assigned agency debt ratings that would have normally precluded capital market access, found themselves in the funding driver's seat, able to dictate incredibly unrestrictive terms to investors who scooped up this flimsy paper. It was all about maximizing yield and little else. With the crunch, the pendulum swung to and remained at the opposite extreme as the punishing downturn hit companies across the ratings spectrum. In July, the market remained shut to the lowest rated companies. In July of 2008, even the

---

70. In Wall Street speak, one who behaves in 180 degree opposition to the prevailing wisdom.

decently rated companies, with credit profiles earning ratings at the high end of non-investment grade, were unable to source new funds. This was a departure from previous downturns when the market could be tapped by these companies, albeit at somewhat elevated interest rates. (Market access had since improved for these companies, though at still elevated rates.)

All of a sudden, leveraged finance was dead and Lehman, in successive rounds of lay-offs, reduced the headcount in this area, either through outright firings or by transferring some of the most highly regarded LevFin bankers to other areas that at least registered an intermittent revenue pulse. In high grade, *i.e.*, investment grade markets, companies had an easier time issuing, though the size of debt securities offerings was often constrained. And even for these companies with extremely solid ratings, cost of issuance increased.

These difficult market conditions made for glum morale. One can always conjure meetings with and pitches to clients, presenting them with M&A or financing ideas. But as we cast our line to hook some form of revenue, really *any* revenue, nibbles were few and far between. Fish taking the hook were even rarer. We were also about a year into the downturn, not a happy anniversary. While there had been a few windows of opportunity over these twelve months, prospects remained dismal, with no discernable end in sight.

The previous autumn, after the initial meltdown of credit markets, there was cause for optimism in the days after Labor Day. All of Wall Street had anticipated that markets could well begin to rebound. The debt of several large LBO's sitting as losses on investment banking balance sheets was floated, not at the favorable rates anticipated when we committed to the underwritings, but better to lock in some level of loss and begin to unclog our balance sheets. This low rated debt had in a heartbeat become an anachronism. We would need to work through it if we were to unburden ourselves and progress toward business as usual. For the first time in quite a while, at least there was some level of apparent investor appetite. As we all feared too large an offering at one time would doom the issues to price at pitiful levels and even result in outright failure to fill the order book, only a portion of the total underwritings were marketed. Still, we crossed our fingers. The few offerings that debuted were judged

Korean Won Plunges Following Lehman Bankruptcy

SEOUL, SOUTH KOREA - SEPTEMBER 16, 2008: A woman looks at a board showing stock price index at a stock brokerage firm on September 16, 2008 in Seoul, South Korea. The Korean Won has plummeted following the collapse of Lehman Brothers Holdings Inc, the fourth-largest U.S. investment bank. (Photo by Chung Sung-Jun/Getty Images) largely successful. They had sold at no worse than the expected discount and in some cases at less of a discount than anticipated. We were not out of the woods, and these were not profitable transactions, but at least we were beginning to work through the massive backlog. As earlier noted, it was also an institutional and personal point of pride that Lehman had marked down these unsold, underwritten securities so conservatively that we actually realized a gain when they sold, while other firms often took additional write-downs. No one was uncorking the champagne, but again, we had been prudent in our recognition of loss.

Following the post-Labor Day securities offerings, we began to plan additional sales of underwritings sitting on our books, pulling out all the stops to generate investor interest. But post-Labor day deals, recently floated, traded down in a fleetingly resurgent market. Investors bold enough to buy in the post-Labor Day debut of discounted deals found themselves holding paper losses. This led to even worse market conditions than those that existed before Labor Day. In light of these fresh investor losses, cash was increasingly the investor asset of choice. It also did not help that an increasing number of banks were announcing huge losses, further undermining any resurgent confidence; and as more and more financial firms undertook mass firings, these bullets to the head were turning Wall Street into a river of blood.

Meanwhile, on the thirty-first floor of the Lehman tower, Dick Fuld had no greater reason for cheer than the rest of us. In fact, he may have worried more than most, to the extent that he understood the magnitude of Lehman's problems, as Bart and his team certainly did. For the most part Dick spasmodically busied himself with further efforts to raise capital that would keep an increasingly diluted Lehman afloat, but was as yet still unwilling to decisively cede control of the firm. He talked with Ken Lewis, the Bank of America (BofA) CEO, about a merger of Lehman with BofA's second-rate investment banking franchise. Dick proposed that BofA own 40 percent, obviously leaving Lehman, and more specifically Dick, or maybe by this time, Bart, in control of the combined operation. Dick was not yet willing to entertain loss of independence, but was clearly coming to the unavoidable realization that it would be more difficult for Lehman to endure without the access to and backing of a formidable bank balance sheet. Lewis was at best lukewarm to Dick's proposal. He had no designs on Lehman so these talks went nowhere. (Lewis, of course, for some time longed to own Merrill Lynch, an ill-fated dream that would later come true in an acquisition on which Lewis would bet his career.)

Dick also approached HSBC, offering a shareholder stake, news of which quickly circulated within Lehman. But HSBC was not tempted and rebuffed Dick's proposition. On July 9, Dick approached New York Federal Reserve Chairman Geithner (now Obama's tax-dodging Secretary of the Treasury) to investigate whether Lehman might convert its holding company into a commercial bank holding company (versus the investment banking variety) in order to broaden our funding base. Unlike J.P. Morgan Chase, BofA, HSBC, and others, Lehman was not a retail bank with an extensive network through which it could source cheap, stable deposits. Like other pure investment banks, Lehman funded institutionally. This source is the so-called "smart money" that could in the blink of an eye stampede from Lehman's corner like frightened bulls in flight from a tornado. But Geithner displayed little enthusiasm for Dick's proposal to convert to a bank. Geithner failed to see such a move as any sort of panacea for what ailed Lehman. And so, like Dick's other overtures, this one died without eliciting any truly serious consideration.

Lehman's former London communications director, Andrew Gowers, has reported that during the very same days that Dick was working the phone to find a partner, he also told a journalist, who happened to be a Gowers acquaintance, "I will never sell the firm."[xlv] No, he could not yet even begin to decisively let go.

Meanwhile, the short sellers were increasingly pushing down our share price, so that $20, at which a portion of our year-end bonus shares would be valued, now put this planned distribution to employees well under water. The firm locked in at $20 on July 1, 2008 because of what turned out to be blind confidence about Lehman's future. An internal memo emailed throughout the firm noted that this "special off-cycle grant underscores our confidence in Lehman Brothers' future."[xlvi] There were also those who bought additional shares, figuring to pick them up on the cheap and make a handy profit to offset the huge dilution, once the market normalized, once the shorts got bloody noses, and once our market value returned to its deserved level. Lehman was probably the number one short seller target, but by this time, with the entire financial sector's losses mounting, other firms' share prices were coming under pressure from shorts as well as outright sales. The SEC, in a futile gesture, temporarily suspended short-selling of financials. Predictably, this failed to change the fundamental basis for the bearish sentiment, so that the ban was doomed to have no lasting impact.

By August, Lehman was in talks with Korea Development Bank (KDB). As Korean banks are not leading edge global financial institutions, lacking sophisticated operations that can match a Lehman Brothers, the rumors of these talks struck most as at least a bit perplexing. Sure cash was cash, and if KDB were to take a minority stake, did it really matter where the funds were sourced? Still, many wondered what had led Lehman to talks with this Korean government development bank. There was surely no natural strategic fit.

Likely, the connection with KDB was based primarily on links to that bank's CEO, Min Euoo-Sung. Min had been a banker in Lehman's Seoul office in the 1990's, left, returned to head Lehman Seoul, then departed again. Nonetheless, the former head of Lehman's Asian investment banking business had a long, friendly relationship with Min. For Min, an important stake in his former firm may have both appeared a potentially attractive investment worth considering and may also have appealed to his ego. After all, his stake in Lehman would place him in the hierarchy as master to all those who had previously been his bosses. While this is conjecture, it is likely that Min's history at Lehman had much to do with his interest in acquiring a large holding.

KDB initially offered $22 per share for a 25 percent stake in Lehman, but Fuld was resistant, as always, believing Lehman's true value was far higher. Talks deteriorated. By early September, as Lehman's fortunes further waned, and as the KDB talks began to fall apart, the offer was down to $8 per share. Min and his bank indicated the lower offer reflected difficulty in gauging potential write-downs not yet taken by Lehman.

Also, Min, it is widely reported, may never have gotten clear Korean government consent for the investment, certainly a prerequisite for a government bank such as KDB. As a result, he may have continued to lower the offer price as one way to unwind serious talks. In any case, not only Fuld, but McDade also, were both adamant that they would not cede over-all control of Lehman to Min's bank.

Some weeks later, on September 19, after the deal was already ancient history, Min would inform Korea's legislature that Lehman had been unwilling to proceed at the price KDB was willing to pay. Nonetheless, he would be criticized by South Korea's legislature for the Lehman bid. The chairman of the country's Financial Services Commission would tell the body "Min was overzealous and unrealistic."[xlvii]

This dance with KDB reflected Fuld's inconsistent, but growing acknowledgement that Lehman had problems it might well not solve on its own and that his options were now severely limited. At the same time, he fell into his habit of relying on pure will and aggressive representations of Lehman's underlying health, as a means to vanquish the nightmare that stubbornly refused to succumb to his fury. This was plainly visible as he seesawed between growing desperation to sell Lehman, if only to keep his life's work in one piece, and a stubbornness to remain in control. This refusal to cede Lehman to others had sat in his gut for decades, dating back to the days when he worked for Glucksman and considered his former boss's sane vote to sell Lehman to Shearson American Express a deeply dis-turbing betrayal. On a number of summer calls, Paulson pushed Fuld to sell the firm outright, but these words fell on ears muddled by static.

August, like the months that preceded it, brought little cheer for any players in the financial sector. But as the months of write-downs, lay-offs, and anemic business flows accumulated, it seemed both Lehman and the financial system were sliding into shadowy, unknown territory. Conven-tional wisdom was by now out the window. Even a career's worth of expe-rience that should have enabled a long-time banker to assess any circumstance was ignored. There were moments I told myself that I knew nothing. I could analyze and intellectually reason, run every conceivable scenario through my head. But as the velocity of Lehman's slide quick-ened, I had no hook onto which I could hang a well-grounded positive outcome. Indeed, I effectively knew nothing, and a huge part of my life appeared out of control and incomprehensible. I would have been equally at a loss if I had discovered that the world was flat, after all.

* * *

During August, Freddie Mac announced an $821 million loss, triple the consensus (average) loss forecast by financial analysts. The quasi-government mortgage giant took a $2.5 billion write-down and cut its dividend by 80 percent.

* * *

Also in August, it was reported that business bankruptcies in the first half of 2008 had risen by 42 percent as compared to the same period a year earlier. Moreover, the number of Chapter 7 bankruptcies (liquidations) outnumbered the Chapter 11 variety (reorganizations) by a ratio of four to one.

* * *

As August, and Lehman's third quarter came to a close, our stock remained under pressure, and though everyone recognized we were navigating an environment that was probably already unprecedented in our lifetimes, no one was clear that our ship's rudder would soon flail as if made of soft, crumbling rubber, a precursor to complete dissolution.

By now Fuld was calling Paulson daily or nearly so. He was counting on the Secretary as an ally, believed he had built a relationship and bridge; that Paulson would dispense with his principles in order to support Fuld. But this was a mirage. Decades of playing the role of belligerent outsider are not repaired and transformed through a series of calls, particularly when, after many years of hot-headed, explosive resentment, the love that surfaces has so utterly transparent a motive. If Fuld's career was Oedipal Greek tragedy, Paulson was the father he viscerally yearned to kill.

All the while, the rumors of Lehman's impending demise were shrugged off by proud, long-time Lehman employees, who after enduring a very many years of this banter, rejected it by pure impulse. But the wolves' numbers were growing and their circle around Lehman tightening. They grew palpably hungrier for The Brothers' exposed underbelly. Night was falling on our century-and-a-half-old firm. And at last some began to see the hazy yellow eyes of the pack that we knew in our gut was inches away from devouring us. But there were also many within Lehman who looked away or closed their eyes.

CHAPTER 8

No Way

"Alone against everyone."
—LOUIS XIV

September has never been my favorite month. As a child it was a time when all the fun and games, the respite of summer dimmed; when after Labor Day I returned to school, a whole year of books and lessons stretching out like an ocean. The opposite shoreline was unfathomably distant. As you swam toward the other side, the distance was so great, that it was often hard to discern tangible progress. You always reached the other side in June, but in September the summer shoreline seemed an agonizing distance away.

Perhaps September was a bit happier once I reached college age. I would reunite with the best of friends who for the most part had been absent from my summer adventures. But the more carefree months of June, July and August, as when I was younger, also gave way to a far more weighty academic effort than had ever been required in my years at home from grade school through high school.

I would eventually enter the workforce, my head bobbing among the masses, as I purposefully strode toward an office. September was now just another month. And summers, for the most part, became just another expanse of work rather than play, with the occasional warm weather vacation. Very early in my career, before investment banking, weekends became my one fairly constant respite. I could simply flop over a weekend as if it were a large feather bed and sink into the cozy Friday night through Sunday chunk of my week, unbothered by the hectic pace of my job. Septembers were better than some months; at least a 3-day weekend to kick it off, and usually a time when New York weather was at its most pleasant. Once I joined Lehman and became an investment banker, sacrosanct weekends became a thing of the past. Hours were long and I was either in the office or on call 24/7. Septembers became part of a continuum where only the weather distinguished it from other months. And this was less a factor in my life, as the great outdoors were often the few steps from the subway to 745 Seventh Avenue, and before 9/11, to the World Financial Center.

It was after Lehman had been an absolute in my life for some time that Septembers, as in my childhood, became a disagreeable month; in truth became a month with anniversaries to mourn far more than the loss of summer freedom. While Lehman occupied the World Financial Center, September became a nightmare, a month where my life and those all around me were engulfed in the horror of the attacks on the World Trade Center. Days, weeks and probably months pass when I do not think of 9/11, but those of you who were in the nexus of the attack, many far closer to the inferno than I, understand exactly the context in which September, at the very least on 9/11, became a time of bereavement.

It is again in a truly dire September, with the summer heat giving way to the breezes of early autumn, that I pick up where I left off in the last chapter. By the second of the month, reports were surfacing in the press about the surprising ongoing negotiations with KDB, specifically citing the Korean government-owned development bank's interest in obtaining a 25 percent Lehman stake. We mostly clung to the conviction that Lehman would recover from its two quarters of blood-red ink. Still, that we were negotiating at all with KDB appeared an act of desperation. The next day, September 3rd, Min Euoo-Sung, KDB's governor, confirmed to the Seoul press that negotiations discussed in the last chapter were underway, adding that these talks included a consortium of private sources. Nearly concurrent comments from a Seoul regulator left a clear impression that the Korean government was at best somewhat reluctant to see a deal struck.

On September 7, the resignation that Jeremy Isaacs had tendered to Fuld, upon the appointment of his nemesis, McDade, as President and COO, was formally announced. It was also announced that Andrew Morton, one of Gelband's successors as global head of Fixed Income, and another Fixed Income leader with no depth in real estate, was out.

Two days later, news broke that all talks with KDB were suspended. LB shares, once again, plunged. There was talk that Bart McDade had scuttled the KDB deal by refusing to structure a ring-fence around Lehman's bad assets, in part because he feared that a KDB deal would be credited to International chief, Isaacs, who then might leapfrog him to fill the CEO spot of the now wounded Dick Fuld. But this is a rumor that is completely unverified, born as someone's theory. After all, McDade by now well understood how desperately Lehman needed capital to survive. Would he really have undermined a deal that risked leaving him without a firm? Throughout this book, I have generally avoided mentioning such unverified, even fanciful chatter. I mention it now to provide a sense of the atmosphere now suffusing Lehman globally. We had not been here before either. If you worked at Lehman Brothers, external rumors came with the territory. But internal rumors were now becoming as pulpy as those in the most sensational media rags.

With the KDB news out, the cost of a Lehman credit default swap (essentially insurance against loss on an exposure to Lehman) skyrocketed. The now pricey default swaps immediately caused Lehman's numerous hedge fund client/creditors to cut short-term lines. But Lehman had long represented that it maintained liquidity at all times for the next twelve months, so the loss of short term hedge fund liquidity was likely not a fatal blow. The larger problem was that much of Lehman's other funding was in place based on pledges of cash and collateral, and the value of the assets Lehman utilized for this purpose was getting hammered. And so, also on September 9, Lehman's clearing agent, J.P. Morgan Chase, demanded additional collateral to the tune of $5 billion, to make up for the diminution of value in those assets already pledged. Absent the topped-up collateral, J.P. would not transact for Lehman the next day.

Fuld, characteristically, flew into a wild rage, lashing out at McDade, Lowitt, and Vice-Chairman Tom Russo. He carried on that Jamie Dimon,

NEW YORK - SEPTEMBER 14, 2008: The headquarters of the Lehman Brothers investment bank on Sixth Avenue in New York City. The troubled Wall Street investment bank moved closer to collapse today as British bank Barclays pulled out of talks. (Photo by Michael Nagle/Getty Images)

J.P. Morgan Chase's CEO, had instigated the demand, caring not whether it would bring Lehman to its knees. Fuld fumed about the "injustice of it all," saying "here we go again . . . Perception trumps reality once more" and "we've got to act fast . . . so this financial tsunami doesn't wash us away."[xlviii] Fuld was determined not to sit by idly, as had Jimmy Cayne, Bear Stearns' former CEO, like Nero fiddling, in the days just before his firm's end.

Irrespective of Fuld's ranting, the pickle in which Lehman found itself was not baseless. As Dick fumed, it was true that we had a top-notch investment banking franchise, with strength in M&A, equities, our traditional fixed income business, investment management, et al. In fact, on the whole, the business of the firm had never been better placed among our peers. But, with Fuld's unambiguous blessing, Joe Gregory and others, such as Mark Walsh, global head of real estate, who supported the real estate strategy, or merely went along with it to save their own necks or advance their careers, had together bet the bank and lost. Though the inadequately hedged real estate exposure was composed of assets acquired in a number of transactions, taken together, they were a huge, imprudent trade gone south.

Lehman was unlike a firm such as, say, Drexel. Drexel had dissolved due to the LBO meltdown, its sole area of strength, and under the weight of senior insider scandals and corporate illegalities. Drexel's core had gone bad. A worm inside the Drexel apple had devoured its innards. Lehman, on the other hand, while enduring a difficult environment was thriving among our peers. We had become a firm that, like an Ivy League University, enhanced any finance professional's resume. And then, yet again, ironically, we were driven to the edge by the imprudent phalanx of former traders that ran Lehman. We were not a firm broadly divided as in the Peterson/Glucksman days. Still, while Fuld had created "One Firm," few investment bankers were as influential as the top executives who grew up in sales and trading. And we were a firm in which reckless decisions of a few were devastating the whole. This was not the first time that a bad bet had hurt Lehman, not even the first one in which Fuld was involved, but it would be the last.

What prompted J.P. Morgan to demand collateral at that precise time?

They were nervous. It was a commercial decision. Client and counterparty confidence is a prerequisite for a financial institution to maintain its business. When this comes into question, as it had for Lehman in the past, it is only natural that both individual and institutional heartbeats quicken with anxiety that losses could materialize, serious losses to a potential bankruptcy filer. At this point, everyone's primal instinct to flee takes charge, and while the stricken institution fights for its survival, the dollars that maintain its pulse depart, as partners and counterparties reduce exposures or cover their positions through demands for additional security.

The absence of an agent to clear your transactions is not a small annoyance. Who will trade or conduct other business with an institution unable to move funds efficiently? As noted above, the value of Lehman's assets had plummeted. And it was soon clear that the $5 billion J.P. gaping hole was a demand that knocked us to the ground, though only one of a coterie of developments that pushed Lehman to the edge. It is shocking in hindsight that so many of us continued to believe that Lehman would pull through. Having reached Everest's peak and planted our flag, we failed to check our oxygen tanks and take note that we were running critically low on air.

The inner circle, in agreement with Fuld's clear belief that quick action was an imperative, decided to preannounce third quarter earnings, along with plans to keep afloat a Lehman that was taking on water, sinking under the weight of its real estate cargo, rumors, short-selling, and pervasive client jitters.

Lehman preannounced third quarter results on September 10, one week ahead of plan. Ian Lowitt, the CFO who had taken over when Erin Callan vacated the post, led the call. Presumably due to the widespread internal and external criticism of Fuld's absence on the devastating second quarter earnings call—an absence deemed both inappropriate and troubling—Fuld was on hand to participate on this one. The firm announced a $3.9 billion loss for the quarter, due to write-downs amounting to $5.6 billion. These amounts far exceeded the miserable second quarter numbers. Within Lehman, at our headquarters, as we sat at our desks and stared at our screens a collective gasp must have permeated the building. If it was audible, we were all too stunned to notice. I can easily imagine pedestrians on the sidewalks outside surprised by a large sucking sound emitted by the Lehman Brothers building, and at the same precise moment, the high wattage Lehman signage wrapping our headquarters flickering.

We had trusted everything our management told us of Lehman's true financial condition. Yes, we had worried about the second quarter loss, but we were told it was our bottom. Even now, we did not en masse believe the firm was on the brink of disappearing. We believed the pronouncements about twelve months of liquidity always on hand and much more. But the superb risk management that we believed was intrinsic, a virtual trademark, had left the building. As we began to absorb the enormity and potential implications of the loss, plans to auction off a majority stake in our asset management unit were announced as well as plans to create a "bad bank."[71]

The mere suggestion that we create a "bad bank" was an instant wakeup call that the value of our Lehman stock and our firm were far less than most had previously believed. Moreover, a sale of a majority stake of our asset management unit was another unmistakable act of desperation. This unit had outperformed the expectations of most, and had been intrinsic to Lehman's now longstanding strategy to diversify our business. In 2008, it was the one major business line experiencing serious growth. But on the call we were announcing intent to sell the majority of this jewel in the Lehman crown. At the very least it was instantly clear that year-end bonuses would suck. But the scope of our worries was by now vaster than just year-end compensation. Our firm was proposing a partial dismantling of what we had over a number of years constructed, with our stockholdings already badly diluted. It no longer seemed Lehman could possibly emerge from its current troubles stronger than ever. This particular post-IPO tradition was entirely moribund.

---

71. A "bad bank" is a separate legal entity created to hold impaired loans and other assets of a financial institution. This does remove the assets from the balance sheet of the commercial or investment bank that holds them, but the new entity must be capitalized and funded. Tricky to pull off, there are nonetheless precedents for "bad banks" that have successfully cleansed a financial institution of its problem assets, with the bad bank remaining solvent.

Dick Fuld's participation in the call had its own odd twist. Despite all that was apparent to those listening to the call, he nonetheless commented, "We have a long track record of pulling together when times are tough. We are on track to put the last two quarters behind us."[xlix] He also added the Lehman mantra that rang false as it dribbled from his lips. "We have been through adversity before and always come out stronger."[l] While it would have only made matters worse if Fuld balked at participating on this call as he had a quarter earlier, external listeners, in droves, no longer found anything uttered by Richard S. Fuld, the man long perceived to be the corpus of Lehman Brothers, credible. Internally, while we mustered what we could to cheer on our management, Fuld sounded utterly depressed. No longer the crusading Gorilla, he was as tame as if he'd been brought down by a tranquilizer dart. This sullen performance only depressed the thousands employed by the firm. As has been repeated in earlier pages, Fuld was ordinarily not a riveting speaker, but on this day Fuld sounded uncharacteristically defeated. It was also conspicuous that in response to a question on the call, Dick did not entirely rule out a sale of the firm.

While those of us living Lehman like a religion desperately wanted to believe, we had sobered up, at least to some degree, and knew a snake oil salesman when we heard him. We still had hopes Lehman would pull through as an independent firm, understanding that the value of our Lehman shares, under the best of scenarios, had been massively diluted and could not for years return to their lofty former value. Moreover, we knew that a surviving Lehman would be in stabilization mode for some time and would only eventually begin to rebuild businesses sold off as well as our reputation. The Lehman that always outperformed was gone. Our reputation as a low risk-taking industry leader was shattered. In short order, the all too briefly resurrected legacy would be archived, a boxed memory stored in a remote warehouse.

Both Moody's and S&P placed Lehman on review for downgrade. It was the Moody's announcement, however, that was particularly damaging, stating that the agency would downgrade Lehman Brothers unless the firm was able to find a strategic partner. This fed the frenzy swirling round my firm.

Dick, who had been a New York Federal Reserve Board member until Tuesday, September 9, called New York Fed Chairman Geithner. Our cash was disintegrating. He asked Geithner about borrowing at the Fed window, but was told our impaired assets were not adequate to meet the collateral requirements for such a loan.

Thursday was the anniversary of 9/11, the day seven years earlier that had created massive challenges for Lehman. Unlike that time seven years earlier when we had rallied for firm and for country, the days following 9/11/08 would give us little to cheer or feel proud about. Lehman executives were now secretly talking to Bank of America, Barclays, and Nomura. Talk later circulated that as late as Thursday night, Fuld was uttering that he did not think things were as bad as everyone was saying. This seems hardly credible, unless he was having a psychotic break. More likely, he was in shock, but with prodding, Fuld was finally ready to sell. Of course, at this point, his nod was a mere formality. The man who for years ran Lehman as an absolute monarch had become little more than the most powerless of constitutional royals.

CHAPTER 9

Dickless

"Everything is Over."

—Emanuel Lehman, at the outbreak of the Civil War
and severing of communication between Lehman Brothers
operations in Montgomery and New York

By Friday morning, September 12, 745 Seventh Avenue was a
hotbed. I, like many, awoke well-rested and made my way to
Lehman's headquarters for another day at my embattled but unde-
featable firm. Business would be less frantic than normal, as it had been
for all of Wall Street since the summer of 2007. We would struggle to
keep clients engaged on the deals for which we held mandates. With effective client handholding all would be well once our restructuring proceeded. Lehman would be clean. And all of us would hold shares in the Lehman
"bad bank," that frankly most viewed as a good investment. Accounting
rules required us to take losses by marking the "toxic assets" down to current market value. But we believed many of these assets were only temporarily impaired, valued lower than they would be in a healthier market.
Once the market recovered, we stood to realize gains on the sale of the
"bad bank" assets. As for our business, it was invariably crippled by
rumors, but not unsound. We were faring well relative to peers in most
broker-dealer fields of play. Certainly, we had suffered a setback, but we
had the muscle and determination to rise again. This was my thinking.
This is what many thought as they arrived at 745 Seventh Avenue.

Soon, however, everyone knew that Lehman was in discussions with Bank of America and Barclays. Word circulated that government regulators were in the building. Or maybe not. Initially, few knew exactly who at Lehman was talking to our likely suitors and exactly where the discussions were underway.

It was at this point that I finally understood without doubt, and, in hindsight, with naïve shock, that a number of the faces I had seen around Lehman for years would soon be gone. I knew, also, that mine might be one of them. Until Friday, we carried on with work as if it were business as usual, even though clients were clearly exhibiting trepidation about hitching their funding wagon to our capital markets horse. Indeed, this hesitancy was one of the reasons Lehman vanished. Even if our liquidity was adequate, even if our restructuring plans had merit, since our days' earlier announcement of third quarter results, confidence in Lehman dispersed like vapor. This loss of confidence, the most abstract, often wholly subjective attribute underpinning a financial institution's health, felt oddly tangible. Surely as tangible as a wallet you reach for in its usual pocket only to find it missing. Where had it gone? One thing was clear. This was a wallet we knew we would no longer recover on our own. By Friday, for all intents and purposes, we no longer had clients. The buzz about Lehman's woes had become so deafening that as the weeks and then days unfolded, there came a point when no one could consider hiring us, fearing that we would not survive to complete the mandated work. In short, regardless of our financial condition and any economic wherewithal that may have remained on our balance sheet, our clients had left the building. Indeed, Lehman was in a hospice, gasping its final breaths. On Friday, we lacked only a coroner to make the approaching death official.

Initially, we heard that all were negotiating on the vaunted thirty-first floor. Fuld was banished from the talks. Apparently, pacing about the negotiating table, offering unsolicited suggestions, he was sent away without fanfare or acknowledgement to cool his heels in his office. Whether the talks began at Lehman or elsewhere, Dick was excluded. This was a role for which he was ill-prepared. An image of another Dick, Nixon, banished to San Clemente after his resignation comes to mind. Whatever the precise tenor of Fuld's isolation, this much was clear: he was no longer a factor. He had neither a seat at the table nor even a voice. He was, in a word, irrelevant.

For Fuld, this must have been excruciating. Not only was he losing the firm that had been his life, but he was also barred from the talks that would determine the future of its operating units. As Lehman deteriorated, he was so utterly trapped in his own head that this ultimate humiliation was not anything he anticipated. It was as if without noticing he had undergone a radical procedure, a full "Lehmandectomy." With the removal of Lehman, an organ that played as much of a role in pumping his blood as did his heart, one must wonder if he will ever truly live again.

Fuld is just one man. He is the headline. But there were many thousands of others working for Lehman whose lives suddenly went topsy-turvy on that Friday. In the preceding days, while we were all somewhat concerned, only some believed that Lehman's days as an independent firm were surely over. Undoubtedly there must have been employees selling Lehman stock, but I do not know anyone who did. On the other hand, in the weeks preceding this day, I know some who "bought on weakness," looking to make the killing one always made in the past by buying Lehman shares when rumors of its demise echoed through the canyons of Wall Street. I must say that even as I began writing this book, I was less clear-sighted than I am today. On that tumultuous Friday when we learned that Lehman was a goner, I did not believe there was any way I could have truly seen this coming—at least not seen it as a likelihood. From my current vantage point, it is clear that I and others drank management's Kool-Aid by the gallon. Even McDade and his team, as earlier noted, were shocked by what they saw after he became LB's president and examined the books. So maybe I can cut us all a bit of slack to admit that we were blind until the eleventh hour. Equally, I take with a large grain of sea salt the claims of Monday morning quarterbacks who represent that they saw the disaster in the making every step of the way. In the end, we were conned, and rushed toward a corporate cliff like lemmings with gold cufflinks and regulation Hermes ties. Clearly, Dick's hubris, and his contention that the world would always malign Lehman, rubbed off on us all. We had a great culture, characterized by teamwork and unity, but unfortunately, these paranoid beliefs had also subtly bled into the culture. The world was against Lehman. We would always somehow survive. That was simply the way it was, an absolute truth.

Penguins at the South Pole, to achieve collective warmth, form a large circular mass when that continent's winter winds are most killing. For the last time as Lehman, that is precisely what we did on that Friday. The world around us had become icily inhospitable and there was little left to do other than instinctively huddle. We gathered in offices, hallways, and elsewhere throughout the building exchanging the latest news, or in some cases, fiction, that each of us had heard.

Within various groups throughout the firm, everyone conjectured as to which of our potential acquirers would leave our teams most intact. Surely there would be considerably more overlap with Bank of America than with Barclays, as the former, while second tier, was a true factor in the markets. Barclays Capital, outside of its lending and commodities business was not a company that had ever mattered when we looked at Lehman's global competitors. Certainly, there would be overlap in Europe, especially the U.K., but in North America we were much larger and consistently in deals to which they had never gained access. Nomura, the leading Japanese securities house, had apparently been in the mix, but concluded it could not move quickly enough. All of this was obviously just talk. We knew it. But the chatter was unavoidable. The day stretched into one long dialogue where we ran all conceivable scenarios. I and others in my broader group spent portions of the day talking with many others we knew around Lehman. When any one of us hung up the phone or returned from a foray to another Lehman business unit, there was often new intelligence or fodder. It became impossible to distinguish between the two.

In the end, Friday turned out to be only one in a sequence of days when a select few executives discussed Lehman's fate with the interested acquirers and government regulators. Dick, throughout, was not party to these conversations, any more than the rest of us were, from senior level department heads down to the recent college graduates who had started over the summer. Of course, Fuld was more apprised of developments than anyone without an office on the thirty-first floor, but for the first time since he had taken the helm in 1994 it was clear to all that Dick was relegated to the bench, effectively nothing more than a sidelined observer.

No one knew who would prevail in the Lehman auction, but one distracting newsflash was that Treasury Secretary Paulson decreed that the government would provide no support for a Lehman transaction. Still, I, personally, thought he was playing a high stakes game of chicken, that in the end he would consent to and arrange a means for taxpayer dollars to back a transaction if this, in the end, was the only way to prevent a possible LB's bankruptcy. To do otherwise would be insanity, particularly for someone who had spent his career in a capital markets business.

Why?

A Lehman bankruptcy would cause global financial chaos in markets that were already bruised. Government inaction would put the already slowing economy at risk of an unprecedented meltdown, at least one unprecedented in most of our lifetimes. The low likelihood—not just potential—of a government yawn and inaction was so crystal clear, that I and those around me more or less dismissed it as unimaginable. Indeed, as we ran the various scenarios on that awful Friday, the one many ruled out was government intransigence if the alternative was a Lehman bankruptcy filing. Paulson, together with Bernanke and Geithner could not be that inept.

But, as it turned out, Hank Paulson was exactly that. He had an ideological aversion to government bailouts. Moreover, he had just, no doubt with great angst, nationalized two of the world's largest companies, Freddie Mac and Fannie Mae. He was a raging ideologically driven believer in free markets and corporate survival of the fittest. He had been unhappy about the government's role in the Bear Stearns situation, and on the heels of Fannie and Freddie was surely suffering from bailout overload. He believed he had to draw the line and would do so with Lehman. In this way, he would teach all of Wall Street a thing or two about moral hazard. He told himself the fallout could be managed. It would be bad, but contained.

Later, after the damage had been done, Paulson, Bernanke and Geithner would recast what they said on that Friday during the course of the ongoing negotiations over Lehman, and in the immediate aftermath of our filing. Currently articulated reasons for not supporting Lehman are revisionist history. As it became clear that this decision was a mistake, the three have all claimed there were legal impediments to providing support.

Senate Banking Hears Testimony on Fannie Mae, Freddie Mac

WASHINGTON, DC - JULY 15, 2008: Treasury Secretary Henry M. Paulson Jr., Federal Reserve Chairman Ben S. Bernanke, and Securities and Exchange Commission Chairman Christopher Cox testifiy during the Senate Banking hearing on turmoil in the capital markets and the prospective regulation of Fannie Mae and Freddie Mac. (Photo by Scott J. Ferrell/Congressional Quarterly/Getty Images)

Henry Paulson Speaks On The Economy At The Fortune 500 Forum

WASHINGTON - DECEMBER 01, 2008: U.S. Secretary of the Treasury Henry Paulson speaks during the Fortune 500 Forum December 1, 2008 in Washington, D.C. Paulson joined major business leaders to discuss issues most important to big business and updated the current situation of the economy. (Photo by Alex Wong/Getty Images)

If this is to be believed, the barrier had to be unique, given prior government support for the Bear Stearns transaction, as well as Freddie, Fannie, AIG, and others later. Moreover, Bernanke had months earlier defended the government's $29 billion support of Bear Stearns, noting that the fifth largest independent bulge bracket investment bank was "too big to fail." He pointed out that the repercussions of such a failure would have been devastating. In the Bear Stearns case, as later with respect to Lehman, it is technically true the Fed lacked authority to lend directly to the faltering investment bank, as Bear, like Lehman later, lacked sufficient sound assets to post against borrowings. So instead, the government did an end run, lending the funds to J.P. Morgan, which acted as a conduit for the government by infusing Bear with this liquidity. The government then guaranteed J.P. Morgan against many billions of losses in the hastily arranged Bear-J.P. betrothal, a shotgun marriage reluctantly acceded to by Paulson at the urging of Geithner and Bernanke. But in Lehman's case, Paulson proceeded with turgid resolve.

Over the week that followed the Lehman bankruptcy, Paulson is not on record stating that there were legal impediments to a government-financed or government-backed Lehman solution. No, what he did say was, "I never once considered that it was appropriate to put taxpayer money on the line when it came to Lehman Brothers."[li] Certainly, a Bear Stearns style liquidity infusion could have been arranged with a buyer, along with guarantees like the ones bestowed upon J.P. Morgan, or in concert with the private sector support, discussed later, that was ultimately arranged. But Paulson was drawing a line in the sand. And it appears utterly transparent when one compares initial statements with those that followed (once the devastating implications of the Lehman failure cast the world into turmoil), Paulson and his two Musketeers reinvented their story. Whereas they initially told the world that they *refused* to find a government solution for Lehman, they later changed the public tale, *insisting* that they were restricted from doing so. I do not know how much of a reputation Paulson now has to salvage, but the changed story seems to me the most shameful and cowardly of backpedaling in a blatant effort to dodge blame. Moreover, the day Lehman Holdings filed, Paulson declared, "I've got to say our banking system is a safe and a sound one . . . "[lii] One day later, the Fed made an $85 billion dollar emergency loan to AIG, lest it follow Lehman and compound the unrelenting storm ravaging global markets. Ultimately, the government came to own a large majority of AIG and is now, as I write, in the midst of selling its pieces. Paulson, the high priest of moral hazard, had nationalized the country's largest insurer, only to later see it pay outsized bonuses to many of those responsible for AIG's difficulties. Moral hazard?

The former Secretary of the Treasury's key, simplistic miscalculation about Lehman may have been that he believed, in the aftermath of the Bear bankruptcy, the rumors about Lehman circulating for some time; that the market had in some way adjusted for the possibility of a Lehman failure. Further, the Fed facilities, now available to both commercial and investment banks, would facilitate an orderly liquidation of Lehman's assets. On the contrary, any forced liquidation of Lehman assets would invariably place further downward pressure on market prices for similar assets held by numerous financial institutions and others.

It ultimately became clear on that Friday that full negotiations were underway, respectively, with Barclays and Bank of America in separate venues, at separate, major New York law firms with which Lehman had long relationships. One group of Lehman executives was at law firm Simpson Thatcher & Bartlett going over Lehman's books with the Barclays due diligence team. Another was at law firm Sullivan & Cromwell, going through a similar exercise with Bank of America. The focus was on Lehman's impaired assets, and finding a way to deal with these so that one of the two banks would buy our hobbled firm.

In any case, most of us headed home on Friday for a long weekend (not of the three-day variety). I cannot recall what time I left and exactly what I was thinking. But I knew the world I inhabited for so many years was irrevocably changed.

Not everyone headed home. It was crunch time for McDade and his team, who were only beginning a weekend of round-the-clock negotiations in the most important deal of their lives. Fuld spent the weekend in his office, working the phones. On the whole, the reception Dick received, when he dialed for dollars, was the icy one reserved for telemarketers. No doubt, if one existed, many would have added their names to a "Dick Fuld do-not-call" list.

Depending on who you were, that last weekend when Lehman gasped it final breaths, unfolded in fundamentally different venues. For the masses of senior investment bankers the weekend was a frustrating, unfamiliar experience. We were accustomed to seats at the table in the marathon negotiations that determined corporate fates. Yet here we were with negotiations proceeding and, except for a few Lehman executives, no role in the process.

On September 13, Paulson called a meeting at the New York Federal Reserve Building at 6:00 P.M. For Lehman, the key players were McDade and Alex Kirk (head of Principal Investing[72] since he had returned with Gelband). Paulson had organized the session to bring together the Lehman representatives and a group of Wall Street leaders, primarily CEO's of the remaining investment banks and other major finance houses. Merrill Lynch's CEO, John Thain, was among the attendees. Fuld was conspicuously absent. Top government officials specifically instructed Lehman management to bar him from the meeting, regarding him as at best a distraction and, more likely, explosive and possibly irrational.

Once the meeting got under way, Paulson reiterated his determination that the government would not provide any form of financial support for a Lehman transaction. The solid relationship Fuld imagined he had cultivated with Paulson was exposed as naked fantasy. If not clear earlier, it was now abundantly obvious that the Emperor, Fuld, wore no clothes. In fact, Joe Nocera of the *New York Times*, in recounting a Paulson interview said, "When I interviewed the Secretary of Treasury I was really astounded at the vehemence of his reaction to Dick Fuld. He was very angry. And whether that predated him being Treasury Secretary or not I don't know, but he was very, very angry. He said, 'I told Dick Fuld to sell the firm or to look for a buyer because he had a problem, and he wouldn't do it. And he's practically just pounding the table with his fist . . .'"[liii]

Paulson's ideological convictions about moral hazard fueled his determination to let Lehman topple. Moreover, the criticism leveled at him,

---

72. Investment of a firms own money, much like a private equity fund.

after he backed the Bear-J.P. Morgan Chase wedding with taxpayer dollars, also left him gun-shy to again put the American public's money on the table. Instead, he had summoned this *Who's Who* of Wall Street group to point out that they all could be hurt by an outright Lehman failure. As such, he asked the group to come up with a private rescue plan, along the lines of the cooperative funding that had allowed for an orderly unwinding of Long-Term Capital Management when it collapsed in the previous decade. But all of LTCM's tentacles amounted to one or two of Lehman's. Geithner more or less echoed Paulson, telling the gathered heads of America's financial giants that somebody would have to buy Lehman or the firm would become bankrupt. He added that there was zero political will in Washington for another bailout.

As Wall Street executives listened to the Paulson-led trio tell them that it was in all their interests to come up with a plan for dealing with the Lehman crisis in an orderly fashion, John Thain, the former Goldman CFO, then Merrill's CEO, grew anxious. With Bear Stearns a memory, and Lehman about to go down, there was little question that Merrill risked coming under similar pressure. Like the two before it, Merrill had significant real estate exposure. Thain, his heart by now racing, envisioned a Monday plunge in Merrill shares, regardless of what sort of deal was cobbled together for Lehman. One of his lieutenants had already repeatedly whispered in his ear that just such a scenario was likely. And so Thain now rationally foresaw risk that the same ilk of rumors that engulfed Lehman could like a wildfire, just hours hence, destabilize his firm. Before long, like LB, he would have to announce write-downs that would feed the fire so that clients and counterparties would stop doing business with Merrill. In short, he realized, he had to act. And he had to act with dispatch.

By later Friday evening, based on his team's due diligence, Bank of America's reluctant Lehman suitor, Ken Lewis, grew even more reluctant. While he did not attend the meetings at the Fed, Lewis connected with Paulson to tell him that he would only consider a deal if the government would remove $65 billion of specific problem assets from Lehman's balance sheet. Paulson declined, consistent with his ongoing insistence that the government would not play a financial role. With these words, the possibility of a Bank of America acquisition of Lehman ended. Lewis was out. Moral hazard, assignable to just a few Lehman executives, was trumping global financial and economic stability.

This opened the door for talks between Bank of America's Ken Lewis and Merrill's now eager to sell chief, John Thain. Lewis, as earlier mentioned, had for some time mused about a Merrill acquisition. The Wall Street firm's broad retail brokerage network would perfectly complement Bank of America's retail banking one. Merrill was no longer as strong a force in investment banking as it had once been, but combined with BofA's lesser, but meaningful foothold in investment banking, they would be formidable. Universal banking was the future. And Lewis was on record saying that owning Merrill would "round out"[liv] his bank's franchise. This must have seemed like a moment that would come only once, a moment he would have to seize. In no time, the Bank of America team took the short car ride to begin fresh negotiations with Merrill. There was also banter about a possible Goldman investment in Merrill, but this never gained the same traction as the full sale to Bank of America.

Months earlier, as noted, Fuld could have stood in Thain's Goldman-pedigreed shoes and negotiated. But after walking in circles it was too late. He had let his unrealistic passion for Lehman cloud all reason. He had turned away all sane offers and failed to consider or explore others. Only Barclays now remained. Lehman was not negotiating from a position of strength. Truly, the firm was Dickless.

Fuld, the eunuch, banned from the meetings that would decide Lehman's fate, was still determined to play a role. By now, he was also finally desperate for a deal, a sale. Unaware of Lewis' initial limited interest, and the cut-off of negotiations with the Lehman team in favor of the Merrill talks, Fuld impotently persisted in calling Lewis' home. He left messages with Lewis' wife, and by Saturday grew incensed that Lewis ignored him. But Dick no longer had minions upon which to vent his rage.

A series of meetings at the New York Fed continued over the weekend. Just days earlier, on Wednesday, Fuld and Lowitt had talked of marking $40 billion of Lehman commercial real estate assets down to $33 billion. By Saturday, after mortgage securities gurus from Goldman Sachs (the firm Paulson had run, and where Thain was former CFO), Credit Suisse,

Deutsche Bank, and Citigroup had reviewed the portfolio, the consensus was that the actual value was closer to a figure of around $21 billion, though they also felt a mark to $25 billion was doable and sufficiently compliant with accounting requirements. Despite such revelations, by Sunday, the government saw a plan come together in which the various summoned financial firms would backstop a new entity, a "bad bank," that would hold $50 to $60 billion of impaired assets, possibly even $70 billion, and that Barclays Capital would then acquire Lehman Brothers. While this would be costly to the banks participating in the scheme, they correctly feared that the fallout of simply letting Lehman fail would be disastrous.

Paulson, Bernanke, and Geithner could breathe a great sigh of relief. It seemed they had pulled off a neat solution to a difficult predicament. The leading financial houses would put up the money to clean up the mess in their own backyard, and the government trio, with sleight of hand, would avoid any potential criticism for a second mega-billion dollar investment banking salvage operation, and might even earn kudos for stabilizing financial markets without using taxpayer funds.

Sunday morning at about 10:00 A.M., I was at home waiting, channel surfing, and Blackberrying with colleagues as we all searched for some additional crumb of information that would clue us in to our fate. At around this same time, Bart McDade emailed his buddy, Gelband, who was at Simpson Thatcher waist deep in the marathon Barclays diligence, to tell him they had a deal. About fifteen minutes later, Bart tapped another message to Gelband into his Blackberry. There was a problem.

Indeed, there was an apparently insurmountable stumbling block. The U.K.'s Financial Services Authority (FSA) nixed the deal a little over an hour later. Why? The consistent explanation is a technical hitch. Until the "bad bank," or spinco,[73] could be created, Barclays would have to guarantee the impaired assets, just as the U.S. government backed the Bear Stearns impaired assets that went to J.P. Morgan Chase. Barclays' guarantee would be temporary. If the U.K. bank took any losses, presumably it

---

73. Generic term often used to describe a company that is spun out from an existing one, in this case the new entity which would hold the impaired Lehman assets.

would be made whole upon the creation of the spinco bad bank, drawing on the financial backing to which the government had convinced Wall Street to commit. However, U.K. stock exchange rules required shareholder approval even for Barclays to extend this guarantee. Barclays unsuccessfully sought a temporary U.S. government guarantee for the assets that would go to spinco. But Paulson, supported perhaps with trepidation by Bernanke and Geithner, was resolved not to provide financial assistance under any guise—no matter how fleeting, no matter how low the risk that the U.S. government would ever emerge on the hook for a penny.

Leigh Bruce, a Barclays spokesman said, "The only reason it didn't happen is that there was no guarantee from the U.S. government and a technical stock exchange rule required prior shareholder approval for us to make a similar guarantee ourselves. We didn't have the approval, so it wasn't possible for us to do the deal. No U.K. bank could have done it. It was a technical rule that could not be overcome."[lv]

On this same Sunday, in anticipation of the Lehman bankruptcy, an event that would cause Lehman to default on both debt and trading positions, banks and brokers held an extraordinary derivatives netting session. The intent was to allow banks to net, or offset, their Lehman positions, and thereby reduce everyone's total exposure to Lehman default.[74] In short, this session was a Band-Aid applied to staunch the gushing blood of a disemboweled casualty.

Had Paulson and his partners in regulation agreed to a temporary U.S. government guarantee, perhaps in the manner provided for Bear Stearns, though of only fleeting duration, all would have likely moved forward. Barclays would have paid a small amount, around $5/share for Lehman. And spinco, once legally created, would have taken the assets off the bal-

---

74. In simple terms, if one firm has a trade with Lehman where it has promised to pay Lehman the current interest rate if rates go up or down and another firm has a trade where Lehman contracted to pay it the current interest rate regardless of rate movements, then the first firm can simply agree to pay the second firm the current interest rate regardless of rate movements. This is a vast oversimplification, but in principle represents a netting of positions.

ance sheet and out from under the government guarantee. Paulson point-ed his finger at the U.K. regulators. He had spoken with the FSA[75] and portrayed them as hesitant to risk that the problems bedeviling the U.S. financial sector would infect the U.K. As for the U.S. government's refusal to take on the temporary guaranty, Paulson later told the *New York Times*, after the post-Lehman bankruptcy meltdown, that he did not have the legal authority to make that commitment. Earlier, on Monday September 15, the day Lehman filed, Paulson held a White House press conference before the full and lasting implications of a Lehman failure had become clear. Bush's Secretary Paulson, in a distinctly different tone, told the world, "I never once considered that it was appropriate putting taxpayer money on the line in resolving Lehman Brothers. Moral hazard is not something I take lightly." He also looked into the camera and said, "The American people can remain confident in the soundness and resilience of our financial system."[lvi]

The team from Lehman was devastated. It appeared an agreement had come together to save the firm and its employees, only to be snatched from their hands as they readied to ink it. Bart McDade, by Sunday afternoon, called Fuld to deliver the news. Fuld was stunned. I suppose, like many of us at Lehman, he never believed the government would let Lehman fail. In Dick's case, however, it was more personal. He believed that all the months of courting Paulson ensured that Lehman would benefit from a worst-case-scenario safety net. As far back as April, following a dinner with Paulson, Fuld had said we "have huge brand with Treasury."[lvii] At last he understood what other Wall Street CEOs had gleaned that recent Friday evening: Lehman was not considered essential by Paulson.

McDade hustled uptown to 745 Seventh Avenue where both he and Fuld frantically phoned the world for help. Paulson quickly shifted gears and told the financial executives assembled at the Fed that it was time to plan for a world without Lehman. On the one hand, these financial gener-als no longer stared up the barrel of Paulson's gun, with their Lehman bad asset purchase agreement in the shredder. Still, those present speculated about the massive fallout likely to greet them when markets opened the

---

75. Financial Services Authority, the U.K. regulator overseeing financial institutions in the U.K.

next day. Some speculated, in John Thain's presence, volubly devoid of compunction, that Merrill Lynch could be the next to crumble. Thain soon departed, more eager than ever to finalize terms with Ken Lewis and Bank of America. Lehman, meanwhile, in preparing for that which now appeared inevitable, phoned law firm Weil Gotshal to enlist its help in drawing up bankruptcy papers. They might be required to file in a matter of hours. Most likely this would be a Chapter 7, *i.e.* liquidation filing.

McDade and Ian Lowitt revisited the Fed for a last-ditch attempt to secure government support. They walked Paulson through a likely doomsday scenario depicting the raw tundra that would be the world after a Lehman failure. The Secretary was unconvinced and told the two Lehman executives that they were to file for Chapter 7 bankruptcy by 7 P.M. that evening. McDade and Lowitt returned to Lehman to deliver the news to an assembled Board of Directors.

It was not long before word leaked out. Every news broadcast announced the likely filing. Every Lehman Blackberry buzzed incessantly. Many of us made our way to the office that Sunday afternoon and evening. If Lehman filed for liquidation the doors to the building might well be locked the following morning.

These were the most surreal hours of the ordeal in which we were all embroiled since the previous Friday. 745 Seventh Avenue was jumping. We waded through the reporters who had surrounded the building to gain access. Microphones were thrust in our faces for a sound bite. Most ignored this assault and simply headed for their offices. There were personal items to collect. Those most conspicuously taken or left behind were the deal Lucites and "Big Deal" awards. For some, these were hard-earned symbols of what they accomplished during their investment banking careers and could not be discarded, and given the density and collective tonnage of a career's worth of Lucites, the transport of these was quite literally a weighty task for anyone who had spent some years in investment banking. For others, these were bitter emblems of the untimely death of our firm that, at least in those moments, were too heavy, physically or emotionally, to transport. Whatever we each carried away was loaded into the various canvas bags or rolling duffel bags that all had brought. As I paused to gaze at the scene around me, shook hands or hugged friends and colleagues, I was reminded of every movie I have seen where refugees hurriedly flee a village.

Meanwhile, the Board continued to deliberate on Lehman's next move. With the deft, invaluable help of our lawyers, the Board came to a consensus that Paulson could tell us to file for bankruptcy, but could neither control the absolute timing nor the form. He could not force Lehman to file under Chapter 7 liquidation.

Then word came that the Fed was expanding the range of collateral that could be pledged by broker-dealers to borrow. If this was true, if they would accept the crap collateral we had left to post, this might still buy us time to work a deal. When The Brothers called the Fed to check, the daunting reply was that, yes, the news was true, but "we're doing that for everybody else but you. We're going to let you guys go."[lviii]

At home that evening, I pondered my next steps and mourned the passing of my firm into total oblivion, an eventuality that now appeared a near-term certainty. Sometime around midnight I went to bed, expecting to wake up to a Chapter 7 filing and no need to head to 745 Seventh Avenue. When I closed my eyes, Lehman still had a pulse, but for how long?

Around this same time there were a few, including Fuld, still with pencils in hand in the Lehman tower. A plan was being hatched, the brainchild of Lehman's counsel, Weil Gotshal, to file only the holding company[76] for bankruptcy under Chapter 11, reorganization, together with the toxic assets that had ruined the firm. A call went out to Bob Diamond, Barclays president, who was the key Barclays executive in the Lehman-BarCap negotiations. He expressed how disappointed he was that despite everyone's superhuman efforts a deal had not been achieved. Next, Diamond listened as the plan for Chapter 11 was described. It was hoped that the broker-dealer would be preserved, and that this cleansed entity could be sold to Barclays. A new wrinkle.

Bob Diamond was interested.

---

76. Legal entity that generally does not conduct operations, but owns operating units of an enterprise. Lehman Holdings was the Lehman holding company, while the actual broker-dealer, as well as certain other units, were subsidiaries owned by Lehman Holdings.

CHAPTER 10

Paulson's Folly

*"I particularly appreciate the efforts of market
participants who came together this weekend and
initiated a set of steps to facilitate orderliness
and stability in our financial markets . . ."[lix]*

—Henry Paulson, former Secretary of the Treasury

As best I can remember, I woke up at my usual time on Monday morning, September 15, 2008. However, I do not recall whether I woke to my alarm, or stirred by my anxieties over Lehman's demise, opened my eyes a few minutes before the clock radio would rouse me. I do know that upon waking, I immediately turned on the television and grabbed my Blackberry for an update on the status of Lehman's Chapter 7 bankruptcy filing. It was unlikely that I had a job at 745 Seventh Avenue, but I was curious whether I could even enter the building. If Lehman had died in my sleep, as expected, I still wanted to retrieve a few items, and more importantly, see my colleagues one last time.

The Brothers seemed to be the only show on television that morning, and so I quickly learned they had, as expected, died peacefully in my sleep. Yet while Lehman filed for bankruptcy, it did not file for Chapter 7, liquidation. Instead, the firm had filed for Chapter 11 bankruptcy protection, technically a reorganization. This was a wrinkle, that like Diamond, I did not expect. Apparently, only Lehman Holdings had filed, and the operating units were on life support. There was no announced resumption of talks with Barclays or any other potential buyer, and there was no suggestion that the operating units would survive. For the moment, unaware of what was afoot, I figured this meant the operating unit was now on true, critical life support, with preservation and sale of the Lehman business as the endgame. Rather, I assumed that the Chapter 11 filing was just a legal technicality. But I was uncertain. There were zillions of Blackberry messages, but nothing any more informative or encouraging than what I saw on TV. In any case, since the investment bank itself had not yet officially filed, 745 would be open. I was naturally eager to reach the office and learn exactly what the Chapter 11 filing was about, though I would not allow myself hope. If it turned out to be nothing more than a meaningless technicality, once at 745, I figured I could at least say my goodbyes. Still, why Chapter 11?

Oddly, I do not remember whether I donned a jacket and tie that day, only that I was eager to get to the office as quickly as possible, to be among those with whom I would share Lehman's presumed hard landing. I do, however, remember that most investment bankers did wear suits and, most of those on the trading floors did not. On Lehman's last day, banker's looked like it was business as usual. Traders looked more casual, and in many cases, were unshaven. My take on the investment banking attire is that everyone was very proud of what Lehman's Investment Banking Division had accomplished, and wanted to walk out the doors of 745 Seventh Avenue with honor, like soldiers who proudly wear their uniforms into battle although the war is lost. The traders' lazy weekend attire was equally expressive in its own way. And indeed, *all this was right.* If you who read this now worked at Lehman on 9/11, you understand exactly what these words mean. If you joined Lehman after that very hard date, you still have a sure sense of it. If you work in the industry, but did not work at Lehman on 9/11 or thereafter, I honestly do not know how much of this you can truly *get.* And, if you are anyone else, even now, you may think that investment bankers are just a hoard of greedy, spoiled assholes; as a group, a singularly unsympathetic lot. If this book captures the eyes of many, then this last group is in the majority. To you, then, I say, suspend all predispositions. Think only of what it means to be marginalized, a laughed-about underdog. Then consider that in whatever it is that you do, positive developments provide a promising, infinitesimal toehold. It does not matter why. The Berlin Wall comes down or you simply get a new boss. But then, somewhere along the line, you endure a seminal event with the people you see every day. You experience firsthand, together, something of great magnitude, like 9/11, experienced by many and yet by few in the larger world. And from that experience a bond develops that propels you with purpose you have never seen in the context of your day-to-day text. You succeed beyond all expectation. Once maligned, you are now collectively in your prime, surpassing all goals that you have set for yourselves. And then a very few make some very poor decisions, and the glorious landscape that is the collective collage you have worked at for a very many years simply falls like light timber through a backyard chipper. You and yours meet for a last day or two. This was Monday for me and the many others with whom I built a house.

Monday at Lehman, or whatever one might call my firm in total limbo, was quite a day. Getting into the building was even more difficult than it had been the previous day, as the media throng had mushroomed, with live broadcasts of employees making their way into the building and some leaving with boxes, duffels or totes. Like most others, I dodged microphones, though of course reporters found some eager to express themselves. I recall hearing of one colleague laughing to a group inside 745 that when a young female reporter had pushed a microphone into his face for comment, rather than duck and dodge, he stopped, looked at her, and with his tongue at his knees, told her "You know, you're really hot." That was one way to say "fuck off" to the press and dash hopes for some juicy human interest. The cliché, one had to laugh or cry, easily characterizes moments like this one. Naturally, there were many like these. But, of course, I also saw colleagues who were not laughing. The image of one on the trading floor, whom I have known for years, sticks in my memory. He shook my hand, at once gentle and firmly serious. We uttered a few words. But in comfortable clothes and with an unshaven, straight-mouthed grimace, he stared off over the trading floor, like a mournful sailor staring off over an infinite sea.

During the first hours of the workday, farewell emails trickled into the inbox of my PC and my Blackberry. Everyone was resigned. We were dead men and women walking. I told myself that I had dodged a few bullets over the years. Until now I had been lucky; the bullets whistled past my ears. And I had joined Lehman when it was weak, only to luck into a career at a financial institution that would see its performance and reputation ascend. I long ago lost count of how many rounds of layoffs I survived during my career, and while I would like to believe this was a reflection of the quality of my contribution, I have seen some very talented and productive investment bankers lose their jobs. And so I have got to credit dumb luck, in part, for my absence from the periodic executioners' lists. Now unemployed, it would have been easier to look for new work in finance or start over completely as a younger man than I am today, but this sort of thought would not serve me well. I had finally been dealt a really shitty hand. I had no choice but to play it.

In the midst of all this, out of nowhere, word began to circulate that Barclays was back. Apparently, despite all that preceded this moment, rigor mortis had not yet set in. Bart and his team were hunkered down with Bob Diamond and his, as well as the entourage of lawyers, *et. al.* negotiating to snatch us back from death's door. That Chapter 11 filing that had taken me by surprise had to be intrinsic to the basis for resumption of talks. What I learned, as the details emerged from the haze, was that the bankruptcy filing of the holding company only, and not the operating units, was a legal stratagem to throw the New York Stock Exchange listed parent, Lehman Holdings, under the bus with all the tainted, poor assets. The rest was to be preserved, hoping that Barclays would now be able to buy spick and span businesses, cleansed of their soiled loans and securities. In effect, they would pick up the people, along with the sounder assets and liabilities funding them. This is precisely what they had wanted from the outset. We assumed they would be eager to acquire our building as well. We could not be stuffed into the far smaller BarCap premises. About this and much more, there was endless conjecture. What it all boiled down to was that hope returned. A small flame extinguished just a day earlier was relit. Still, there was no hard and fast deal. And up until now, Murphy's Law had prevailed: everything that could go wrong would go wrong. Also, the message trickling from the thirty-first floor was that a deal was still a long-shot. But we had a discernible faint pulse. We were all, however, keenly aware that the pulse would flatline if the reconvened negotiations were not expeditiously completed. Cardiac arrest would shortly ensue. No defibrillator on the planet would have the juice to resuscitate us.

As all of this was happening, rumors began to rage that our most productive bankers were already fielding offers with attractive bonus guarantees from other firms. Some of these rumors were very specific. If we could not come to terms with BarCap quickly, these heads would be out the door, and with them Barclays' interest in a deal. After all, much of the client franchise our suitor coveted could depart in the portfolios of fleeing rainmakers with whom our clients had long done business. And even if we reached an agreement, there would be redundancies. There always are, even when there is as little overlap as that which existed between Lehman and BarCap. In the current environment, this was bound to be more painful than a deal reached in more prosperous times. And honestly we did not know how bad the markets would get. U.S. stock exchanges had opened and quickly followed global markets into a bottomless well. Despite news of renewed talks, farewell emails continued to appear intermittently in my inbox. For many, it was easiest to assume the worst. Having been long-time believers in Lehman's endurance through the fires of Hell, recent events gave rise to a new caution to resist the seductive hope now dangling within reach.

By afternoon, we were both restless and numb. Even those clinging to the small hope revealed early in the day were emotionally spent. We were expecting to hear something definitive on that Monday, but the hours passed with a rattling silence. Outside our building, there was nothing but noise: 745 was still under siege by reporters, and by a few headhunters, who like sleazy ambulance-chasing lawyers, stood at Lehman's entrance handing out cards. A massive sort of board, an effigy of Dick Fuld, was erected in front of the building as a place for people to pen messages. It steadily accumulated a litany of epitaphs, with the mobbed structure reminding me of the statue of Saddam Hussein toppled after the American invasion of Baghdad.

As the stock market trading day drew to a close, we still had no deal. But the Dow had fallen 504 points, its worst single day decline since 9/11. The Lehman bankruptcy also ignited a surge in bank borrowing rates, and a global run on both banks and money market funds. It was about this time that I came to loathe Henry Paulson. I was not a fan of Bernanke or Geithner at this point either, but it was evident that the former Goldman Sachs chief had led the government in its handling of the Lehman crisis. It was also evident that this seasoned Wall Street executive, with an unmatched pedigree from the industry's most admired, and surely most constantly profitable firm, had tragically miscalculated.

There were naturally those who speculated that Paulson's handling of both the Bear Stearns and the Lehman meltdowns was designed to eliminate two of his former firm's competitors. One can also speculate that, to some extent, the decision to abandon Lehman, leaving it to twist in the wind, was driven by a personal element. Yes, Fuld had erroneously believed he had created "brand," a valuable relationship with the Treasury Secretary that would, in a pinch, serve Lehman well. However Fuld's unwavering refusal to sell when the Secretary had urged him to do so left Paulson livid. Moreover, decades of animosity between the explosive, pugnacious Fuld and many of Wall Street's leaders were not easily erased. Regardless of what they may have thought about Dick professionally, his peers at other firms did not seem to like him personally. With Fuld's name fully synonymous with Lehman Brothers, one could reasonably ask whether there was also a punctuated reluctance to save Dick Fuld: *i.e.,* the man *and* his firm.

While it was tempting to sink my teeth into these infectious contentions, it is difficult to seriously conclude that such pettiness was behind Lehman's end. Paulson, by all appearances, entirely loathes Dick Fuld, but he was primarily driven by his rigid, narrow ideology, and was reacting to public and congressional disapproval of the government's role in the Bear Stearns solution, not to mention the recent rescue of Fannie and Freddie. By the time the Lehman crisis erupted he was feeling considerable pressure to avoid providing what many regarded as a government check for greedy, obscenely wealthy investment bankers. He wanted to see Lehman sold, not bankrupt. Of course, he was surely furious with Fuld for his failure to lucidly assess Lehman's options and act decisively at an earlier stage. Still, despite all of this, it is difficult to imagine that Paulson would have permitted the bankruptcy if he had more lucidly anticipated what would follow. But, as is now painfully clear, Paulson was not an oracle. Still, it is disturbing that our Treasury

Secretary was so blind to the inevitable global meltdown that predictably ensued as he directed Lehman to file, with a firm shove on a figurative Dick Fuld's back. This was a monumental and historic lapse in judgment. Surely, Paulson could not have desired to create a legacy in which he would be assigned much of the blame for a global financial and economic Armageddon, a disaster of biblical proportions that would cause millions, perhaps billions, around the world future pain. And while Paulson truly appeared oblivious to the prospect that the fallout of the Lehman bankruptcy would prove so costly, one has to question whether he would have countenanced a similar fate for Goldman Sachs. At least in this, there was a fundamental conflict of interest.

I do not remember what time I left the office that hopeful Monday, but I do know I left without Lehman and Barclays coming to terms. The ensuing evening was spent again surfing the widescreen, with Lehman featured on any number of concurrent, ongoing broadcasts, but with no definitive news forthcoming—just regurgitations of less than what I had learned that morning and afternoon inside the walls of 745 Seventh Avenue. The rest was just the usual pundit talking heads exhaustively, repetitiously, speculating as to every possible outcome. I could not stop watching.

Another personal and prominent feature that evening, and for several more, was the ringing telephone. The last time I can recall it beckoning so frequently, so urgently, was on 9/11/01. The sheer volume of calls that crowded my answering machine had only that one precedent. Once I was home, I answered when it rang, at least for a bit. But I soon resorted to screening calls or ignored them. It was, of course, thoughtful that each of the callers wanted to see how I was in the wake of the bankruptcy. And support of those in one's life is always appreciated. Honestly, though, the calls were exhausting. I was living the drama, and repetitiously reciting my story, answering the same questions, became increasingly draining. Again, it was lovely that people called. I was, however, unprepared for the breadth of dialers. People came out of the woodwork, much as they do when someone dies.

Later, comparing notes with others at Lehman, I found that my telephone experience was similar to everyone's. Oddly, we would not have been surprised to receive flowers, fruit baskets and casseroles at our front doors. While the accumulating volume of phone messages became a daunting, digitally compiled and preserved tome, I do anonymously thank everyone who called me, and I suppose anyone else at Lehman. I also thank those who chose not to call me, concerned that it might not be the best of times to do so. This was equally thoughtful.

That the prevailing environment became funereal was unexpected. A company, not a human being, had died—with the possible exception of Dick Fuld in a figurative sense. There are protocols for human death instilled in all the world's cultures, but there is no rulebook for consoling casualties of a corporate demise. I suppose, however, when a job loss plays out on national television, one is bound to receive more attention than would be the case upon quietly receiving a pink slip one Friday afternoon in a small five-person office. After all, we are a society tethered to mass media, and through it, to one another, so that the concerned calls I received on 9/11/01, and then again, beginning on 9/15/08, were both spurred by the endless news coverage of these two very different events. To that point, calls did not similarly accumulate when my position at BarCap was eliminated without fanfare.

I lay in bed Monday night no more enlightened than I had been soon after I learned negotiations had resumed. The only other development was that markets in Asia had opened for another sell-off. As I drifted toward sleep, I mused that events could lead to an unexpectedly ironic outcome. If Barclays did in fact acquire Lehman, not all, but many jobs would be saved. On the other hand, with Lehman safely tucked into the sturdy Barclays, the rest of the world would likely continue its descent into a greater financial chaos. In the end, Lehman could disappear as an independent firm. The century-and-a-half-old name could be tossed in the rubbish bin. But vestiges of the firm might endure while the world paid the price for mistakes of Lehman's management, the U.S. government, rating agencies and others—for the murder of Lehman through negligence, faulty judgment, greed and bad timing.

I pondered Paulson's contention that he takes moral hazard so very seriously. This position is devoid of both humane and practical considerations. Good God, I thought to myself as I neared sleep, Paulson is a zealot who has triggered an off-the-Richter-scale earthquake to punish a few villains,

NEW YORK - SEPTEMBER 15, 2008: Members of the press attempt to interview an employee of Lehman Brothers Holdings Inc. as he carries a box out of the company's headquarters and hails a cab in New York City. Lehman Brothers filed a Chapter 11 bankruptcy petition in U.S. Bankruptcy Court after attempts to rescue the storied financial firm failed.
(Photo by Chris Hondros/Getty Images)

Former Lehman Brothers CEO Auctions Off
Part Of His Art Collection

NEW YORK - NOVEMBER 12, 2008: Christie's employees take bids over the phone during a post-war and contemporary art sale, which includes a collection owned by Richard Fuld Jr., formerly chairman and CEO of the bankrupt investment bank Lehman Brothers, and his wife Kathy Fuld, at Christie's auction house in New York City. Fuld's collection is expected to bring in about $20 million. (Photo by Ramin Talaie/Getty Images) but in doing so crushed millions of innocent souls. Collateral damage.

I woke up Tuesday, and, by now you know before I tell you, went directly to the repetitious news broadcasts and my schizoid humming Blackberry. Still there was no outcome. Not long after I arrived at 745 Seventh Avenue, noting the electronic Times Square Lehman graphics still wrapping the building, I learned that we had apparently reached an agreement with Barclays, were just ironing out last minor wrinkles. Spirits rose, but we still held our breath. By no means had the fat lady sung.

Soon I heard there was actually disagreement about Barclays' outright purchase of our headquarters and two data centers across the Hudson River in New Jersey. Possibly, Barclays was concerned that owning the building made no financial sense in a soft real estate environment poised to soften further. The exact details of this snag never became clear. But here we were again, with the deal in jeopardy.

Man, we all intoned, it simply cannot come down to this. *Barclays, buy the fucking building* I found myself wanting to shout. I was not alone. If the deal died because Barclays balked at purchasing our headquarters, I would not have been especially surprised to see a few Lehman lifers leap from the roof.

* * *

As we waited, we continued to observe that financial markets were in a tailspin. The U.K. market was pushing through levels that purged three year lows. In New York, the Dow had opened down 1.5 percent after Monday's historic plunge.

* * *

At last, word arrived that Lehman and Barclays had reached a firm deal. There was much shaking of hands. But no one was quite ready to uncork the champagne. While it seemed that bankruptcy court approval of BarCap's Lehman acquisition would be a slam dunk, the hearing was days off. No one's elevated pulse would moderate to its normal rate until we were through that process. Moreover, I noted in documents to which I had access, that the acquisition was contingent on retention of a limited number of key employees. I do not recall the exact number, but it was in the neighborhood of, say, ten. There were another couple of hundred key executives of which a high set percentage would have to be retained for the deal to close. Certainly, the handful, the ten or so individuals that had to all formally commit to stay for the acquisition to close, had already consented. But many individuals and even groups around the firm were actively shopping themselves to other financial houses. There was a top executive management full court press on all the named individuals to stay put, but there was simply no absolute guarantee we would meet the required numbers.

So as the Tuesday work day wound down, there was much about which to feel optimistic. But there were still risks the deal could implode or be irrationally rejected by bankruptcy court. The potential pitfalls were unlikely to occur, but then so was Paulson's folly. I took nothing for granted and would not rest until I saw the Barclays banner had replaced Lehman on the electronic dashboard that lit the outside of our iconic building.

There was also the cold reality of what Lehman's murder, by removal of critical life support, had set in motion. Even if we were sucked into Barclays, Paulson and company had unwittingly devestated world markets and economies, and no one in a financial job would live without worry for quite some time. Of that I was sure. And depending on just how bad the whole morass became, the pain could spread like a diaspora across all of global industry and commerce.

At least Paulson and the handful of others in our government who had decided to hang Lehman out to dry were not so stubborn that they ignored the worldwide market implosion that greeted them on Monday. The fallout in Asia, already into market trading days, began the instant it became public Lehman had filed. Europe followed suit. And then finally, New York, as Monday made its way around the globe. The Lehman mushroom cloud in a matter of hours smothered the world. Seeing all this, the harsh beginning of a financial nuclear winter, Paulson unexpectedly found himself out on a limb.

Finally rational, the Treasury secretary and the government did an abrupt one-eighty, and on Tuesday dug into taxpayers' public pockets to lend $85 billion to prevent the failure of a teetering American International Group (AIG).[77] Shortly *after* this was accomplished (with no mention of legal obstacles that Paulson and company later explained as the basis for their inaction in the Lehman crisis), Paulson and Bernanke turned to Congress for $700 billion to buy assets of banks under pressure. According to U.S. Senator Christopher Dodd, in an urgently arranged meeting with Congressional finance committee members from both houses, Paulson told the assembled group, "unless you act, the financial system of this country and the world will melt down in a matter of days."[lx] Paulson had found religion, or at least saw his chosen one was ridiculously faulty and led to irretrievable missteps. All other institutions of scale that would later come under pressure would without exception be deemed "too big to fail," with the government using taxpayer funds to stabilize each of them, to avoid another Lehman-like blunder. Paulson's moral hazard doctrine was out the window. It was likely as hard for him to let go of this principle by which he ruled as it had been for Dick Fuld to let go of Lehman. After all, with doctrinaire conviction, rather than common sense, dominating his decision to let Lehman file for bankruptcy, Paulson must have felt the abandonment of his guiding moral hazard principle was a near sacrilegious act, a betrayal of his bedrock beliefs. In a televised White House press conference, as he later readied to inject government capital into a number of banks, he told the public, "The government owning a stake in any private company is objectionable to most Americans, me included." To call the move "objectionable," was surely for him a fantastic understatement. More likely, Paulson felt like a public school educator forced to abandon preaching creationism in favor of teaching evolution.

Digressing for a paragraph, it should now be clear to any who wondered why the government only allowed Lehman to die, that this was in large part a simple matter of bad timing. After the government role in Bear Stearns, Freddie and Fannie played out, the Paulson trio called it a day on bailouts. They would send a message that if you played, you most definitely paid. Certainly bailouts were contrary to Paulson's capitalist moral reasoning. But he also plainly worried that unless he established that moral

---

77. America's largest insurer, like Lehman, with deep and complex entanglements in global markets. Larger than Lehman.

hazard could in fact bring down a major firm, all of Wall Street would presume that the worst-case scenario for engaging in high stakes poker was a government rescue. He believed it imperative he transmit the message that this was not the case, and in doing so provide greater disincentive for taking on imprudent risk. Few can challenge Paulson's thinking from a strictly ethical standpoint. Individuals should, in a perfect world, suffer the consequences of irresponsibly risky behavior. Unfortunately for us all, however, the moral hazard doctrine was not a sensible playbook for our real, rather imperfect circumstances.

If instead of Lehman, another investment bank experienced the same collapse of confidence precisely when The Brothers did, absent a buyer, Paulson would have encouraged it to file for bankruptcy (with the probable exception of Goldman Sachs). Of course, subsequently witnessing the nuclear fallout of this misstep, he undoubtedly would have wanted to turn back the clock. And if Lehman, on the heels of such a public policy disaster, was the next one to teeter, Paulson would then have ensured LB remained afloat, just as he ensured that others did not follow my former firm into bankruptcy. Unfortunately, for Lehman, and certainly its creditors and transaction counterparties, bad timing and simple bad luck was one of many critical factors that led to the firm's undoing.

For Lehman employees, whether Barclays acquired our firm with government support, or, as it turned out, post-bankruptcy without government backing, the result would have been similar, except for the fact that we would have received distressed, minimal value for our shares. Absorbed by another financial organization, in a world ravaged by Paulson's blunder, like the rest of Wall Street, we would still have struggled to generate profits.

* * *

Lehman and Barclays publicly announced BarCap's acquisition of The Brothers on Tuesday, September 16. However, BarCap was not acquiring all of Lehman, only its North American operations, and not even all of those. I worried for my colleagues in other markets. If the Barclays acquisition moved ahead would they all be out of work? And what of those posted overseas by Lehman? Were they now stranded without a flotation device, left to find work far from home, or finance their own return to the U.S. where they would have to search for employment in an industry that was rapidly downsizing?

Barclays was to pay $250 million for the Lehman business units, *i.e.,* pocket change. The figure was a fraction of the firm's quarterly profit in a sound operating environment. In fact, the year-end bonuses BarCap would have to pay its former Lehman employees to simply retain them when markets would improve, albeit substantially below everyone's 2007 number, would exceed the $250 million by a large multiple. Also acquired, as noted, was the headquarters building at 745 Seventh Avenue, plus two data centers in New Jersey, for $1.29 billion. Right, even the real estate was more highly valued than the living, breathing people, the associated franchise, and a cleansed balance sheet. The primary businesses acquired were investment banking, both fixed income and equity sales and trading, and research. Businesses most conspicuously absent from the purchase were Neuberger Berman and the rest of Lehman's Investment Management Division. In total, there were roughly ten thousand Lehman employees integrated into BarCap out of about 24,000 Lehman employees globally.

In announcing the Lehman acquisition, Diamond called it a "once in a lifetime opportunity"[lxi] for BarCap. Fuld and McDade were also quoted, as one would expect, lauding the transaction. And the U.K.'s FSA was no longer sufficiently concerned to scuttle the agreement.

To keep Lehman operations afloat until the desired bankruptcy approval would be received, and the acquisition could then close, Barclays extended $450 million of debtor-in-possession (DIP)[78] financing to

---

78. Typically, financing for a bankrupt entity, generally extended to enable a bankrupt company to continue to operate, to keep the lights on. This lending normally ranks ahead of other indebtedness of the bankrupt company, and therefore is first in line to recover amounts lent if the bankrupt company should cease operations and liquidate its assets for the benefit of creditors. The aim of DIP financing is to avoid a disorderly liquidation at fire sale prices. Existing creditors will normally benefit from a DIP financing, as more value is preserved by allowing for an orderly liquidation or a restructuring that permits the company to emerge from bankruptcy, with either accommodations from creditors and/or a sale of the business. Additionally, if the company is able to continue to operate, this maintains employment for at least a substantial number of pre-bankruptcy employees.

Lehman. This facility required formal approval by bankruptcy judge James Peck, sought on Wednesday, September 17, in a debtor's motion to borrow from Barclays bank. Lehman's Weil Gotshal attorney told the judge that without a cash infusion, Lehman would exhaust its liquid funds, and have no choice but to shut down, to turn off the lights. Of the $450 million, an initial drawdown of $200 million was proposed. It was to be repaid by the proceeds of the sale of Lehman businesses and assets to BarCap. Ian Lowitt, Lehman's then CFO, told the judge that the terms of the Barclays credit facility were without question more attractive than any they might find elsewhere, if indeed they could even find another lender. Judge Peck readily approved the proposed facility.

The asset purchase agreement spelling out these terms was also filed on September 16. The credit agreement was dated September 17. Terms of agreements continued to be tweaked in real time all week, so that documents ultimately submitted to the court were covered with hand-written changes. Even the words "execution copy" had been handwritten, with "draft" crossed out on the same page.

In the period between the announcement of the transaction and Friday bankruptcy hearing, my colleagues and I were in an extended state of limbo. Year-to-date, the combined company was the top book runner[79] for global debt underwriting. This week, however, there was no new business to augment that total. Lacking our usual, all-consuming business focus, people's thoughts and conversations strayed to resentment over the significant premium above market value that Bank of America paid to acquire Merrill Lynch, versus the complete erasure of Lehman's stock value. There was also news that colleagues who lost their jobs during several rounds of layoffs that occurred before Lehman's filing were immediately to lose any remaining severance payments and benefits. About five thousand former Lehman employees were smacked in the face with this byproduct of the

---

79. The lead underwriter that manages the books of a securities offering. The majority of deals have more than one book runner, however the one listed farthest to the left on the cover of offering documents is considered deal captain. Book runners capture the largest part of underwriting fees on an offering, with other underwriters individually capturing a considerably smaller piece of the fee pie.

bankruptcy filing. As obligations of the bankrupt holding company, Lehman Holdings, Inc., all these payments, along with those to creditors, ended the very moment that Lehman filed. The severance benefits rank behind more senior obligations, so that it is unlikely these former Lehman employees will see another nickel. This is particularly tough on ex-Lehmanites who lost their jobs shortly before the bankruptcy filing—particularly lower-level workers who surely have less of a financial cushion than many others.

For the moment, those of us left standing sort of had jobs. With the Friday court session several days off, we could not yet exhale. And of course we still mourned Lehman and the fallout impacting so many we knew personally. Expressing the feelings of many, a Lehman research analyst sent clients a farewell email on Monday afternoon, writing that he was "very saddened by the outcome for our firm . . . and for the loss of a truly great franchise." He later commented to the press that the experience "has been an emotional roller-coaster."[lxii] Again, because so much had gone wrong that should have gone right there was palpable trepidation as we neared the Friday court date. There was talk that the firm's acting leaders might try to pack the courtroom and the area just outside with Lehman employees, holding placards, imploring the court to save jobs. As we thought about this, there was general consensus that sending a bunch of spoiled bankers wearing impeccable high-end suits would generate little sympathy—could even backfire. Clearly, support staff was the way to go. Their numbers were a multiple of the rock star rainmakers now scorned by most Americans and, unquestionably, the "average-Joe" staff would be more sympathetically received. In the end, though, this was all just talk by many with little to do but wait. No Lehman bus transported forlorn, desperate employees, en masse, downtown to the federal court.

Finally, it was Friday, D-Day for Lehman Brothers, and exactly one week after the traumatic Friday when we learned Lehman was up for grabs or about to disappear. The court proceedings were scheduled to begin in the late afternoon, so nail-biters were well occupied chiseling their fingers throughout official working hours. Dick Fuld would not be present in court. For him it was a very different day than for both

Lehman's acting leaders and everyone else at the firm. No doubt, he hoped the acquisition would be approved, though it was of little direct consequence to his personal situation. The sun had set on his exalted professional years. The media was only just beginning to paint him as a villain and monster. With his diminished, but still enormous personal wealth, he will never need a job, unless lawsuits somehow empty his many pockets. About this, he consulted with attorneys to assess his liability to creditors of Lehman Holdings seeking redress. Whatever they told him, he must not have been pleased if he saw the Bloomberg item that ran that Friday, noting he likely was personally liable. A Harvard and University of California professor was quoted saying that bankruptcy law allows for recovery from senior executives if the value of their service was less than they were paid. In 2007, Fuld had received a pay package of about $34 million. Lynn LoPucki, the law professor, was quoted saying that "[t]he value of the services of a CEO who runs a company into bankruptcy is less than $34 million.[lxiii] But this vast amount is only a fraction of Fuld's net worth, and much of that figure was paid in Lehman stock. Only over time will his personal consequences for the Lehman failure unfold.

At last it was 4:00 P.M. when bankruptcy court was scheduled to begin its consideration of the BarCap acquisition of Lehman Brothers. As this would likely drag on for some hours, there was little reason to remain in the office. Like many others, I headed home with my Blackberry secured in its holster at my hip. Recent days made me quicker on the draw than ever. It seemed to always be high noon.

I was definitely not up for dinner out or any sort of social gathering. Small talk would be painful; I would be preoccupied. This was not one of those times when a bit of distraction or diversion would do me good. Plus, like others, I was utterly spent, so that even if a favorable decision had already been reached, I would not make for lively company that night. The only thing for me to do was spend a quiet evening at home, ignoring the telephone, and wait out the hours of legal rhetoric ricocheting around the bankruptcy courtroom. I felt like I was hunkered in a storm cellar, waiting out a hurricane, wondering if my house would be intact when I emerged through the cellar door.

The scene in Courtroom 601 in the Alexander Hamilton Custom House in lower Manhattan was entirely different. The room was jam-packed with literally hundreds of lawyers and creditors who had begun arriving an hour ahead of the scheduled start to score a seat. Many present were doomed to stand throughout the lengthy proceedings. These would be overseen by Judge Peck, the U.S. Bankruptcy Court Judge for the Southern District of New York who had approved the Barclays loan a couple of days earlier. The agreement for sale of assets in this, the then-largest bankruptcy in U.S. history (four times larger than runner up WorldCom), had been so hurriedly crafted that changes were still made both inside and outside the courtroom while it was in session. And this session was to last an exhausting eight-and-a-half hours. Few witnesses testified: only one from Lehman, Bart McDade, our president. Team Lehman nonetheless hammered at a set of core points. First, failure to approve the BarCap acquisition would lead to even more devastating financial fallout than was already occurring, dealing another harsh blow to world markets and economies. Second, it was BarCap or no one. The Paulson-sponsored arrangements the past weekend had failed. No other buyer would magically materialize, certainly not a timely one. Finally, should the acquisition be disallowed, thousands would be out of work, and not just wealthy bankers, but people at all income levels.

Creditors raised objections, which the judge tolerated up to a point. Most argued that insufficient effort had been exerted to ensure that creditors were getting top dollar on the assets being sold, that there was no semblance of a normal process for ensuring the price paid was fair.

The judge reacted by casting aside these contentions as "preposterous."[lxiv] The only saleable assets were the buildings. Other balance sheet assets and liabilities that were to be assumed by Barclays had dropped from $72 billion and $68 billion, respectively, earlier in the week to $47.4 billion and $45.5 billion by the time court was in session, quite simply reflecting the rapidly shrinking value of Lehman's and others' securities over this short period. Further, any value that remained in the franchise would vanish in liquidation, as this was wholly vested in Lehman's employees who would soon scatter if the court failed to approve the acquisition.

Finally, around half-past midnight, a fatigued Judge Peck issued find-
ings most deemed preordained, in favor of the sale of Lehman to BarCap
as described in the hand scribbled execution copy of the asset sale agreement on hand. Peck said, "I have to approve this transaction because it is
the only available transaction . . . in the most momentous bankruptcy
hearing I have ever sat through. Lehman Brothers became a victim, in
effect the only true icon to fall in a tsunami that has befallen the credit
markets."[lxv] He continued, "I have a responsibility to the creditors, to all
the employees, to all the customers and to all of you. This is not a question of due process being denied. Rather, to wait, would be reckless."[lxvi]

The creditors committee would drop objections to the decision, as they
too satisfied themselves that there was no realistic viable alternative at this
juncture. Had the government handled the crisis differently from the outset they may have ultimately stood to recover a great deal more of the
Lehman debt owed to them, but they were never in the driver's seat and
could not rewrite history. They were helpless backseat passengers, with
Paulson DUI.

Just after the court decision was handed down, my Blackberry began to
buzz as incessantly as the beating of a hummingbird's wings. The news
was good. Moments later all was confirmed on television. It had been an
exhausting night both for those in court and for me isolated on the island
that was my couch. But there were no more hoops through which to jump.
After a week in perpetual crisis mode, it now seemed extraordinarily
unnatural to be free of worry that the deal would not come to fruition. On
Monday, September 22, I would approach 745 Seventh Avenue and see the
green Lehman electronic tableau that wrapped the building replaced by a
now reassuring Barclays blue motif.

And so it was. In an exceptionally dramatic transition, on Friday we
were Lehman, in some misshapen form, and on Monday, September 22
we were BarCap. Enough of the preferred list bankers had stayed to prevent the deal from disintegrating. Bob Diamond delivered a rousing
speech to the army of Lehman bankers that packed the lower level auditorium at 745 Seventh Avenue, overflowing into the hall outside where
video screens displayed our new chief rallying his vastly enlarged investment banking army. He spoke of the round-the-clock effort that had

brought us to this positive conclusion, and praised the tireless efforts of McDade and his team. Fuld was not mentioned. (Dick's final direct communiqué to employees had been an internal email distributed to all letting us know that he felt "horrible" about our losses.) Bonuses, Diamond told us, would be paid in cash—no more stock that could vaporize—and would be commensurate with salaries on the street. At the time, no one knew how bad things would get at other firms, substantially lowering the bonus bar. So all cheered, as at the time we believed bonuses might not be as bad as those that were eventually distributed. The biggest cheer sounded when Diamond pronounced that the two firms, now one, through superhuman efforts had managed to save ten thousand jobs.

Of course, there were the other fourteen thousand. Some of those were in asset management, most notably, at Neuberger Berman. No doubt that firm would seamlessly continue to operate with different owners since its business continued to thrive. Our thoughts were with our colleagues in Europe and Asia, many local hires, as well as the many expats, previously mentioned, who had been moved by Lehman for an overseas stint.

On Monday, September 22nd, the same day we had morphed into BarCap, Nomura announced that it had reached an agreement to buy up most of Lehman's Asian business. The following day Nomura announced it was buying most of Lehman's operations in Europe and the Middle East. Not all my former colleagues were retained, but then Barclays would institute a series of cuts as well, reflective of both the overlap, albeit limited, and as the year progressed, of distressed markets with anemic business flows.

This ends the tale of how Lehman precipitously fell from a leading position on Wall Street, breaking into pieces that a sturdier financial institution was able to pick up like scrap metal in a junkyard. But what the failure of Lehman unleashed by no means ends here. In early 2009, when many of the traditional best and worst lists of the previous year in the financial world appeared across the Internet and other media venues, the decision to allow Lehman to file for bankruptcy is most often listed as the number one gaff. While I understand Hank Paulson's ideological bent, I have few kind words about the former Secretary. The Lehman collapse was not a time when ideology should have overtaken sound reason. His effective inaction over the critical September weekend shall be noted by economic historians as an error unleashing a cataclysm that clutched the world in a stranglehold, while simultaneously delivering a knee to its kidney. We will never know whether all that followed was inevitable, but few now doubt that while Henry Paulson did not cause Lehman's problems, his decision to let it file was a monumental mistake. Paulson's illustrious career as a Goldman banker and CEO is now a perfunctory footnote in his bio. His legacy will be that he managed the financial crisis without a consistent, sound strategy. He was "reacting not acting."[lxvii] In the end, he appeared decisively lost—at best ineffective—with his ill-conceived moves utter folly that needlessly spread misery.

CHAPTER 11

Addiction Interrupted

*"The difference between Lehman Brothers
and crack is that crack is forever."*

—JOE TIBMAN

As noted in the opening section of this book, I am a former Lehman banker. Little that I tell you from this point forward will be as personal as events in the rest of the book, as I have not been involved. I will not be discussing the circumstances or precise timing of my Lehman/Barclays departure because, as noted in the forward, I wish to remain anonymous and fully preserve my employability in investment banking, to which, I must admit, I am hopelessly addicted.

I wrote in my Foreword that with this book I am taking an unexpected stab at a literary career. At the same time it is hard to imagine life without the rush of "a deal." In this I am far from alone. Investment bankers are a singular breed, with a capacity to not only cope with the business' extreme demands, but to actually thrive on the adrenaline pumping journey that is a major investment banking deal. I have never experienced an easy transaction. In this, too, I am far from alone. Each deal or project has unanticipated problems and unique hurdles. Sometimes deals blow up. But more often, with relentless energy, we investment bankers immerse ourselves, body and soul, into the work at hand, knowing no limits. As deals heat up, virtually 24/7 we cope with a barrage of meetings, calls, emails, documentation, faxes, flights, complaints, unforeseen stumbling blocks of every stripe, and, well, so much more. The deal becomes a marathon in which we are always sprinting, driven by the pure rush that this exhausting, yet exhilarating work on high profile, high revenue transactions induces. Invariably, when a deal is successfully completed, we bask in the glory, but are immediately, like a crack addict, craving the next fix.

In the current financial environment, investment bankers, accustomed to the brisk deal pace that ended in the summer of 2007, are like addicts that can only occasionally score. And those out of work, in addition to financial hardship (in many but not all cases), are in forced detox.

Dick Fuld, the ultimate addict, occupied his office at 745 Seventh Avenue for a couple of weeks after the bankruptcy. There were press reports that he had been punched and knocked out cold by an angry former Lehman, now Barclays, employee in the company gym, but this was fictitious pulp. If this happened, the news would have spread as quickly as an email blasted firm-wide. It did not. And none of my former colleagues have suggested that there has been subsequent talk on the subject. This is not to say that there would not be a long line of takers to angrily beat on him. But it did not happen. In reality, while he did occupy his office on thirty-one for a couple of weeks after the bankruptcy filing, he maintained a low profile. There were few Fuld sightings.

On Monday, September 29, Dick and a few other senior Lehman executives without BarCap jobs moved to far less posh offices on the forty-fifth floor of 1271 Sixth Avenue, the Time-Life Building. Dick, in name only, remained CEO of the bankrupt Lehman holdings until December 31, 2008. In all fairness, Fuld magnanimously offered to work, to help without pay during a transitional period. Of course, this may have also served as a framework for him to mourn the loss of his firm, and to disengage less abruptly than if he had been entirely barred from all Lehman premises as soon as the ink was dry on the purchase agreement with Barclays. Spending time at the bankrupt Lehman Holdings with his distressed assets must have been a bit morbid. These assets are Lehman's corpse, so that Fuld, unlike most people, attended at least part of his own funeral.

Bryan Marsal, an executive quickly hired for his skill in managing liquidation, assumed true command of the bankrupt Lehman Holdings, from the outset including the weeks during which Fuld was still present. Fortunately, Marsal did not launch a quick fire sale of the distressed assets. He understood that if he rushed their sale at a time when market appetite was weak, the ultimate value he would deliver to creditors would be sub-optimal, as any interested investors would only buy at highly distressed prices. Additionally, a rapid sale of Lehman's underwater assets would be of such scale, that it would likely further undermine values—not only on Lehman's bankrupt balance sheet, but in the broader markets, as well. And so, much of the portfolio has and will simply remain inventoried while those entrusted to sell it wait for improved conditions, and avoid flooding the market by selling down the portfolio all at once.

* * *

At the new Barclays Capital, the firm's senior executives were immediately deep into the process of integrating legacy Barclays Capital and legacy Lehman Brothers. An integration of this magnitude would typically be planned over a period of some months, ahead of the actual close of the acquisition. Because of the extraordinary circumstances that led to the Lehman combination, BarCap had no opportunity for such pre-acquisition planning. Instead everything was happening real time, with the two firms already legally one. There were surprisingly few hiccups, though at the same time employees often found themselves starved for information, and often unclear as to what aspect of the integration was currently underway. The most visible aspect of the combination, quite literally, was the quick removal of all things cosmetically Lehman. Any Lehman signage was replaced with BarCap equivalents. And the Lehman green motif was changed to blue, wherever possible. (From what I understand, as certain floors undergo minor refurbishment, green Lehman carpet is replaced with new blue pile.) Still, there was minimal disruption to the business, aided by the fact that the business of all financial players had slowed to a near halt in the aftermath of the Lehman bankruptcy. Though all would have preferred the greater stability that existed before Lehman filed, the market freeze that followed that folly had the unintended silver lining of allowing BarCap time to integrate while there was little business to be lost. By the time business would begin to truly resume, the integration would be sufficiently advanced to enable BarCap to ably compete.

* * *

As BarCap was working 24/7 to get its fundamentally changed house renovated and rewired, former Lehman executives were confronting their own challenges. The earliest and most high profile of these was Dick Fuld's October appearance in Washington, D.C. before the House Committee on Oversight and Reform. Out of work former Lehman employees and those now at BarCap nearly all tuned in to C-Span for the nauseating event. Clearly, Fuld would not be fielding questions from a panel of admirers. Accordingly, he surely prepared and braced himself for a battery of angry questions. Dick would naturally have conferred with his private counsel ahead of this session, both to anticipate and script responses. In particular, he would have searched for ways to appear as responsive and contrite as possible, while at the same time not conceding fault that would strengthen the hands of those government bodies investigating his conduct, or the people who would surely name him in lawsuits.

Walking this fine line, in his opening statement Dick said, "No one realized the extent and magnitude of . . . problems, nor how the deterioration of mortgage-backed assets would infect other types of assets and threaten our entire system. In April 2006, Chairman Bernanke predicted that the housing market would most likely experience a gradual cooling rather than a sharp slowdown. In March 2007, he stated 'the impact on the broader economy and financial markets of the problems in the subprime market seems likely to be contained.' Similarly, Secretary Paulson said in June 2007 that the crisis in the mortgage markets 'will not affect the economy overall,' echoing the views of the International Monetary Fund. And at Lehman Brothers' annual shareholder meeting, I too said what I absolutely believed to be true at the time—that the worst of the impact to the financial markets was behind us. With the benefit of hindsight, I can now say that I and many others were wrong." With these words, as expected, Fuld was quick to admit mistakes had been made, but repeatedly pointed out that he was not unique in his erroneous pre-crisis views, thereby accepting responsibility while casting off blame or any suggestion of wrong-doing.

Insisting he worked single-mindedly to avoid the disintegration of

Lehman Brothers, Dick added, "We did everything we could to protect the Firm, including: closing down our mortgage origination business; reducing our leveraged loan exposure; reducing our total assets by $188 billion, specifically reducing residential mortgage and commercial real-estate assets by 38%; and dramatically reducing our net leverage so by the end of the third quarter in 2008 it was 10.5 times, one of the best leverage ratios on Wall Street at the time. We raised capital. We made changes to our senior management team and reduced expenses. We sought strategic investors for a sale of all or part of the Firm. We called on regulators to clamp down on abusive short selling practices." These words portrayed the Lehman management team as working to right the business, as they certainly did when the Lehman name came under pressure, but ignored any mention of the imprudent and highly risky build-up in commercial and Alt-A real estate exposures that irresponsibly bet the firm and led to its undoing. While one might debate whether taking a risk position based on a market view is prudent, few would endorse a position so large that it could lead to accidental corporate suicide. Dick also notably pointed a finger at a favorite target, short-sellers. No doubt, rumors and short-selling can unjustly bring down a financial institution. Still, there are times when betting a firm's share price will fall is a rational, even ethical investment strategy, if it is truly based on weaknesses that are not reflected in the share price, as was the case with Lehman, given its crumbling real estate-risk portfolio.

My expectations for Fuld's tone throughout the session, as reflected in his opening statement, were spot on. I also expected the harsh grilling that followed. Those questioning him predictably seethed with outrage, whether real or conjured, in at least some cases pandering to constituencies who surely did not find Richard Fuld a sympathetic figure. Asked why Fuld thought AIG was rescued, but not Lehman, he replied "Until the day they put me in the ground, I will wonder." When he also said, "This is a pain that will stay with me the rest of my life . . ." I doubt there was much empathy among those across America who witnessed the testimony on their television screens and those who saw these words in summary news reports. Personally, my emotions were mixed, leaving me numb with indifference.

* * *

Forgetting about Dick and what became of Lehman, what most appalled me about the session was not the expected dance, similar to many congressional hearings of this ilk. Rather, what deeply troubled me was the absolute ignorance about financial markets and economics displayed without exception by the congressional panel busy lobbing incendiary questions. This session, and similar ones with other financial sector leaders that would follow, left most finance professionals shaking their heads and decrying the sheer ineptitude of the committee conducting these hearings. Indeed, it was, and still is, terribly frightening. After all, these congressional representatives constitute the small number of individuals charged with creating laws and structures that will enable our financial system and economy to flourish, that will enable sound and proper regulation of the financial capitalists whose nature it is to drink their own Kool-Aid, and at regular intervals.

With such a financially ignorant group writing our laws, how can we possibly hope to navigate and legislate our country into a more effective regulatory framework than the one that has failed us? Our Congress is largely clueless as to what is required to manage the financial sector and the economy. Perhaps when Greenspan said he thought financial institutions could best manage their own risk it was because he knew all too well that legislators were ill-prepared to design effective regulation. All right, I do not really believe this was Greenspan's thinking, but the notion is not insane that self-regulation could be the lesser of two evils. None of this should surprise us. Few in Congress have meaningful financial or economic training and backgrounds, in contrast to the multitudes that do, but never seek elective office. When a lone senator, such as Phil Gramm, does have a background in finance and economics, he is able to dominate the discourse and legislative agenda by bullying those who cannot even begin to understand the technical terminology that sounds to most like arcane mumbo-jumbo. Until people of intelligence with relevant backgrounds and divergent philosophies and sensibilities engage in the legislative discourse, providing fundamental and extensive input into the governance of finance and the economy, it is unlikely that we will see systemic improvements that can both work and endure. Moreover, the world will continue to change, and so we must have capable voices in both political parties who can write legislation that evolves with changing times and new challenges.

* * *

Fuld's hearing ultimately deteriorated into a stilted and largely meaningless debate over the proportion of Fuld's wealth, certainly a topic to win Fuld's interrogators kudos for labeling and admonishing this fallen giant as a creature of audacious greed. But how important is it, really, for Congress to nail down the precise number that represents Richard Fuld's net worth? He is less rich than he once was, but still obscenely rich. Do we really need to yank out our calculators?

For his part, Fuld summed up his record as CEO stating that the various actions he and his top management team took "were both prudent and appropriate" based on what they knew at any given point in time. Undermining Fuld's contention is an internal 2008 company analysis, now public, that plainly states there were "warning signs," but that management "did not move early/fast enough."[lxviii] Those of us, former Lehman people, who either attended the hearings or watched the videotape on television news spots saw our former chief, the man so many—until the very recent past—heralded as one of America's great senior executives, heckled by the angry crowd outside the capital building as he walked to his private limousine. In a less civilized time, or without police protection, the crowd might have publicly stoned him.

* * *

The next day, October 5, Congress passed the $700 billion rescue plan that they had in an earlier form rejected. The Federal Reserve, on the same day, utilized its principal tool for managing the economy by lowering its reference interest rate by 1 percent, a substantial adjustment in comparison to most Fed interest rate changes. By October 8, as BarCap continued to work toward unifying and rationalizing the old BarCap and Lehman, Fortune magazine estimated that layoffs at the combined company numbered three thousand. When markets closed for the week, at the end of the trading day on Friday, October 10, the Dow Jones index had declined by about 15 percent for the week, its worst week in a hundred years.

* * *

Mike Gelband, the Lehman executive whom Bart McDade brought back to Lehman, one of those who had opposed the heavy investment in commercial real estate, received a pre-global crisis-sized pay package to remain at BarCap. This compensation package, as it came into public focus, garnered virulent criticism from the government and others who viewed this as continuation of the excesses of Wall Street. Within Lehman, many were resentful of the fact that a handful of leaders were to be disproportionately re-enriched, re-equitized; in short, they would regain their pre-bankruptcy wealth to a much greater extent than most legacy Lehman BarCap employees. However, it was the external criticism of the Gelband package that placed BarCap on the hot seat. Around mid-October, Gelband, in effect, solved the problem by accepting an offer to move to Millennium Management LLC to run its global fixed income business. This difficulty in granting an out-sized pay package was new. Wall Street has changed. It will continue to sail into uncharted waters.

* * *

Also during October it came to light that Federal prosecutors in Brooklyn, Manhattan and New Jersey, as well as the FBI, were investigating Lehman's collapse. Little information about these investigations has been revealed. However, it is evident that much of the activity focuses on whether Lehman executives misled the public, most especially investors, which includes the firm's own employees, as to the financial condition of The Brothers. Inherent in this is an examination of whether assets were properly valued. At least a dozen former Lehman senior executives have been subpoenaed. Some reports put the number as high as seventeen. From the outset, it was clear that Fuld was on the list. Over time, three other names have been added in various reports: Joe Gregory, Erin Callan, and Ian Lowitt. Lowitt, who replaced Callan as CFO and did most of the talking on Lehman's third quarter earnings call during the week preceding the firm's bankruptcy filing, is the only executive among the four to be employed by BarCap, with initial responsibility for the integration process. Erin Callan, in February, as mentioned earlier, took an extended leave of absence from CSFB, a financial firm she joined about four months prior. Most speculate that the leave is intended to allow her to focus on the various investigations; she has retained counsel.

On November 5, the bankrupt Lehman Brothers Holdings made public that Dick Fuld was not only forgoing pay as he remained CEO through December 31, but would also receive no severance or bonus upon his departure. Of course, no other option would have been acceptable to any of the interested parties with an eye on the Lehman holding company's liquidation process.

The precise scale of this liquidation came into sharper focus as precise numbers were assigned to the easily foreseen enormity of the liquidation task so many assumed the government would move heaven and earth to prevent. For example, about one million intercompany derivative transactions and about 450 thousand external ones with around eight thousand counterparties would need to be analyzed. The job is so vast that the bankrupt entity has been swamped with the résumés of out-of-work financial professionals, and has indeed hired a number of them for work that is anticipated to span two years, subject to revision.

* * *

At the beginning of November, Barclays PLC, the large bank that owns BarCap, raised a substantial amount of new capital from Middle Eastern investors. With all banks in the U.K. suffering from the growing global financial fallout, most had tapped U.K. government funds. Why did Barclays instead strengthen its capital position through private sources? Firstly, it could. Many weaker institutions would have been unable to attract private investment. Secondly, Barclays eschewed government money because it would come with strings attached. While the bank remains subject to all banking sector regulation, partial government ownership could subject it to greater government meddling and constraints, inhibiting its ability to pursue its strategic and financial goals.

* * *

During the first half of November, Bob Diamond announced that Bart McDade, the final Lehman president who had done so much to enable the BarCap acquisition of his firm, would resign at the end of the month. No one has disputed that Bart's intent from the outset was to remain at Bar-Cap for a limited period only, to assist in the integration. Diamond's internal memo emailed to all BarCap employees suggested that the integration was proceeding ahead of schedule. Alex Kirk, the other executive McDade had brought back along with Mike Gelband when he assumed the Lehman presidency, left around the same time.

* * *

In mid-November, San Mateo County in California initiated a lawsuit against former Lehman Brothers Executives, naming Fuld, O'Meara (the CFO, who became global Risk Management chief when Erin Callan assumed the CFO slot), Callan, Gregory, and some of the firm's directors. The county lost about $150 million on investments in Lehman bonds and will no doubt allege that these former Lehman executives misled them regarding Lehman's financial health. Of course, this is only one of the lawsuits filed to date. There are others. More will undoubtedly follow. Bankruptcy court generally protects Lehman Holdings from lawsuits, but former executives are fair game.

* * *

In December, I was bemused to read in the papers that Dick Fuld was not planning to retire. Rather, it was reported he intended to start an advisory boutique. While I have pointed out that Fuld was frequently a talented and effective Lehman leader, it is hard to envision a long client list after his devastating fall from grace. Regardless, I assumed he would be otherwise occupied for some time with the government investigations and private lawsuits currently underway, and those that will surely and perhaps endlessly materialize.

* * *

Bankrupt Lehman Holdings in early December chose a management buyout bidder as winner in the sale of Neuberger Berman, Lehman's gem asset management subsidiary. The Neuberger management team beat out competing bids from private equity houses, Bain Capital and Hellman Friedman. The proceeds will of course go to Lehman creditors.

* * *

Also during December, the Federal Reserve, to encourage lending and ease the cost of financing for borrowers, lowered its target reference interest rate to 0-0.25 percent. Investors rushed to buy short-term Treasury debt issues yielding 0 percent. With this latest interest rate action, the Federal Reserve exhausted its primary instrument for managing the economy. There are others in its toolbox, but certainly its policy choices now became fundamentally constrained.

* * *

Around mid-December, Goldman Sachs reported its first quarterly loss since becoming a public company in 1999. As earlier noted, its bet against subprime had a finite shelf life. Indeed, Goldman posted a $3.5 billion loss on real-estate related assets. Not long after its loss announcement, Moody's downgraded Goldman's credit ratings, with the agency commenting, "This crisis has demonstrated that the business model of wholesale investment banks is not as resilient as it appeared."[lxix] Just days earlier, Goldman announced new rules that would lengthen the time necessary for employees to qualify for a complete retirement package. In the first quarter of 2009, Goldman would bounce back and post enviable profits.

* * *

Not very long after the announcement of the Bank of America acquisition of Merrill Lynch, last discussed in these pages in the context of the weekend when Lehman declared bankruptcy, problems arose. John Thain, Merrill's CEO and former Goldman CFO, ahead of the merger, paid out bonuses in excess of $1 million to about 700 employees. He did this at an earlier date than bonuses had ever been paid previously. By December, it became clear that losses at Merrill far exceeded expectations, soaring to ever higher levels. Ken Lewis, the Bank of America CEO, reportedly told

Paulson and Bernanke that he was reconsidering the acquisition, but both these government officials forcefully pressed Lewis to proceed. Additionally, BofA, having been one of nine banks to receive government funds to the tune of $25 billion in the fall of 2008, now secured government provision of another $20 billion to offset losses on $118 billion of impaired assets. Yes, Paulson had insisted the government would not financially support a Lehman solution. This set the stage for the Bank of America acquisition of Merrill for a price well in excess of Merrill's then-current market value, and without the benefit of government support. In the end, government assistance to BofA has amounted to $45 billion and counting. *Moral hazard?*

* * *

In January, Barclays cut roughly 2000 jobs, about 7 percent of global employees. About 1300 of these were at Barclays Capital.

* * *

Days later, Barak Obama was sworn in as President. His choice for Treasury Secretary, Timothy Geithner, the chairman of the New York Federal Reserve who had participated with Paulson and Bernanke in eleventh hour talks over Lehman's fate, sat before Congress for hearings to approve his installation into this key cabinet post. Geithner acknowledged that the Lehman bankruptcy had been an unmitigated disaster. However, he attributed this to the same revisionist explanation proffered earlier by Paulson and Bernanke: that they had lacked a legal basis for financially supporting a Lehman solution with government funds. Amazingly, no one on the panel interrogating him questioned this explanation. No one asked why a solution similar to the Bear Stearns one had not been attempted for Lehman. Certainly, there is widespread speculation that Geithner was at least somewhat uncomfortable with Paulson's insistence that the government would not financially participate in facilitating a Lehman salvage operation. But here was Geithner repeating the same revised explanation that Paulson had uttered once it was plainly apparent that the government's Lehman decisions were catastrophic. Had everyone on this panel forgotten the trio's original explanation? Did they feel complicit? Or were they all simply too focused on questioning Geithner's flimsy excuse for not paying all his back taxes until weeks before his nomination to the Treasury post? In any case, he took office as the man who could solve our economic problems.

* * *

Toward the end of January 2009, Dick Fuld sold his Florida mansion to his wife for $100. He would have done better on eBay. But, of course, he was not looking for a profit. He bought the property in 2004 for $13.3 million. It is widely believed that the transaction is intended to shield a portion of his wealth from the various investigations and lawsuits that might siphon away his vast assets. Florida law shields a primary residence from the claims of creditors and plaintiffs. Was the sale intended to ensure that if the Fuld's lost most of their other wealth, they would be optimally positioned to retreat to a shack they consider livable in the Sunshine State?

* * *

By early February, Bank of America's stock reached a twenty-four-year low amid speculation that the government might seize the bank. This speculation subsequently faded, though jitters about BofA's condition remained. The congressional oversight panel that monitors the Troubled Asset Relief Program (TARP) in early February 2009 reported that Paulson's team received only sixty-six cents on the dollar for the troubled assets it bought, translating to a $78 billion loss on the first $254 billion spent.

* * *

Around the same time, the SEC announced new rules governing rating agency activities. Most of these rules seem of little meaningful substance. The one key rule that does mandate a healthy change is a ban on rating agencies suggesting structures to achieve specific ratings. This quite obviously is intended to address the rating agencies' role in determining the financial architecture for many structured financings, a segment that includes subprime mortgage securitizations.

* * *

In early February, Judge Peck, who oversaw the Lehman bankruptcy charges, was arrested on misdemeanor assault charges. Apparently, he was unhappy about a ladder his wife of more than forty years had stored in his closet. According to the judge, when he began to move it to another location his wife slapped him. He then, allegedly, slapped her back causing some bruising. The charges were later dropped in March, with multiple reports indicating the judge's wife was not cooperating with prosecutors.

* * *

In February, Barclays PLC announced 2008 profits that represented a substantial decline from year-earlier results, but surpassed the single most optimistic earnings estimate. The primary reason for this upside surprise was a £2.3 billion gain stemming from the Lehman brothers acquisition. Having paid a mere $250 million for everything other than the real estate it purchased, Barclays was able to write up both the value of the operations as well as the on-balance sheet assets of the business. This is value that neither Lehman's creditors nor former employees will ever see.

* * *

In early March, Jon Stewart of Comedy Central's "The Daily Show" traded barbs with Jim Cramer of CNBC's "Mad Money." Stewart alleged that Cramer acted irresponsibly by not using his platform to accurately portray the cancer spreading through the body of Wall Street. Finally, amidst frenzied media coverage of the war of words, Cramer appeared on Stewart's show. Stewart for the most part checked his comedy at the studio door and hammered away at Cramer in a sober interview. Defending himself, Cramer insisted that many CEO's misled him. He even singled out one by name. Noting that he had known Lehman's former CEO for twenty years, Cramer told Stewart and the world that Dick Fuld "lied o me, lied to me, lied to me."

* * *

March also brought news that AIG had paid huge bonuses to a large number of employees. This was particularly notable since many of these individuals worked in the AIG unit that had put the insurer in hot water. This news was even more stunning as the government now owns about 80 percent of AIG. The revelation, a worthy follow-up to the excessive bonuses paid out by Merrill Lynch before its sale to BofA closed, takes government ineptitude to a whole new level. Not only is our legislated regulatory structure and oversight of our nation's purse strings a mind-bending failure, but our government is not even competent to soundly administer a company it owns. We can be grateful that rather then oversee it, our government will sell it piece by piece.

* * *

The definition of irony: In early April it was announced that Dick Fuld found himself a new job at Matrix Advisors, a hedge fund. You will recall that Dick considered these firms the gutless animals he long blamed for short-selling Lehman's stock. *"When I find a short-seller, I want to tear his heart out and eat it before his eyes while he's still alive."* These were Dick's words. Has the man who raged against hedge funds and other short-sellers been born again as one of them? Or is this simply a highly visible display of self-loathing? On the other hand, perhaps Fuld intends to exact retribution, to do what he can to bring down Matrix Advisors, just as he brought down Lehman. Whatever his impetus, it would be prudent for him to remove all the mirrors in his many houses. What, if anything, Fuld will actually be doing at Matrix is unclear. Surely he is as least as tied up with investigative and legal matters as the furloughed Erin Callan. A hedge fund hiring Fuld could be the ultimate trading floor gallows chuckle.

* * *

On April 16, 2009, the *Wall Street Journal* on its front page reported that Weil Gotshal, the law firm representing Lehman Holdings in bankruptcy proceedings, had requested court sanction for quarterly fees in excess of $50 million for its work. It is anticipated that the firm could profit to the tune of $200 million or more by the time the bankruptcy process is complete.

* * *

In a sense, while Lehman is now gone, its story continues to unfold, as its former employees, even with ongoing rounds of layoffs, far outnumber their legacy Barclays colleagues in BarCap. Of course, over time, the sense of BarCap as little more than Lehman Brothers in blue drag, rather than the traditional Lehman green, will fade. As markets ultimately recover, as employees gradually lose the deep, nearly intractable impulse to introduce themselves as so and so from Lehman, and as the people populating the firm change over time, the vestiges of the Lehman name and history, the moments of triumph and excellence, will be lost in the finance world's cobwebbed archives. The sad confluence of trespasses and faulty industry and regulatory architecture that serendipitously came together, as neatly as a well orchestrated conspiracy, slitting the firm's throat and left it for dead, shall be forgotten. The details of the negligent homicide of Lehman Brothers by protagonists both inside and outside the firm, and Lehman's often glorious "storied" history, will surely be replaced by a one-dimensional, cautionary fable of avarice on Wall Street.

Endnotes

i. Keith Dovkants, "The Godfather, a man they call the Gorilla and how a banking legend was lost," www.thisislondon.co.uk/standard/article-23556046-details/The+ Godfather,+a+man+they+call+the+Gorilla+and++how+a+banking+legend+was+lost/article .do, September 16, 2008

ii.   Knowledge@Wharton, http://knowledge.wharton.upenn.edu/article.cfm?articleid=1631, January 10, 2007

iii. Ken Auletta, "Greed and Glory on Wall Street: The Fall of the House of Lehman," Warner Books, 1986

iv. Ken Auletta, "Power, Greed and Glory On Wall Street: The Fall of the Lehman Brothers, Top of Form. http://select.nytimes.com/search/restricted/article?res=F20B1EF93F 5D0C748DDDAB0894DD484D81, February 17, 1985

v. Ken Auletta, http://select.nytimes.com/search/restricted/article?res=F20B1EF93F5 D0C748DDDAB0894DD484D81

vi. Ken Auletta, Warner Books

vii. Ken Auletta, Warner Books

viii. Ken Auletta, Warner Books

ix. Ken Auletta, Warner Books

x. Ken Auletta, Warner Books

xi. Ken Auletta, Warner Books

xii. Ken Auletta, Warner Books

xiii. Steve Fishman, "Burning Down His House" http://nymag.com/news/business/ 52603/, November 30, 2008,

xiv. Fishman

xv. Andy Sewer, "The Improbable Power Broker: How Dick Fuld transformed Lehman from Wall Street also-ran to super-hot machine" http://money.cnn.com/magazines/fortune/ fortune_archive/2006/04/17/8374342/index.htm, April 13, 2006

xvi. Lewis S. Rosenbloom and Dean C. Gramlich, "Trolling for the Deep Pockets in the

Subprime Lending Crisis: The Ninth Circuit's First Alliance Decision" Real Estate Law Journal, Fall 2007

xvii. Michael Hudson, "How Wall Street Stoked The Mortgage Meltdown," www.real estatejournal.com/buysell/mortgages/20070628-hudson.html?refresh=on June 28, 2007

xviii. Michael Hudson

xix. Michael Hudson

xx. Michael Hudson

xxi. The Reckoning: Debt Watchdogs: Tamed or Caught Napping?" The New York Times, December 7, 2008

xxii. "The Department of the Treasury Blueprint for a Modernized Financial Regulatory Structure" www.treas.gov/press/releases/reports/Blueprint.pdf, March, 2008

xxiii. Scott Cohn "Investigation: SEC Failed in Bear Stearns Probe" www.cnbc.com/id/27123485, October 10, 2008

xxiv. DAVID GLOVIN & JESSE WESTBROOK, "Madoff Under House Arrest as SEC Says It Missed Signs" www.mindfully.org/Industry/2008/Madoff-House-Arrest17dec08.htm, December 17, 2008

xxv. Fishman

xxvi. Andrew Gower, "Exposed: Dick Fuld, the man who brought the world to its knees" http://business.timesonline.co.uk/tol/business/industry_sectors/banking_and_finance/article5336179.ece, December 14, 2008

xxvii. Yalman Onaran and John Helyar "Fuld Sought Buffett Offer He Refused as Lehman Sank" www.bloomberg.com/apps/news?pid=20601109&refer=home&sid=aMQJV3iJ5M8c, 11/10/09

xxviii. Andrew Gower

xxix. Fishman

xxx. Yalman Onaran and John Helyar "Fuld Sought Buffett Offer He Refused as Lehman Sank"

xxxi. Gower

xxxii. Jon C. Ogg, "Lehman Beats on Mixed Bag,,"www.247wallst.com/2007/12/lehman-beats-on.html, December 13, 2007

xxxiii. Lloyd Blankfein, "Do not destroy the essential catalyst of risk," www.ft.com/cms/s/0/0a0f1132-f600-11dd-a9ed-0000779fd2ac.html, February 8 2009

xxxiv. "CEO Richard Fuld on Lehman Brothers' Evolution from Internal Turmoil to Teamwork" http://knowledge.wharton.upenn.edu/article.cfm?articleid=1631

xxxv. PBS

xxxvi. Andrew Clark and Jill Treanor, "We won't be next to fall, says Lehman" www.guardian.co.uk/business/2008/mar/18/creditcrunch.useconomy, March 18, 2008

xxxvii. PBS

xxxviii. "U.S. Banking Giant Soothes Investors' Nerves" The Guardian March 18, 2008

xxxix. "Barclays makes its U.S. move as rivals are weakened" www.telegraph.co.uk/finance/markets/2786197/Barclays-makes-its-US-move-as-rivals-are-weakened.html March 19, 2008

xl. "The Department of the Treasury Blueprint for a Modernized Financial Regulatory Structure"

xli . www.youtube.com/watch?v=dib2-HBsF08

xlii. Yalman Onaran and John Helyar "The Fall Of Lehman, Part 2" www.nzherald.co.nz/business/news/article.cfm?c_id=3&objectid=10549901&pnum=0, 11/29/08

xliii. Yalman Onaran and John Helyar "The Fall Of Lehman, Part 2"

xliv. Fishman

xlv. Gower

xlvi. Bill Condie, "Lehman Staff Paid in Shares," www.thisismoney.co.uk/investing-and-markets/article.html?in_article_id=445323&in_page_id=3, July 3, 2008

xlvii. Bomi Lim, "Lehman Spurned KDB's Offer of $6.40 a share, Min says" www.bloomberg.com/apps/news?pid=20601080&sid=aX2LXoyhpXjE&refer=asia, September 18, 2008

xlviii. Yalman Onaran and John Helyar "Fuld Sought Buffett Offer He Refused as Lehman Sank"

xlix. "Yalman Onaran and John Helyar "Fuld Sought Buffett Offer He Refused as Lehman Sank"

l. "$6 billion bid to rescue Lehman" The *Guardian*, September 3, 2008

li. Aaron Smith, "Paulson: Banking system is 'sound," http://money.cnn.com/2008/09/15/news/economy/bush_economy/index.htm, YAHOO! BUZZ
• DIGG
• FACEBOOK
• DEL.ICIO.US
• REDDIT
• STUMBLE UPON
• MYSPACE
• MIXX IT
Subscribe to Economy
feed://rss.cnn.com/rss/money_news_economy.rss
Paste this link into your favorite RSS desktop reader
See all CNNMoney.com RSS FEEDS (close) September 21, 2008

lii. Sam Youngman "Paulson says Americans can be 'confident' in banks," http://thehill.com/leading-the-news/paulson-says-americans-can-be-confident-in-banks-2008-09-15.html, September 15, 2008.

liii. PBS

liv. William Cohan, "Three Days That Shook the World," http://money.cnn.com/2008/12/12/magazines/fortune/3days_1.fortune/index.htm, September 16, 2008.

lv. "Yalman Onaran and John Helyar "Fuld Sought Buffett Offer He Refused as Lehman Sank"

lvi. William Cohan

lvii. William Cohan

lviii. William Cohan

lix. "Paulson Statement on SEC and Federal Reserve Actions Surrounding Lehman Brothers" www.treas.gov/press/releases/hp1134.htm September 14, 2008

lx. PBS

lxi. "Barclays to Acquire Lehman Brothers Business and Assets" www.lehman.com/press/pdf_2008/0916_barclays_acquisition.pdf, 9/1608

lxii. Randall Smith, Diya Gullapalli and Jeffrey Mccracken "Lehman Workers Receive a Reprieve" http://online.wsj.com/article/SB122163100282247355.html, September 17, 2008

lxiii. "Linda Sandler and Tiffany Kary, "Lehman Creditors Can Try to Recover Fuld's Pay," www.bloomberg.com/apps/news?pid=20601103&sid=aM8r4dakjoQk&refer=news, September 19, 2009

lxiv. Matt Miller, "Inside Lehman's Courtroom," www.thedeal.com/servlet/Content Server?cid=1221081370605&pagename=TheDeal%2FNWStArticle&c=TDDArticle, September 22, 2008

lxv. "Court approves Lehman sale to Barclays" www.upi.com/Business_News/2008/09/20/Court_approves_Lehman_sale_to_Barclays/UPI-60061221925756/, Sept. 20, 2008

lxvi. Matt Miller

lxvii. PBS

lxviii. Daniel Schulman, "The Gorilla in the Hearing Room" *Mother Jones*, October 6, 2008

lxix. Greg Farrell & Francesco Guererra "Goldman Sachs falls to $2.12bn loss" http://us.ft.com/ftgateway/superpage.ft?news_id=fto121620080951088206

Bibliography

Aldrick, Philip, "Barclays makes its U.S. move as rivals are weakened." www.telegraph.co.uk/finance/markets/2786197/Barclays-makes-its-US-move-as-rivals-are-weakened.html, 3/19/08

Antilla, Susan, "Wall Street; Ousting Hotshots From the Street," http://query.nytimes.com/gst/fullpage.html?res=9F0CE2D61238F937A35757C0A965958260, April 4, 1993

Associated Press, "With JPMorgan deal to rescue Bear Stearns, market wonders what's next," HTTP://WWW.CNBC.COM/ID/23663919, Monday, March 17th 2008

Associated Press, "Paulson: "After Bear, Regulations Need Review" CBS News Timeline: Credit Crunch," http://wcbstv.com/business/treasury.secretary.paulson.2. 685089.html, Mar 26, 2008, (AP),

Auletta, Ken "POWER, GREED AND GLORY ON WALL STREET: THE FALL OF THE LEHMAN BROTHERS," The *New York Times* Magazine, 2/17/85

Benner, Katie, *Fortune* "I was lucky to get out" September 26, 2008

Bill Clinton Takes Aim At Rising Foreclosures, http://online.wsj.com/article/SB1208 14636821612223.html?mod=todays_us_page_one, April 14, 2008

Bilodeau, Otis, "SEC's Cox Tightens Reins on Enforcement Division," www.bloomberg.com/apps/news?pid=20601087&sid=aodWCvu220YE&refer=home, April 13, 2007

"Bradley H. Jack," http://investing.businessweek.com/businessweek/research/stocks/people/person.asp?personId=548104&capId=473285&previousCapId=3609766&previousTitle=Synta%20Pharmaceuticals%20Corp.

Chernov, Ron, The House of Morgan: An American Banking Dynasty and the Rise of Modern Finance, Grove Press September 2001

cityfile new york, http://cityfile.com/profiles/pete-peterson

Class Notes and News, http://www2.aya.yale.edu/classes/yc1957/notes2003.html

Cohan, William, *Fortune*, "Three Days that Shook the World," December 16, 2008

Cohn, Scott, "Investigation: SEC Failed in Bear Stearns Probe," *CNBC* www.cnbc.com/id/27123485, Oct 10, 2008

Daily News, "Lehman Brothers cuts hit 140 traders" www.nydailynews.com/money/2008/01/25/2008-01-25_lehman_brothers_cuts_hit_140_traders.html, January 25th 2008,

Dovkants, Keith, "The Godfather, a man they call the Gorilla and how a banking legend was lost," www.thisislondon.co.uk/standard/article-23556046-details/The+Godfather%2C+a+man+they+call+the+Gorilla+and++how+a+banking+legend+was+lost/article.do 9/16/08

Downing, Larry "Cox's reign seen denting own image, SEC's future" July 24, 2008; www.boston.com/news/nation/washington/articles/2009/01/04/coxs_reign_seen_denting_own_image_secs_future/

Eichenwald, Kurt "An Albatross Named Shearson," http://query.nytimes.com/gst/fullpage.html?res=9C0CE3D6143CF936A25754C0A966958260, July 15, 1990

Eisenberg, Carol, "Erin Callan dubbed Wall Street's alpha female," http://news.muckety.com/2008/03/27/erin-callan/1582, March 27, 2008

"Erin Callan," www.mahalo.com/Erin_Callan

Financial Times, "Broken brothers: How brinkmanship was not enough to

save Lehman," September 15 2008

Fishman, Steven "Burning Down His House" http://nymag.com/news/business/52603/, November 30, 2008,

Fishman, Steve, "Remember the Sheriff?" http://nymag.com/news/intelligencer/51831/, Nov 2, 2008

"Frederick L. Ehrman," The Daniel E. Koshland Jr. Page, www.smokershistory.com/koshland.htm;

Freedman, Richard D. Vohr, Jill Goldman Sachs / Lehman Brothers,, New York University Stern School of Business, Revised September 1999, www.stern.nyu.edu/mgt/private_file/mo/rfreedma_ca/goldman.pdf

"Frontline," PBS broadcast, "Inside the Meltdown" February 17, 2009

Geisst, Charles R., The Last Partnerships, Chapter II, Our Crowd: The Seligmans, Lehman Brothers, and Kuhn Loeb; http://books.google.com/books?id=tE2RMBKGItgC&pg=PA49&lpg=PA49&dq=The+Case+of+the+Lehmans+and+the+Seligmans&source=bl&ots=P3TbkgOs_L&sig=aMy0d7iambkTYz-1zLAOppW5MRc&hl=en&ei=zL6hSZ-TCuPetgfMhv35DA&sa=X&oi=book_result&resnum=7&ct=result

Glovin, David & Westbrook, Jesse "Madoff Under House Arrest as SEC Says It Missed Signs" Bloomberg www.mindfully.org/Industry/2008/Madoff-House-Arrest17dec08.htm, December 17, 2008

Gordon, Marcy, "Madoff fraud case raises questions about SEC," www.wtopnews.com/? nid=111&sid=1548169, December 12, 2008

Harvard Business School Leadership Database, www.hbs.edu/leadership/database/leaders/ philip_lehman.html;

Harvard Business School, Lehman Brothers Collection, Twentieth Century Business archives, www.library.hbs.edu/hc/lehman/history.html

Henriques, Diana B., & Bergman, Lowell "MORTGAGED LIVES: A special report.; Profiting From Fine Print With Wall Street's Help" http://query.nytimes.com/gst/ fullpage.html?res=9E06EFDE1E3BF936A25750C0A9669C8B63 March 15, 2000

Hudson, Michael, "How Wall Street Stoked The Mortgage Meltdown," www.realestate journal.com/buysell/mortgages/20070628-hudson.html?refresh=on, June 28, 2007

"Impact of 9/11 on Lehman Brothers, Merrill Lynch and American Express" CIO, http://www4.cio.com/article/31296/Impact_of_on_Lehman_Brothers_Merrill_Lynch_ and_American_Express, September 1, 2002

Investorwords.com

Kim, Jim, www.fiercefinance.com/story/future-richard-fuld/2008-09-11, 9/11/08,

Knee, Jonathan A "The Accidental Investment Banker: Inside the Decade that trans-formed Wall Street" www.fundinguniverse.com/company-histories/Shearson-Lehman-Brothers-Holdings-Inc-Company-History.html;

Labaton, Stephen "SEC Concedes oversight flaws fueled collapse" The *International Her-ald Tribune*, September 28, 2008

La Monica, Paul R. "Lehman: Too Big To Fail?" http://money.cnn.com/2008/09/10/ markets/thebuzz/index.htm September 10, 2008

Landler, Mark & Stolberg, Sheryl Gay "Finger-Pointing in Financial Crisis Is Directed at Bush" www.nytimes.com/2008/09/20/business/20prexy.html?ref=politics, September 19, 2008

"Lehman Brothers," AbsoluteAstronomy.com www.absoluteastronomy.com/topics/ Lehman_Brothers

"Lehman Brothers Certificate Vignette" www.scripophily.net/lebronewistf.html

"Lehman Brothers: The Rise and Fall of Lehman Brothers. A History that Goes Beyond the Great Depression". www.doctorhousingbubble.com/lehman-brothers-the-rise-and-fall-of-lehman-brothers-a-history-that-goes-beyond-the-great-depression, 12/15/08

Lehman Brothers bankruptcy news, Bankruptcy Creditors' Service, Inc, Issue Number 4, September 18, 2008

Lehman Brothers press release, "Barclays to Acquire Lehman Brothers Business and Assets" September 16, 2008

Lehman Brothers: The Wall Street giant that survived the 1929 Crash, but couldn't weather the credit crunch, Daily Mail, September 15, 2008, www.dailymail.co.uk/news/article-1055850/Lehman-Brothers-The-Wall-Street-giant-survived-1929-Crash-weather-credit-crunch.html

Leibs, Scott, *CFO Magazine*, "The Year That Was: A look back at the lows and ultra-lows of an all-too-historic year." January 2009

Lewis L. Glucksman" Business Week online executive profiles, http://investing.business week.com/businessweek/research/stocks/people/person.asp?personId=673820&capId=34 6919&previousCapId=368278&previousTitle=Boston%20Properties%20Inc

Lipton, Eric & Labaton, Stephen "The Reckoning: Deregulator Looks Back, Unswayed" www.nytimes.com/2008/11/17/business/economy/17gramm.html?_r=1&scp=1&sq=the %20reckoning%20lipton&st=cse, November 16, 2008

Miller, Matt, "Inside Lehman's Courtroom," TheDeal.com, September 22, 2008

Minard, Lawrence "Charity For None, Avarice For All," http://query.nytimes.com/gst/fullpage.html?res=9B0DE4D9153BF93AA25752C0A960948260&scp=2&sq=lehman &st=nyt

The *New York Post* www.nypost.com/seven/09182008/gossip/pagesix/lehman_heiress_late_lament_129566.htm, September 18, 2008

The *New York Times*, "Debt Watchdogs: Tamed or Caught Napping?" December 7, 2008

The *New York Times*, "In Lehman Fallout, Two Stars are Given Lesser Roles" June 13, 2008

Onaran, Yalman and Helyar, John, "Fuld Sought Buffett Offer He Refused as Lehman Sank" www.bloomberg.com/apps/news?pid=20601109&refer=home&sid=aMQJV3iJ5M8c, November 10, 2008

Onaran, Yalman, "Lehman Fault-Finding Points to Last Man Fuld as Shares Languish," www.bloomberg.com/apps/news?pid=20601109&refer=home&sid=aKlvv3EUW8lk, July 22, 2008

Onaran, Yalman "Lehman's Gelband to return as Capital Markets Chief," www.bloomberg.com/apps/news?pid=20601087&sid=aoRiFfHNHNdo&refer=home June 24, 2008

Orpheum Theater: a Brief History, www.orphinc.org/html/history.htm,

"Paltrow, Scott, "S.E.C. No Evil" www.portfolio.com/executives/features/2008/09/18/Profile-of-SEC-Chief-Christopher-Cox/?refer=email, October 2008

Peter G. Peterson" The Peterson Institute for International Economics, www.peterson institute.org/institute/peterson-bio.cfm

Pressler, Jessica "Dick Fuld Kind of a Crybaby, Says Former Lehman CFO" http://nymag.com/daily/intel/2008/09/dick_fuld_kind_of_a_crybaby_sa.html, September 26, 2008

Quint, Michael "Lehman Without Shearson Can Still Be a Wall St. Force,"
http://query.nytimes.com/gst/fullpage.html?res=9F0CE5DD1031F936A25750C0A965
958260&n=Top/Reference/Times%20Topics/Subjects/F/Finances, March 15, 1993

Reuters, "JP Morgan agrees to Buy Bear Stearns for $2 a Share," www.cnbc.com/id/
23663919, March 17, 2008

"Richard S. Fuld Jr.," 1946-www.referenceforbusiness.com/biography/F-L/Fuld-Richard-
S-Jr-1946.html

Rosenbloom, Lewis S. Rosenbloom and Gramlich, Dean C., "Trolling for the Deep Pockets in the

Ross, Brian & Schwartz, Rhonda "Report: SEC Gave "Preferential Treatment" to Wall
Street CEO, Attempts to Question Morgan Stanley's John Mack "Connected" to Firing
of SEC Lawyer", ABC News http://abcnews.go.com/Blotter/Story?id=5970263&page=1,
October 6, 2008,

Rothman, Claudette, "Judge James Peck arrested for slapping his wife," http://theoriginal
greenwichdiva.com/2009/02/03/judge-james-peck-arrested-for-slapping-his-wife-
judith-peck/, February 3, 2009

Rubinstein, Dana, "Mark Walsh, Lehman's Unluckiest Gambler," The *New York Observer*, October 1, 2008

Sandler, Linda and Kay, Tiffany "Lehman Creditors Can Try to Recover Fuld's Pay"
www.bloomberg.com/apps/news?pid=20601103&sid=aM8r4dakjoQk&refer=news September 19, 2009

Securities & Exchange Commission Form 8-K, Lehman Brothers Holdings, Inc, Item
1.01 Entry into Material Definitive Agreement, Asset Purchase Agreement with Barclays
Capital, Inc.

Sewer, Andy, "The Improbable Power Broker: How Dick Fuld transformed Lehman from
Wall Street also-ran to super-hot machine," http://money.cnn.com/magazines/fortune/
fortune_archive/2006/04/17/8374342/index.htm, April 13, 2006:

STATEMENT OF RICHARD S. FULD, JR. BEFORE THE UNITED STATES
HOUSE OF REPRESENTATIVES COMMITTEE ON OVERSIGHT AND GOVERN-
MENT REFORM, OCTOBER 6, 2008, http://oversight.house.gov/documents/
20081006125839.pdf;

"States lose to U.S. over regulating some banks," Associated Press, April 18, 2007

Subprime Lending Crisis: The Ninth Circuit's First Alliance Decision" Real Estate Law
Journal, Fall 2007

The *Australian*, "Richard Fuld: Architect of the Rise and Fall of Lehman" September 20,
2008

"The Department of the Treasury Blueprint for a Modernized Financial Regulatory Structure" March, 2008

"The Hard Sell: Combating Home Equity Lending Fraud in California, PART II, The Subprime Lending Industry: Explosion and Retreat," www.consumersunion.org/pub/core_newmoney/005285.html

The Sunday *Times*, "Exposed: Dick Fuld, the man who brought the world to its knees" http://business.timesonline.co.uk/tol/business/industry_sectors/banking_and_finance/article5336179.ece, December 14, 2008,

Thomas, Owen "Lehman Boss' Weekend from Hell" http://gawker.com/5119969/lehman-bosss-weekend-from-hell, December 29, 2008

United Press International, "Court approves Lehman sale to Barclays," www.upi.com/Business_News/2008/09/20/Court_approves_Lehman_sale_to_Barclays/UPI-60061221925756/. Sept. 20, 2008

Walsh, Amy "New SEC Enforcement Manual: Better Late Than Never," New York Law Journal, November 5, 2008, www.law.com/jsp/ihc/PubArticleIHC.jsp?id= 1202425785835

The *Wall Street Journal*, "Lehman's Straight Shooter, Finance Chief Callan Brings Cool Jolt of Confidence To Credit-Rattled Street" May 17, 2008

The *Wall Street Journal*, NOVEMBER 7, 2008, "SEC Won't Discipline Its Enforcement Chief " KARA SCANNELL

The *Washington Post* "Lehman Employees Lost $10 Billion," www.washingtonpost.com/wp-dyn/content/article/2008/06/13/AR2008061303298.html, April 13, 2008

The *Washington Post* "SEC Enforcement Cases Decline 9%,Staff Reduced Because of Budget Crunch," www.washingtonpost.com/wp-dyn/content/article/2006/11/02/AR200611 0201701. html November 3, 2006

Wall Street *Deal Journal*, "Barclays to buy Lehman Investment Bank, Save at least 9000 jobs" Heidi N. Moore,

The *Wall Street Journal* Europe, "Lehman Workers Receive a Reprieve" 9/17/08

Acknowledgements

I am grateful to the many people at Lehman with whom it was my privilege to work for many years. The life of an investment banker is extreme; one spends enormous amounts of time with colleagues, often working under pressure. I was fortunate to spend all this time with people I like.

I am in great debt to my publisher and editor, who generously permitted me, a first time author, to tell the Lehman story in my own words without the help of a proven writer. The publishing of a book is for me a new experience, and I have been fortunate to collaborate with someone who both guided me through the process, and was open to the suggestions of a novice.

I thank my literary attorney who took a keen early interest in my book. He did much more than superb legal work.

I am much indebted to my agent, whose early frank input improved the book. His years of experience and sharp literary mind were consistently helpful.

I am grateful to the small circle of those close to me who provided all sorts of advice and input. This, too, made for a better, smarter book. I am fortunate to have talented and insightful friends and family.
I want to thank the two artists who created the book cover. Because they are both people in my life, its collaborative design and execution was a labor of love and, for me, makes this more than just a book cover.

Most of all, I thank my immediate family. It is not enough to dedicate my book to them. They have had the misfortune to have a husband/father whose time belonged to an investment bank – meaning that I was always on call. On top of that, they endured the months when I was entirely MIA writing this book. Sequestered in a room with a computer, I am lucky to have family whose love was generous, permitting me this time to be entirely selfish. They are my greatest joy.

For sales, editorial information, subsidiary rights information

or a catalog, please write or phone or e-mail

Brick Tower Press

1230 Park Avenue

New York, NY 10128, U.S.

Sales: 1-800-68-BRICK

Tel: 212-427-7139 Fax: 212-860-8852

www.BrickTowerPress.com

email: bricktower@aol.com.

For sales in the United States, please contact

National Book Network

nbnbooks.com

Orders: 800-462-6420

Fax: 800-338-4550

custserv@nbnbooks.com

For sales in the U.K. and Europe please contact our distributor,

Gazelle Book Services

Falcon House, Queens Square

Lancaster, LA1 1RN, UK

Tel: (01524) 68765 Fax: (01524) 63232

email: gazelle4go@aol.com.

For Australian and New Zealand sales please contact

Bookwise International

174 Cormack Road, Wingfield, 5013, South Australia

Tel: 61 (0) 419 340056 Fax: 61 (0)8 8268 1010

email: karen.emmerson@bookwise.com.au